Collaborative
Teaching
in
Elementary Schools

Collaborative Teaching

in
Elementary Schools

Making the Co-Teaching
Marriage Work!

Wendy W. Murawski

CORWIN
A SAGE Company

For information:

Corwin
A SAGE Company
2455 Teller Road
Thousand Oaks, California 91320
(800) 233-9936
Fax: (800) 417-2466
www.corwinpress.com

SAGE Ltd.
1 Oliver's Yard
55 City Road
London EC1Y 1SP
United Kingdom

SAGE India Pvt. Ltd.
B 1/I 1 Mohan Cooperative
    Industrial Area
Mathura Road, New Delhi 110 044
India

SAGE Asia-Pacific Pte. Ltd.
33 Pekin Street #02-01
Far East Square
Singapore 048763

Printed in the United States of America

Library of Congress Cataloging-in-Publication Data

Murawski, Wendy W.
Collaborative teaching in elementary schools: making the co-teaching marriage work!/Wendy W. Murawski.
    p. cm.
Includes bibliographical references and index.
ISBN 978-1-4129-6808-9 (cloth: alk. paper)
ISBN 978-1-4129-6809-6 (pbk.: alk. paper)
    1. Teaching teams. 2. Education, Elementary. 3. Classroom management. I. Title.

LB1029.T4M86 2010
372.133'4—dc22   2009035689

This book is printed on acid-free paper.

14 15 16 10 9 8 7 6 5 4

Acquisitions Editor:	David Chao
Editorial Assistant:	Sarah Bartlett
Production Editor:	Libby Larson
Copy Editor:	Tomara Kafka
Typesetter:	C&M Digitals (P) Ltd.
Proofreader:	Wendy Jo Dymond
Indexer:	Sheila Bodell
Cover Designers:	Anthony Paular and Lisa Riley

Contents

Publisher's Acknowledgments   vii

About the Author   viii

Introduction: Why This Book?   1

PART I: THE DATING SCENE   5

1. Understanding What It Means to Be in a Relationship   6

Defining the Terms   6
Changing the Minds of the Commitment-Phobic   13

2. Dating, Living Together, and Marriage   21

Recognizing the Continuum of Options   21
Going in With Eyes Wide Open   23
Do's and Don'ts of Co-Teaching   31

3. General Educators Are From Jupiter;
Special Service Providers Are From Saturn   42

Recognizing Different Frames of Reference   42
The Second Time Around: Getting Over Bad Experiences   49
Self-Assessment 1: Are We Ready to Date?   57

4. Matchmaker, Matchmaker: The Role of the Administrator   62

To Marry Them or Not to Marry Them:
    Determining Whether to Use Co-Teaching   62

PART II: THE ENGAGEMENT   67

5. Getting to Know Your Partner   68

Drinking Out of the Carton (and Other Pet Peeves)   68
Ensuring Parity   70
Who'll Do the Laundry? Setting Roles and Responsibilities   75

6. Registering for the Wedding   78

Identifying Our Needs   78
Communicating With Stakeholders   78

7. Discussing the Future   98

Establishing Schoolwide Improvement Goals   98
Establishing Individual Team Improvement Goals   103
Self-Assessment 2: Are We Ready to Get Engaged?   107

8. Matchmaker, Matchmaker: The Role of the Administrator   108

Avoiding Arranged Marriages: The Search for Soul Mates   108

PART III: THE WEDDING   **117**

   **9. For Better or Worse: Establishing Norms
      for Behavior and Academics**   **118**

      Physical Issues   119
      Classroom Management Issues   121
      Instructional and Assessment Issues   135

  10. For Richer or Poorer: Sharing Space and Materials   **140**

      Sharing Space   141
      Sharing Materials   144

  11. Planning Quality Time Together: Why, When, and How to Plan   **147**

      Why Should We Co-Plan?   147
      When Should We Co-Plan?   152
      How Should We Co-Plan?   163
      Self-Assessment 3: Are We Ready to Marry?   173

  12. Matchmaker, Matchmaker: The Role of the Administrator   **174**

      Avoiding Polygamy: Too Many Is Simply
         Too Many (When Scheduling)   174

PART IV: THE MARRIAGE   **193**

  13. Working Together to Wrangle the Li'l Rascals   **194**

      Five Practical Approaches for Co-Instruction   194
      Approach 1: One Teach, One Support   195
      Approach 2: Parallel Teaching   198
      Approach 3: Station Teaching   202
      Approach 4: Alternative Teaching   205
      Approach 5: Team Teaching   209

  14. Teaching the Seven Dwarves   **213**

      Understanding Differentiation   213
      Practical Strategies for Differentiation   220

  15. Are We Successful Yet?   **225**

      Co-Assessing Us and Them   225

  16. Playing Nicely With the Other Parents   **240**

      Co-Teaching's Role With Other School-Improvement Initiatives   240
      Reading First   241
      Cooperative Learning   243
      Twenty-First-Century Technology   243
      Universal Design for Learning   246
      Response to Intervention   247
      Self-Assessment 4: Will We Be Able to Celebrate Our Anniversary? 250

  17. Matchmaker, Matchmaker: The Role of the Administrator   **251**

      Is It Time for a Divorce?   251
      Building an Effective Program: Making More Matches   257

Appendix: Keeping the Honeymoon Going   **261**

References   **265**

Index   **275**

Publisher's Acknowledgments

Corwin gratefully acknowledges the contributions of the following individuals:

James Becker, ESL Teacher
Saint Paul Public Schools
Saint Paul, MN

Mari Gates, Special Education
Co-Teacher
Henry B. Burkland Intermediate
School
Middleboro, MA

Iris Goldberg, Director of Early
Childhood/Childhood Education
Westchester Graduate Campus
Long Island University
Brooklyn, NY

Susan Hott, Special Education Teacher
Davis Elementary School
Plano, TX

Rob Kuchta, Science Teacher
Chippewa Falls Senior High School
Chippewa Falls, WI

Margaret T. McLane, Chair
Department of Literacy and Special
Education
The College of Saint Rose
Albany, NY

Melissa Miller, Sixth-Grade Teacher
Randall G. Lynch Middle School
Farmington, AR

Sylvia Rockwell, Professor of
Special Education
St. Leo University
Palm Harbor, FL

Sharon Shores, Fourth-Grade Teacher
Oglethorpe Avenue Elementary
Athens, GA

Amy Trenkle, Eighth-Grade U.S.
History Teacher
District of Columbia Public Schools
Washington, DC

About the Author

Wendy W. Murawski is an associate professor and graduate coordinator at California State University, Northridge, in the Department of Special Education. She is an experienced co-teacher (for K–12 and university, general and special education) and an accomplished presenter. She is often requested to work with state departments, districts, and schools; present keynote addresses at conferences; and provide training seminars. Murawski has won prestigious awards including the Dissertation Award from the Division of Learning Disabilities and a Publication Award from the Division of Research for the Council for Exceptional Children, and she was the 2004 California Teacher Educator of the Year. Murawski's research in the area of co-teaching has been widely disseminated through her numerous publications. Murawski is the author of *Co-Teaching in the Inclusive Classroom: Working Together to Help ALL Your Students Find Success*, an extensive resource handbook on co-teaching, as well as the co-creator of the CTSS (Co-Teach Solutions System) software. Her educational consulting company, 2 TEACH LLC, was created to provide professional development specifically in the areas of inclusive education, collaboration, and co-teaching. Murawski is a dynamic speaker who utilizes humor, personal experience, and research-based methods in her seminars while keeping them in the context of practical, ready-to-use strategies for general and special educators to implement in their inclusive classrooms. Murawski holds a master's degree in special education, an EdS in educational administration, and a PhD in special education with an emphasis in research, collaboration, and co-teaching. She lives in southern California with her husband, son, cat, and a really mean fish.

Introduction

Why This Book?

The big question is always, "*Why?*"

This book is intended to be practical, easy-to-use and easy-to-read for busy educators interested in jumping right into co-teaching. Numerous forms, worksheets, and examples are included. I use humor and an informal tone to make the information interesting and personal. That said, however, it is critical that I first explain why you need this type of handbook, what precipitated the writing of it, and then introduce you to the concepts of inclusion and co-teaching so that we are all on the same figurative and, in this case also, literal page.

The advent of No Child Left Behind (2001) with its mandate of more accountability for all children, including those with disabilities and its emphasis on the need for "highly qualified" teachers, has greatly impacted the makeup of today's typical classroom. In addition, the reauthorization of the Individuals with Disabilities Education Improvement Act (2004) continues the emphasis on least restrictive environment for students with disabilities while supporting the need for access to the general education curriculum for all students. These laws have led to a complete paradigm shift in the way students with disabilities are educated and, subsequently, how teachers in schools are utilized to meet those needs in an inclusive environment.

One of the key ways that schools are addressing these needs is through pairing general education teachers and special service providers in general education classrooms in a technique known as co-teaching. By pairing educators with differing areas of expertise, teachers are able to better collaborate and differentiate. This also ensures that students are exposed to the general education curriculum and higher academic standards. Co-teaching is considered a viable option for ensuring that students have a "highly qualified" teacher in the room for the content, while also ensuring that all students' individualized educational needs are met by having an instructor who is highly qualified in differentiation and individualization. Please note that while I frequently refer to the general education teacher co-teaching with a special education teacher, co-teaching can occur with any professional educators. Special service providers include special educators, Title I teachers, teachers of English language learners, teachers of the gifted, speech language pathologists, school psychologists, and so on. It does not include paraprofessionals, volunteers, and student assistants, for reasons I will explain later.

You will notice the theme of marriage evident in the title and chapter names; this is for a very good reason. The concept of having two equal adults paired together for a lengthy time to share in the education and raising of children—to include behavior management, social skills, academics, and emotional support—sure does sound like another relationship we are all familiar with in one way or another, doesn't it? So, rather than focusing on how co-teaching is new and different in the educational arena, I have chosen to focus on how we can take what we know about successful, productive, and healthy marriages and relate that knowledge to the realm of co-teaching. Don't worry though—no ministers or fieldtrips to city hall are required for this particular arrangement.

Despite the growing use of co-teaching, studies continue to reveal a lack of training regarding this service delivery model. Very little has been done in many districts to genuinely prepare teachers to collaborate in the same classroom. While many textbooks refer to collaboration and briefly address co-teaching, the practicalities of how to prepare for co-teaching and how to ensure that teachers have the strategies they need to do it successfully are lacking. Districts are clamoring for more information on how to use collaboration and co-teaching effectively, thus clearly demonstrating that this is an area of increasing importance. This text will address these needs by providing readers with a practical, easy-to-use manual on how to set up, conduct, and successfully maintain co-teaching at any school interested in supporting inclusive practices.

My intent is to provide readers with a detailed, comprehensive treatment of co-teaching, in a practical and easy-to-access format. The book is useful as a Co-Teaching 101 reference for schools that have no experience with co-teaching and want to begin to set it up. At the same time, it provides sufficient practical differentiation and application strategies for districts that already have implemented co-teaching to help improve their current programs. Numerous templates and models are provided so that schools and districts can follow the steps to make co-teaching a feasible strategy for addressing diverse needs in the inclusive classroom. Each section has call-out boxes letting readers know where in the book they can go when they *want more on a topic*. There are EZ Reference pages designed to provide quick references for copying, sharing, and reminding educators of important topics. Each of the four parts also has a section titled Self-Assessment to aid in reflection and readiness evaluation, as well as a chapter titled Matchmaker, Matchmaker designed to provide administrators with helpful information regarding their role in creating, supporting, and evaluating co-teaching. In addition, a wide variety of resources and references have been provided throughout the text for those sites interested in reading further or learning about the theoretical and research base supporting the various sections. Because all organizations, districts, schools, and individuals are unique and have their own cultures, strengths, and needs, feel free to tweak and adapt as needed.

This book has been divided into four major parts: Dating, Engagement, Wedding, and Marriage. Sorry, no honeymoon details here. Within each of the four parts, there are chapters related to improving co-teaching effectiveness. Each chapter's title relates to the marriage analogy and the subtitles clue you in to its relation to co-teaching. Don't let the cutesy titles throw you; the information in each chapter is actually grounded in educational research and literature. You will find that the analogy works very well in taking a concept that is rather new and confusing (i.e., co-teaching) and putting it into a paradigm with which we are quite familiar (i.e., marriage). I have also found that humor encodes learning, and this analogy invites a variety of comedic comparisons.

While I have used the marriage comparison for years and am certainly not the only one to do so (e.g., Wasserman, 2008), I would like to recognize the many co-teachers who routinely go above and beyond in their daily interactions with children and with each other. Many co-teachers gave me permission to come into their classes and to use their pictures. Special thanks to those teachers at the CHIME Institute (preschool, elementary and middle schools), Granada Hills Charter High School, Montebello School District and Lincoln County School District. Thanks to the many professionals who have contributed to the concept of co-teaching, but especially to those good friends who have helped me as I conceptualized my contribution to the field over the years: Lisa Dieker, Claire Hughes, Sally Spencer, Rachel Friedman Narr, Wendy Lochner, Jeni Huber, and Lynne Cook. A special "shout-out" goes to Sally Spencer who actually tried to co-teach with me during the writing of this book; in retrospect, not something I would recommend. Luckily, we had a solid relationship and, many laughs and groans later, our marriage stood up to a very rocky semester. In addition, I would like to thank Dr. Linda Hutchinson, my very first co-teacher. Not only did Linda give me a wonderful experience co-teaching, which has led to my focus and research over the past 17 years, she also gave me her son in marriage. So, if you begin to doubt that successful co-teaching can exist, just remind yourself that I did it—with my mother-in-law no less! (For those of you who are single and looking, I highly recommend finding a co-teacher who has an available and very good-looking son, daughter, or friend. Whatever works for you.) Finally, I must also acknowledge my own family. My mom is my very own cheerleader, not to mention my business manager, who really helped me coordinate writing, teaching, traveling, and parenting. My son, Kiernan, is now four years old and is ready for Mommy to be "all done with that book!" My husband, Christien, has provided me with a solid, positive, and strong marriage to use as an exemplar for this book. Every day, we co-plan, co-instruct, and co-assess—some days better than others, but always with a common goal and vision. Lucky for us, our classroom only has one student in it. Wouldn't it be nice if you and your co-teacher could just start with one also? That would make your new relationship so much easier. Given how unlikely that is, however, I recommend that you read on for tips, strategies, and guidelines to make your own co-teaching marriage a successful one.

Part I

The Dating Scene

Teachers who get along can make the co-taught classroom a fun learning environment for all students.

1

Understanding What It Means to Be in a Relationship

■ DEFINING THE TERMS

In order that we begin this book on the same page, literally and figuratively, I think it is important that we have a clear understanding of the philosophy, terms, and definitions of co-teaching and how they relate to inclusion and collaboration. I'm just making sure here that all of us (me as the author, you as the reader, your co-teachers, and your administrators) are all sharing the same language and understanding of the issues so that there are no miscommunications. For example, let me begin by saying that while I delight in comparing two co-teachers to a married couple, and their administrator to a marriage counselor, I will not go as far as to consider myself the mother-in-law or justice of the peace or anything like that. I am merely the author of your *Co-Teaching Marriage Self-Help* book.

Defining Inclusion

Throughout the years, various civil rights acts have led to providing students with diverse needs a more rigorous academic education in an inclusive setting. In 1975, the Education of All Handicapped Children Act (Public Law 94–142) was passed. It was rewritten as the Individuals with Disabilities Education Act (IDEA) in 1990 and was reauthorized in 1997 and 2004 as the Individuals with Disabilities Education Improvement Act (IDEIA). Because of IDEIA and the No Child Left Behind Act (NCLB) of 2001, more and more students with disabilities are being taught in general education classrooms (Magiera, Smith, Zigmond, & Gebauer, 2005; Thousand, Villa, & Nevin, 2006b). IDEIA supports the notion of a Free and Appropriate Public Education for students with disabilities and mandates that these students be educated with their peers without disabilities to the maximum extent appropriate, in what is known as the Least Restrictive Environment (LRE) (Katsiyannis, Yell, & Bradley, 2001). For most children, the general education classroom is what is considered their LRE.

The practice of providing supports and services to students with disabilities in a general education setting is referred to as inclusion. Inclusion is "the understanding that all students—those who are academically gifted, those who are average learners, and those who struggle to learn for any reason—should be fully welcomed members of their school communities and that all professionals in a school share responsibility for their learning" (Friend & Pope, 2005, p. 57). The evolving movement of including students with diverse needs into general education classes is designed to provide them and typically developing students with systematic instruction and the opportunity to interact with one another (Lamar-Dukes & Dukes, 2005). However, some critics argue that "the increased reliance of general educators to assume responsibility to disabled or at-risk children demands an effective support system that takes into consideration shared input and resources, responsibility, and decision making between general and special educators—a support system which is not in place in many educational settings" (Miller, Wienke, & Savage, 2000, p. 14). Is this support system in place at your school? If not, what is lacking? The collaboration of general educators and special service providers is one of the predominant ways that schools are using to ensure this type of support system exists for students—and for teachers.

In the past century, there has been a substantial increase in the number of students included in the general education classroom (Burstein, Sears, Wilcoxen, Cabello, & Spagna, 2004). With the increased number of students with disabilities as well as increased educational reforms, schools are looking into instructional delivery services to meet the needs of diverse students in the general education classroom. Miller et al. (2000) caution that, while shared input and resources are part of the proposed benefits of inclusive settings and collaborative instruction, in order for this to occur, "general educators must increase their willingness to open traditionally private classrooms to special educators" (p. 35). For students, families, educators, and schools to benefit from inclusive practices, it is imperative that educators are (a) open to the notion of fully integrating students with disabilities into the general education classes, (b) willing to collaborate with their colleagues to do so, and (c) aware of the characteristics, components, and strategies necessary to make inclusion successful for all. This book tackles these issues and provides readers with the information needed to create a successful co-taught program.

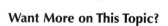

Want More on This Topic?

Find out about the research-identified benefits to inclusive education on the following pages.

Why Include *Those* Kids?

Check out these research-based benefits to inclusive education!

- *Inclusive schools provide opportunities.* These include opportunities for students with disabilities to make friends with a more diverse group of students, to include those without disabilities; opportunities for students to learn tolerance for those who are different; opportunities for teachers to learn skills from one another; and opportunities for communities to build on and support a collaborative culture.

- *Inclusive schools help avoid labels/stigma.* As teachers work collaboratively to meet the needs of all students, there is a reduction of stigma attributed to *those* kids (e.g., the ones who are separated and taught in the small room down the hall).

- *Inclusive schools increase an acceptance of diversity.* As students and faculty work with one another and learn about each other's strengths and weaknesses, there is a stronger emphasis on the importance of diversity. Students see teachers modeling collaboration and respecting one another's differences and are able to learn those skills, ultimately bringing that acceptance—and celebration—of diversity with them when they enter society as contributing members.

- *Inclusive schools help build relationships.* As general educators work more closely with special service providers (e.g., academic coaches, special education teachers, Title I teachers, and speech-language pathologists), they forge relationships that can support them in the future. Similarly, students continue to build relationships with other students who are different than they are.

- *Inclusive schools consider the future.* Society is diverse and all types of individuals are necessary to make it function. Bringing various individuals together to learn from one another and to recognize the strengths of each individual, rather than working from a deficit model, helps positively impact the future of our society.

- *Inclusive schools result in improved instruction.* As teachers collaborate, they are able to provide each other with both support and strategies to ensure that students are provided with high quality instruction based in best practices pedagogy. Access to the general education content enables students with disabilities to have a chance at learning what their peers who are nondisabled are learning.

- *Inclusive schools result in improved assessment results.* Schools that have embraced inclusive practices over a period of years report having positive results on informal and formal assessments. Students with disabilities are able to participate in standardized assessments and their scores are increasing due to the access to general education content that inclusion affords them.

- *Inclusive schools support self-advocacy.* When students feel comfortable that diversity and differences are acceptable, they are more willing to self-advocate. They recognize that each person is an individual with differing needs and that it is important to be able to know and explain one's areas of strength and need.

- *Inclusive schools uphold the law.* The Individuals with Disabilities Education Improvement Act (IDEIA) of 2004 states that children with disabilities need to be educated in the least restrictive environment, which for most students is typically determined to be the general education classroom. The No Child Left Behind Act (NCLB) of 2001 encourages the standardized assessment of all students, including those with disabilities, and requires that all children receive content instruction from a highly qualified content teacher. In order to meet both of these items, teachers need to include students in the general education class and ensure that their needs are being met.

- *Inclusive schools increase collaboration.* The inclusion of students with disabilities cannot be successful unless stakeholders are collaborating. Parents need to work with educators, general and special education teachers need to work together, teachers need to work with administrators, and everyone needs to include the child. In inclusive schools, all of these individuals have the opportunity to positively interact in order to do what is best for the child—a true testament to collaboration.

Defining Collaboration

Because numerous school reforms seek to ensure systematic, valuable instruction for all students in the general education setting, *collaboration* has been a popular buzzword in schools. Dr. Marilyn Friend (2000) shared that there are numerous myths about collaboration, and she includes the misconception that collaboration is occurring every time two or more individuals interact. The requirements for collaboration are more than engagement among individuals of group. Collaboration requires interaction, to be sure, but it is much more than that. Just as we would not label any two people we see interacting as *married*, so must we realize that professionals who are interacting are not necessarily collaborating. Collaboration is a very specific relationship. Collaboration refers to "a style for direct interaction between at least two coequal parties voluntarily engaged in shared decision making as they work toward a common goal" (Friend & Cook, 2007, p. 4). Collaboration can occur in almost any context where people are interacting; equally important, however, is the understanding that it may *not* be occurring, whether or not the label is applied. . . . All too often, schools label their programs 'collaborative' without having the elements in place to guarantee that authentic partnerships exist" (Friedman Narr, Murawski, & Spencer, 2007, p. 9).

Idol, Paolucci-Whitcomb, and Nevin (1986) defined collaboration by describing the importance of differing areas of expertise that collaborators would bring to the table. Their definition highlights the importance that diverse areas of expertise can play when problem solving. My friend and colleague, Claire Hughes, and I define collaboration more narrowly in an article we wrote on co-teaching for gifted education. We define collaboration as "a style for interaction, which includes dialogue, planning, shared and creative decision making, and follow-up between at least two coequal professionals with diverse expertise, in which the goal of the interaction is to provide appropriate services for students, including high achieving and gifted students" (Hughes & Murawski, 2001, p. 196). While our specificity may not work for collaboration in all instances, we believe it is highly appropriate when discussing collaboration in inclusive schools where differentiation and addressing students' individual and diverse needs is the goal. And shouldn't this be the goal of all schools?

Why is collaboration so popular in schools these days? Why aren't teachers allowed to just continue doing what they have done for years—shut their doors and teach their own ways as they see fit? To begin with, society has become more and more collaborative and interactive. Fortune 500 companies identified the top skills required for their incoming employees; their top five skills were (1) teamwork, (2) problem solving, (3) interpersonal skills, (4) oral communication, and (5) listening. Where did Reading, 'Riting, and 'Rithmetic fall? Writing was #10, computation was #12, and reading was #13. Social networking is key in most jobs and certainly requires strong collaboration and communication skills. The educational research literature also cites numerous benefits as to why students and teachers need to learn to play nicely with each other. For example, any time there is a need to shift an organizational paradigm, such as what is required for inclusive education to take hold in a school, collaboration is a necessary component for success (Hourcade & Bauwens, 2003; Villa, Thousand, Nevin, & Malgeri, 1996). Teachers who cringe at being asked to meet the diverse needs in the classroom have found that collaborating with other educators increases their ability to meet those needs (Mastropieri & Scruggs, 2007; Purcell & Leppien, 1998). Hughes and Murawski (2001) and Pugach and Johnson (1995) reported that collaboration among students and faculty helped achieve more complex goals, improve social interactions, and even increase creativity. Therein lies the adage, "two heads are better than one."

Another important benefit of teacher collaboration is that teachers can better assist one another with problem solving (Foley & Mundschenk, 1997; Snell & Janney, 2000). Given how often problems arise in the everyday classroom, this is certainly a valuable asset. In addition, teachers who collaborate with other educators found that they were more able to model and communicate the value of collaborative behaviors to their students (Villa et al., 1996; Weinstein, 2003). Instead of telling students how they should interact with others, we can now show them. Modeling behavior is certainly a key element to instruction in the elementary classroom.

Let me emphasize that collaboration is *not* about watering down the curriculum for students with disabilities; it is about working with colleagues to problem solve and meet goals. Are you a sports fan? Then collaboration is not about moving the goal posts; it is about raising the bar. This can include providing enrichment opportunities to students who need challenge, as well as additional depth or breadth to their curriculum and instruction (Hughes & Murawski, 2001; Purcell & Leppien, 1998). Finally, another benefit I have experienced is that in those schools where collaboration is more common and evident, administrators and teachers actually encourage the interaction of university and K–12 faculty for data collection and research (Murawski, 2003). What this means is that instead of having a moat between the ivory tower concepts that university professors may espouse (yours truly excepted here, of course) and what is actually occurring in PreK–12 schools, there is a clear connection between theory and practice (Murawski, 2002b).

How do we become more collaborative? For starters, training. Professional development is a critical element in providing a clear vision of the roles and responsibilities of participating in an inclusive and collaborative program (Friend, 2000). For collaboration to be an effective approach across the spectrum of an inclusive program, it is essential that professionals acquire the skills and knowledge of what constitutes effective collaboration (Fennick & Liddy, 2001; Friend, 2000). In addition, the educational literature supports the importance of a mutual commitment and willingness among active participants to promote a positive collaborative atmosphere (Friend & Cook, 2007; Weiner & Murawski, 2005). As participants develop an understanding of collaboration, it is more likely they will share common visions and goals, thereby developing more cohesive inclusive programs for students with and without disabilities (Fennick & Liddy, 2001; Friend, 2000; Weiner & Murawski, 2005).

Inclusion and collaboration are not going away. Due to IDEIA requiring collaboration as part of special education services, schools are shifting toward a collaborative inclusive model wherein instructional partnerships between general and special educators are essential in delivering services to students with disabilities in the general education classroom (Friend & Cook, 2007; Weiss & Lloyd, 2003). Thus, successful implementation of services and support needs to be delivered through the qualified and positive collaboration of general and special education teachers, among others. Friend and Cook (2007) reference different structures that require collaboration (i.e., consultation, teaming, and co-teaching). Each of these structures can assist general and special education teachers in providing the educational services students need to succeed. An easy reference is provided here to help clarify the many special education–related terms and acronyms that can get confusing.

Clarifying Terminology

Regular Education Initiative (REI). First major movement to put all children with disabilities into the general education classroom (Will, 1986)

Mainstreaming. The placement of students with disabilities into general education classes, usually part-time and without any additional services

Collaboration. A style of interaction in which two or more professionals work together toward a common goal (Friend & Cook, 2003)

Consultation. An interaction in which one party provides assistance and expertise to assist another party

Inclusion. A philosophy that states that students with disabilities have the right to receive their education in a general education classroom, with necessary supports and services provided in that setting

Least Restrictive Environment (LRE). A legal specification from the Individuals with Disabilities Education Act (IDEA) that students with disabilities are to be educated *to the greatest extent* possible with their general education peers

Teaming. When educators collaborate and communicate regarding the same group(s) of students without necessarily teaching in the same classroom

Job Sharing. When educators work part-time and take alternate days to instruct the same group of students

Team Teaching. A method of co-instruction by which both educators co-facilitate a lesson at the same time, one of the five co-teaching approaches identified by Cook & Friend (1995)

Co-Teaching. When two or more educators *co-plan, co-instruct, and co-assess* a group of students with diverse needs in the same general education classroom (Murawski, 2003)

EZ Reference

Figure 1.1   Clarifying Terminology

EZ Reference

> ## Clarifying Acronyms
>
> - **IDEIA or IDEA**: The Individuals with Disabilities Education (Improvement) Act
> - **NCLB**: No Child Left Behind Act
> - **GET**: General education teacher
> - **SET**: Special education teacher
> - **SSP**: Special service provider (e.g., provider of services like special education, Title I, English Language Learner program, gifted education, speech/language, occupational or physical therapy, adapted physical education, and so on)
> - **IEP**: Individualized education program
> - **RTI**: Response to intervention (or instruction)
> - **LD**: Learning disability
> - **EBD**: Emotional and behavioral disorder
> - **CPP**: Content, process, product (components for differentiation)
> - **HALO**: High achieving, average achieving, low achieving, other
> - **PBS**: Positive behavior support
> - **LRE**: Least restrictive environment

Figure 1.2 Clarifying Acronyms

For the purpose of this text, co-teaching is the collaborative model of focus. In fact, it is often cited as one of the most common service delivery approaches gaining in use in schools for students with disabilities (e.g., Dieker & Murawski, 2003; Fennick & Liddy, 2001; Murawski & Swanson, 2001; Thousand et al., 2006b; Weiss & Lloyd, 2003). Before we venture further into this book, we need to clearly define co-teaching. Naturally, since we have a whole book devoted to co-teaching, this next part provides an overview; details of who, what, when, where, why and especially *how* are covered in subsequent chapters.

Defining Co-Teaching

As schools are shifting to provide more inclusive programs, due in great part to the IDEIA 2004 emphasis on providing more systematic academic opportunities to students with disabilities, general and special education teachers are being pressured (did I say pressured? I meant sweetly encouraged) to jointly and effectively deliver services to all students in the general education classroom (Weiss & Lloyd, 2002; Wischnowski, Salmon, & Eaton, 2004). A popular service delivery model that is frequently being suggested in meeting academic needs of students with disabilities in the general education classroom is—*you guessed it*—co-teaching. Co-teaching is also called collaborative teaching, team teaching or cooperative teaching but, regardless of which term is used, we are describing two or more professionals who deliver quality instruction to students with and without disabilities in a classroom (Dieker & Barnett, 1996; Friend & Cook, 2007). Furthermore, co-teaching is also referred to as the key for bringing people with diverse backgrounds and interests together to share knowledge and skills as they individualize learning for students

(Thousand, Villa, & Nevin, 2006a). Collaborative teaching provides general and special educators a greater opportunity to ensure that students with disabilities obtain a more structured and appropriate education within their community. If you have chosen—or have been chosen—to embark upon this professional marriage, congratulations! You and your partner must now get ready to work together to *raise* some very special students. This quick litmus test (Figure 1.3) will help you determine if you are already co-teaching.

Co-Teaching Litmus Test

Are you a professional educator?	☐ yes	☐ no
Are you working in the same classroom at the same time as another professional educator on a regular basis?	☐ yes	☐ no
Do you and your colleague co-plan (jointly determining what you will teach and how)?	☐ yes	☐ no
Do you and your colleague co-instruct (teach the students together, sharing roles)?	☐ yes	☐ no
Do you and your colleague co-assess (share in evaluation and determining grades)?	☐ yes	☐ no

If you have any no's, you are *not yet successfully co-teaching*. Read on to determine what you need to be doing.)

If you only have yes's, *congratulations!* You are co-teaching successfully. Read on to determine how you can continue to improve.

Figure 1.3   Co-Teaching Litmus Test

CHANGING THE MINDS ■
OF THE COMMITMENT-PHOBIC

It is important for those interested in supporting inclusive education to recognize that some educators will be, and often rightfully so, resistant to change. So many new theories, practices, initiatives, and programs have come and gone in education that many veterans are skeptical of change. They are the ones who often question the rationale for new policies and who tend to hold firm to practices that they find tried and true. Rather than avoiding, overlooking, or even talking negatively about these individuals and their resistance to change (Friend & Cook, 2007), inclusion supporters should recognize these veteran educators' reluctance and address it directly. For example, some teachers may appear *commitment-phobic* when in truth they are merely concerned that all students will not get their needs met in an inclusive environment. They, like the rest of us, truly want what is best for students; they may, however, disagree with how to accomplish that. We become possessive and territorial rather than open and collaborative. For inclusive practices to be embraced and for relationships and commitments to grow, all stakeholders need to be educated as to the rationale and research behind inclusive education and the various service delivery options that might be used in schools to make inclusion successful.

History and Rationale of Inclusion

According to Sindelar, Shearer, Yendol-Hoppey, and Liebert (2006), the concept of inclusion is over 30 years old. We can look to the principle of normalization espoused by Wolfensberger in the 1970s for its impetus. Focusing on the education of individuals with disabilities, Kavale and Forness (2000) report that special education started as a program separate from general education. This is different from the concept of inclusion. Inclusive education seeks to meet individual needs as well as to provide universal education for all students. In fact, Universal Design for Learning (UDL) is inclusive in nature and is increasing in popularity. UDL calls for multiple means of representation, multiple means of action and expression, and multiple means of engagement (www.cast.org/research/udl/index.html). If learning can be universally designed, why then were students with disabilities historically served in segregated settings?

Want More on This Topic?

Learn more about UDL and its relation to co-teaching in Part IV: The Marriage.

The purported advantages of segregated programs include smaller class sizes, more individual instruction, and specially trained teachers. However, even back in 1968, Lloyd Dunn wrote an article that questioned the ethical and legal implications of excluding special education students from general education. Kavale and Forness (2000) suggest that this article was the impetus for including students with disabilities in general education. In addition, a look at current special education programs calls into question the assumption of smaller class sizes, individualized attention, and specially trained, highly qualified teachers. I personally had the experience one year of teaching 24 students with identified disabilities in a special education resource class, while my general education colleagues enjoyed a class-size reduction initiative that mandated certain general education classes have no more than 20 students. The district had not thought to include special education classes in that initiative. Ironically, the majority of the students in my class were there because their individualized education programs (IEPs) stated that a special education class was required in order to provide more intensive, individualized, small-group instruction in their areas of disability. So, ultimately, those students were pulled out of a 20:1 class with a highly qualified teacher to come to a class with a 24:1 ratio and a teacher trying to address multiple subjects, grade levels, and disability issues in the same class at the same time.

Renzaglia, Karvonen, Drasgow, and Stoxen (2003) concur that inclusion comes from the concept of normalization. Although their research primarily addresses individuals with severe disabilities, the normalization concept suggests that *all* individuals with disabilities should have lives similar to people without disabilities. It also suggests that *all* individuals with disabilities should be free to create better lives according to their personal situations. The concept of civil rights and the notion that "separate is not equal" are lines of reasoning that have been frequently argued as advocates work to promote inclusive education.

Alper, Schloss, Etscheidt, and MacFarlane (1995) clarified the principles of inclusion in their book *Inclusion: Are We Abandoning or Helping Students?* Look at Figure 1.4 on page 16 as you think about your own school site and situation.

How does your site demonstrate—or *not* demonstrate—these principles? Are some of the principles easier to agree with than others? Why? What concerns do you have related to these principles or to taking these principles from theory into practice? Take a few minutes to share these principles with others at your school and discuss their reactions to them. If you already know who your co-teacher is or will be, make sure to get his take on these principles and questions also. Communicating about big ideas is an excellent start to a collaborative relationship.

Having special and general educators communicate regularly can help faculty embrace the notion of inclusion.

Individuals with disabilities should be considered the same as individuals without disabilities and have the same rights. This means that all individuals with disabilities should have the right to participate in the same activities and routines as individuals without disabilities in their communities, including having jobs and friends without disabilities. Although this idea has been supported by many advocates of individuals with disabilities, the question of how best to meet the needs of students who need special education services continues to challenge parents, advocates, and educators.

Before 1975, there was very little reform in special education. It took vocal parents and parent organizations to prompt the government to act. When President Gerald Ford signed Public Law 94–142 into law (first called the Education for All Handicapped Children Act and later reauthorized as the

Principles of Inclusive Practices
(1) Students are more alike than not alike.
(2) Learning can occur through participation with and modeling of competent peers.
(3) The supplementary instructional support needed to help students succeed can be provided in a general education classroom.
(4) Everyone benefits from having students with different learning styles and behavioral traits in the same classroom.

As a school, discuss the above and answer the following questions:

- Do you agree with all four principles? Why or why not? If there is a principle you do not agree with, why not? What needs to occur to change your opinion?

- What actions do faculty and staff take at your school to demonstrate these principles?

- Do students and families appear to recognize and support these principles? Why or why not?

- What additional actions can be taken to further promote these principles and to share these principles with students, their families, and other stakeholders?

Figure 1.4 Principles of Inclusive Practices

SOURCE: Adapted from Alper et al. (1995).

Individuals with Disabilities Education Act or IDEA), the way was paved for more students with disabilities to be served in general education. The law states that *all* children, regardless of disability, be provided with educational services (Lipskey, 2005). School districts were required to develop and implement IEPs for each child identified as having a disability. Kavale and Forness (2000) define inclusion as a " movement seeking to create schools that meet the needs of all students by establishing learning communities for students with and without disabilities, educated together in age-appropriate general education classrooms in neighborhood schools" (p. 279). Burstein et al. (2004) add to this definition by including the phrase "with the supports and accommodations needed" (p. 104). McLeskey and Waldron (2002) emphasize that inclusion involves *all* students and teachers. It is not just a special education issue. If inclusion is going to be successful, the educational practices of all teachers must change. Inclusive schools go through a process. See Figure 1.5 for a typical progression of meeting the needs of students with disabilities over the years. Even after schools embrace the philosophy of inclusion, it takes time and baby steps to successfully implement inclusive principles (Murawski, 2005b). It does not happen overnight or all at once.

Obviously, this is not an easy task. As might have been expected, the inclusive movement marked the beginning of a series of laws and lawsuits designed to challenge the idea of increased integration of students with disabilities in general education. The next section of this review discusses some of the important legislation that continues to change the face of special education. Administrators and teacher leaders who are planning to lead their schools in moving toward more inclusive practices must be aware of these laws and their subsequent impact on today's districts.

Special schools	"Keep 'em separated"
Special classes	"Little room down the hall"
Pull-out model	"Only *we* can teach them"
Mainstreaming	"Here ya' go!"
Inclusion	"Let's do this together"

Why is inclusion the goal for so many schools?

What does the literature tell us about the results of inclusive practices?

What have your experiences been as related to the above table?

Less

Figure 1.5   The Progression

SOURCE: Murawski, W. W. (2008a).

[handwritten margin notes: Mostly Inclusion, pour, cluster classes, mainstream - some classes]

Laws Related to Inclusion

Katsiyannis et al. (2001) credit the civil rights victory in *Brown v. Board of Education* in 1954 for leading many parents and advocates of students with disabilities to demand full inclusion in general education. *Brown v. Board of Education* ruled that separate was not equal and caused many parents and advocates to question the educational placement of students with disabilities. Certainly, institutions, special schools, and even classrooms down the hall were all very separate areas for educating—or let's face it, in many cases, not educating but simply parking—individuals with disabilities. Labeling a child as having a disability guaranteed that the child would receive a separate education.

Much special education legislation was passed over the next 20 years, including the 1965 Elementary and Secondary Education Act (ESEA), the first effort by the federal government to provide funds for special education. However, the law that most significantly changed special education was Public Law 94–142 in 1975, the first act to exclusively address students with disabilities (Smith, 2005). Smith also reports that while there were many provisions to PL 94–142, the following addressed the inclusion of students with disabilities in general education:

- *FAPE.* Ensuring a *free appropriate public education* for all children with disabilities that focuses on providing special education and related services to meet their individual needs.
- *Child Find.* Schools have to find children with disabilities and start the referral process to determine eligibility.
- *IEP.* Every child in special education must have an *individual education program* identifying the child's needs, goals, and objectives.
- *LRE.* To the maximum extent possible, children with disabilities should be educated with their nondisabled peers in the *least restrictive environment*. This provision resulted in the increased inclusion of students with disabilities and created years of debate about the placement of individuals with disabilities.

Katsiyannis et al. (2001) also reported that due to the many changes in the law, special education is the most litigated area of education. There have been many important laws, but the Education for All Handicapped Children Act (EAHCA) and its subsequent amendments continue to push the agenda of inclusive education for all students. In 1990, EAHCA was amended and renamed Individuals with Disabilities Education Act (or IDEA). One of the most controversial issues in IDEA is the FAPE requirement that students with disabilities be provided a free appropriate public education in the least restrictive environment (Yell & Katsiyannis, 2004). This means to the maximum degree possible, students with disabilities are educated in the general education classroom and when general education settings are not appropriate, in the least segregated setting appropriate. It also addressed placement of students who were not appropriate for general

Want More on This Topic?

The continuum of placement options is addressed further in Chapters 2 and 4.

education by providing a continuum of alternative placement options. The controversial provision of LRE continued in succeeding reauthorizations of IDEA in 1997 and 2004 (Smith, 2005). What this means for us in terms of co-teaching is that more and more students with disabilities continue to be in the general education classroom, and it is expected that their educational, behavioral, and social needs will be met in that environment.

According to Zigmond (2003), while the IDEA amendments continue to push for inclusion, the focus moved from providing access for students with disabilities to be with their nondisabled peers for a social purpose, to a new focus defined in terms of their access to the general education curriculum. With the additional requirement that students with disabilities participate in all statewide assessments and accountability procedures, educators face increased pressure to choose a service delivery model that includes all students in the educational process.

Another requirement emerged to add to the confusing paradigm shift—one that presumably offered higher expectations and better instruction for students, and one that also resulted in increased co-teaching. This new requirement in IDEIA 2004 directed all special education teachers to meet the "highly qualified" mandate of No Child Left Behind (NCLB) (Smith, 2005). This required all special education teachers to meet NCLB requirements, have a state special education certification (not a temporary, emergency, or provisional certification), and at least a bachelor's degree. It also meant that a special education teacher teaching core academic subjects in Title I schools, and listed as the teacher of record, must possess a teaching credential in that content area (Müller & Burdette, 2007). This created major problems in special education (Smith, 2005), especially at the secondary level. With the current shortage of special education teachers, the new *highly qualified* standards discouraged some otherwise qualified teachers from pursuing special education teaching credentials. Additional requirements in some states mandated that general education teachers take more special education courses than they previously had to during their credentialing process. At the elementary level, many teachers across the nation are becoming *dually certified* in both special education and multiple subjects (general education) by completing programs that have special education teacher licensing requirements aligned with those of general education teachers (Müller & Burdette, 2007).

One solution many schools have selected is to have a general education subject area teacher and a special education teacher teach in the same classroom at the same time by using the service delivery option we are focused on in this book—co-teaching. In fact, some states (e.g., Alabama) do not require special educators who are working collaboratively in general education classes to obtain content knowledge specialization; by having a general educator in the room who is highly qualified in the content, the special educator can continue to focus on providing specialized support (Müller & Burdette, 2007). Yet, though we will be concentrating on the what, why, and how of co-teaching for the majority of this text, it is equally important that educators (and families as well) realize that co-teaching is just one option on the continuum of service options provided to students in the inclusive classroom. Understanding that continuum can also help educators and parents collaborate to determine what supports a child really needs in order to be successful in the general education classroom. This requires an explanation of the various options available on that continuum and how educators can collaborate to determine what is best for each individual child.

2

Dating, Living Together, and Marriage

RECOGNIZING THE ■ CONTINUUM OF OPTIONS

One of the requirements of the Individuals with Disabilities Education Improvement Act (IDEIA, 2004) mandates that students with disabilities are educated with their nondisabled peers in the least restrictive environment (LRE) as much as possible. However, the Free Appropriate Public Education (FAPE) concept also considers the possibility that not all students benefit from full inclusion. Some students need a more restrictive, specialized environment. Katsiyannis, Yell, and Bradley (2001) discuss the IDEA provision that allows students with disabilities to be removed from general education classes if the nature or severity of their disabilities is such that they cannot receive an appropriate education, with support and accommodations, in that setting.

IDEIA ensures that students are educated in the LRE by mandating school districts to provide a continuum of alternative placements. These services range from settings that are least restrictive to those that are more restrictive and specialized. The least restrictive setting is typically considered the general education classroom, followed in restrictiveness by resource rooms and then the more restrictive special classes, schools and hospitals, and institutions. As previously stated, the goal is to have students with disabilities with their grade-level peers and in their home schools as much as possible.

After decades of litigation, laws, and expectations, Lipsky (2005) reports that while society has achieved some access to public education for students with disabilities, a system of dual education continues. According to Lipsky, great efforts have been made to address this dual system. This includes the enactment of both IDEIA and NCLB. Both laws emphasize access for all students to the general education curriculum and the inclusion of all but a few students in general education assessments and reports with the opportunity to provide alternative assessments for students with disabilities. In addition, both IDEIA and NCLB indicate a strong preference for students with disabilities to be educated with their typically developing peers. Thus, students are expected to be taught and assessed together, while concurrently having their individualized needs met. This apparent dichotomy of mandates has led to much confusion on the part of educators. This confusion is also compounded by the fact that the issues of inclusion may differ from elementary school to high school.

Co-teaching is the focus of this text but, as you may know from experience, it is not realistic to assume that all teachers will co-teach and that all students will be co-taught. In fact, I would like to note here very clearly that not all students need to be in a co-taught class. If you take a look at Figure 2.1, Understanding the Differences in Support Along the Collaborative Continuum, you will see that co-teaching provides a significant amount of support. That is not the ultimate goal of education. The ultimate goal of education is that students learn independence and are able to become productive members of society (Friedman Narr, Murawski, & Spencer, 2007). While some individuals will always need more support than others, in school and even after graduation, educators and family members alike should closely monitor how much support a child is receiving and work to only provide what is necessary.

Friedman Narr et al. (2007) present a model of a continuum of service delivery options, all of which involve collaboration between parties and are tied closely to placement decisions. They state,

> The continuum is a dynamic model that doesn't view a child's placement as static—for example, a child is not designated as "a [self-contained] student" or "a Resource student." Instead, a student's needs are examined separately in each of the academic subjects, the best service delivery option is chosen for each given subject, and the level of collaboration needed to sustain that option is decided upon. The type of collaboration needed to help a student achieve maximum independence will change according to his or her strengths and needs in any given content area. (p. 9)

The continuum provided in Figure 2.1 shows that some children in special education may only need "monitoring" in a general education class, while others may need a completely separate environment. While "full inclusionists" may argue that offering a separate setting works against inclusive education by providing teachers, students, and parents with alternatives to the general education setting, the reality is that these alternatives are mandated by law. When I talk more about scheduling, I will clarify how to determine whether or not a student should be in a co-taught class or a different environment. For now, I would like to quote my mentor and a noted expert in co-teaching, Dr. Lynne Cook, when she stated, "Co-teaching is not a panacea." While it is a valuable option when done well, and while the rest of this

Want More on This Topic?

Additional information on scheduling is provided in Part III: The Wedding.

text concentrates on helping you know *how* to do it well, be aware that there will be times when co-teaching is simply not the most appropriate option.

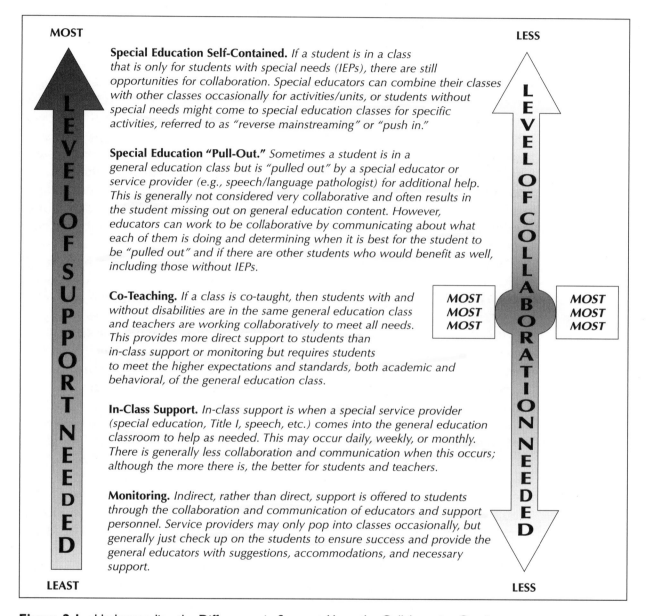

Figure 2.1   Understanding the Differences in Support Along the Collaborative Continuum

GOING IN WITH EYES WIDE OPEN ■

Definition, Benefits, and Barriers to Co-Teaching

You completed the Co-Teaching Litmus Test in Figure 1.3 on page 13 and at least one of your responses was *no*. Having worked with co-teachers on the national level for years, I frequently hear both general and special service providers lamenting that they were "thrown into" a collaborative teaching situation with no training, no time for planning, no shared knowledge of content or students, and no true understanding of the goal or rationale for this professional marriage. In essence, there is an *arranged marriage* wherein two people show up at the same school and are told they are married—without really even knowing what their marriage is supposed to look like or having the benefit of a ceremony and reception. (I should mention here that my colleague Dr. Sharon DeFur clarified for me that actual arranged marriages are culturally based and that there is a large amount of research that goes in proactively as families get to know one another and determine if there is a good match. My arranged marriage analogy assumes no such research so it is culturally inaccurate.) It is no surprise that researchers like Weiss and Lloyd (2003) found that, more often than not, special educators who are supposed to be co-teaching are generally taking a support role or even taking students to their own classrooms, effectively going back to a "pull-out" model (see Figure 2.1). They may simply be unaware of what their new role is supposed to entail.

When interviewed, general education teachers often state that they do not know the role of the special service provider nor what they are supposed to do in the co-taught setting. They are concerned about making sure the content is taught, and as the grade-level content specialist and teacher of record, many feel it is their role to provide direct instruction to students while the special service provider walks around, providing proximity control and whatever on-the-spot accommodations are identified as necessary. While general educators are maintaining their position in front of the class, special service providers are concurrently complaining that they are often viewed and treated as a "glorified aide." In other situations, the special service provider is happy to take the support role, unclear as to what else she might do in the class, especially if she is not comfortable teaching the elementary content. It is not unheard of to have teachers question *why* they should be sharing the classroom, rather than allowing the fourth-grade teacher to continue to focus on fourth-grade content in his room while the special educator continues to provide individualized modifications and strategies in her own room, at whatever grade level the students might be functioning developmentally.

I first establish a definition of co-teaching, followed by a rationale and the research-based benefits of engaging in this service delivery option. Teachers are notorious for asking *why*—they want to see for themselves why they are being asked to change and implement new practices. Once I have provided a few definitions and the numerous benefits to reflect upon, I then review the Do's and Don'ts of Co-Teaching in Figure 2.3 on page 41. This form is an easy reference for talking to colleagues and evaluating current co-teaching situations.

Definitions of Co-Teaching

There are many definitions for co-teaching. The first one was provided by Bauwens, Hourcade, and Friend in 1989. They stated that co-teaching is "an educational approach in which two teachers work in a coactive and coordinated fashion to jointly teach academically and behaviorally heterogeneous groups of students in an integrated setting" (p. 18). Building on that work, Dr. Lynne Cook and Dr. Marilyn Friend, authors of *Interactions: Collaboration Skills for School Professionals, 5th Edition* (2007), a well-known educational text in this area, provided a definition that has been the most cited definition of co-teaching in the literature since they first wrote about it in 1995 for *Focus on Exceptional Children*. Their refined definition states that co-teaching involves "two or more professionals delivering substantive instruction to a diverse, or blended, group of students in a single physical space" (Cook & Friend, 1995, p. 1).

Since 1995, others have also worked to provide additional clarification to the definition of co-teaching. One such addition was by Snell and Janney (2000), when they wrote that co-teaching is "two or more team members teaching a class together. When special and general educators teach together, the motivation is often more effective instruction of a diverse group of students" (p. 5). Villa, Thousand, and Nevin (2007) define co-teaching as "two or more people sharing responsibility for teaching some or all of the students assigned to a classroom. It involves the distribution of responsibility among people for planning, instruction and evaluation for a classroom of students" (p. 3).

Bauwens et al. (1989) first mentioned teachers working together; Cook and Friend (1995) opened up the definition to include two or more professionals. Villa and colleagues (2007) broadened the definition to "people"—allowing a variety of individuals, including students, paraprofessionals and family members, to co-teach. Snell and Janney (2000) specifically mentioned special and general educators. In the definition I have crafted, I find it necessary to bring it back to educators. While I certainly agree with Villa and colleagues that there are a variety of collaborative options for including families, paraeducators, and students in the classroom, and I respect the incredible work these three have done related to co-teaching, I disagree with their assessment that co-teaching is really happening in these situations. Let's take a moment to discuss why.

The definition I proposed in 2003 and that I maintain today and for the remainder of this text is the following:

Co-Teaching

When two or more educators *co-plan, co-instruct, and co-assess* a group of students with diverse needs in the same general education classroom (Murawski, 2003)

Notice the emphasis on co-planning, co-instructing and co-assessing. Remember that Figure 1.3 Co-Teaching Litmus Test on page 13? Do these items look familiar? Here's why. Quality teaching cannot occur unless teachers are (1) constantly planning what they are going to do and why, (2) constantly instructing students in the ways they find to be most effective, and (3) constantly assessing how the instruction impacts students (academically, behaviorally, socially, and emotionally). By the same token, I believe that co-teachers need to engage in each of these activities equally. This is not to say that co-teachers can't each have areas of expertise or decide they are going to "divide and conquer" at times. Those are certainly important aspects of co-teaching. However, for true co-teaching to occur, both educators need to be engaged in all aspects of the teaching process and parity needs to be present.

Take a look at these components of *effective* co-teaching, based on the work of Friend and Cook in *Interactions* (2007). Note the word "effective." It deserves added emphasis. While most of us have seen individuals who say they are co-teaching, in fact the literature is replete with example after example of partnerships that did not meet these criteria (e.g., Keefe & Moore, 2004; Trent et al., 2003; Weiss & Lloyd, 2002). For *true* co-teaching to occur, these elements need to be in place. Otherwise, what we will have is a diluted version of co-teaching—one that may not result in the ideal outcomes for students and teachers. Consider the Co-Teaching Component Checklist provided in Figure 2.2. After reading the brief description of each component, do you think your current or past situations (if you've had them) would qualify as effective co-teaching?

For *true* co-teaching, educators need to co-plan, co-instruct, and co-assess.

Co-Teaching Components Checklist

Co-Teaching Component	Description of Component	Check if Present ☑
Two or more adults	Two or more adults are physically in the same room at the same time working with a group of students.	
Both professionals	Both of the adults are considered "professionals." (This is not meant to be a judgment call, by which you look at your colleague and think, "Well, he's not very professional most of the time!") This means that credentialed teachers, speech pathologists, school psychologists, Title I teachers, and ESL teachers would qualify, while paraprofessionals, student teachers, and parent volunteers would not.	
Working collaboratively	Are the two of you engaging in shared decision making and problem solving? Are you "playing nicely," or are you merely physically in the room at the same time, sharing the space?	
Delivering substantive instruction	This is one that is often missing in many "co-taught" classes. Are both of you (not just the general education classroom teacher) actually providing direct instruction to the class? If the special service provider is merely walking around and providing supports, that does not qualify as co-teaching.	
To a heterogeneous group of students	So far, every classroom I've ever been in qualifies for this one. If your class has students with different learning styles, preferences, genders, ethnicities, cultures, languages, or interests, you have a heterogeneous class. Don't wait to have a student with an IEP to consider yourself heterogeneous or inclusive; the typical class requires differentiation also.	
In the same physical space	If you and your partner always take turns in the room (e.g., "during the 20 minutes you are teaching them, I'll go make copies"), you may not be co-teaching. If you split the week, you may be job sharing. If you take "your kids" to "your other room," you are essentially resorting to "pull out."	

EZ Reference

Figure 2.2   Co-Teaching Component Checklist

Benefits of Co-Teaching

Why co-teach? Because there are numerous benefits, of course. Sometimes it is helpful to review those benefits, particularly if you and your colleagues are overwhelmed by the prospect of this paradigm shift. I am providing these in an easy-to-read bullet format but feel free to check out some of the excellent articles and resources for yourself. In addition, while I first provide the benefits to students—which are important, not to mention plentiful—I also provide the reported benefits to teachers. Let's face it, if teachers aren't happy, *ain't* no one happy! (For the language arts teachers reading this text, my apologies. I clearly meant to write, "If teachers are not in high spirits, no one else is exuberant either.") As teachers feel rejuvenated and empowered by the strategies and learning they glean from one another, they too will be more willing to bring those strategies to the classroom to improve the instruction for all students.

Benefits for Students ~

- Access to the general curriculum for students with disabilities (Bauwens & Hourcade, 1997; Cook & Friend, 1995; Murawski, 2005a).
- Positive social outcomes for students with and without disabilities (Hunt, Alwell, Farron-Davis, & Goetz, 1996; Pugach & Wesson, 1995).
- Increased student engagement and increased use of strategies by students (Boudah, Schumaker, & Deshler, 1997).
- More individual attention and more interaction with teachers (Murawski, 2006; Zigmond, Magiera, & Matta, 2003).
- Improves students' social skills and self-concept through the reduction of pull-out situations that are thought to be potentially stigmatizing for students (Jones & Carlier, 1995; Salend et al., 1997; Walther-Thomas, 1997).
- Benefits to students with disabilities include increased self-confidence and self-esteem, enhanced academic performance, increased social skills, and stronger peer relations (Walther-Thomas, 1997; Weichel, 2001).
- Benefits to students without disabilities who participated in co-taught arrangements include improved academic performance, increased time and attention from teachers, increased emphasis on cognitive strategies and study skills, increased emphasis on social skills, and improved classroom communities (Walther-Thomas, 1997; Weichel, 2001).
- Delivery of services and modifications can be provided to students with academic difficulties or who are considered at-risk without requiring those students to be labeled as needing special education (Bauwens & Hourcade, 1997; Salend, et al., 1997).
- Students with disabilities had a more positive attitude, were provided with role models for behavior and learning, interacted more with nondisabled peers, and were exposed to higher level concepts and discussions than was typically found in a segregated special education setting (Dieker, 1998; Murawski, 2006).
- Jones and Carlier (1995) also reflected on the benefits to students with multiple disabilities when engaged in a co-taught setting and found that these students increased the amount of interactions they initiated, exhibited increased self-confidence, decreased aggressive/noncompliant acts, and that students without disabilities interacted "more naturally" (p. 26) with them over time.
- The provision of individualized instruction through the use of differentiated instructional groupings and strategies made possible by having two teachers in the room is a key benefit for students with mild disabilities (Murawski & Dieker, 2004; Walsh & Snyder, 1993).
- Co-teaching approaches for bilingual classrooms have been found to produce significant possibilities for students, to include strong student-student relationships and increased student self-esteem (Bahamonde & Friend, 1999).
- Behavioral and academic expectations remain high for students with and without disabilities (Dieker, 2001; Murawski, 2006).
- Students with disabilities preferred to have co-teachers in content classes they deemed "difficult." They also preferred to have their needs met in general education classes rather than to receive services through a resource setting. Students in inclusive classrooms had higher self-concept in the areas of social skills and academic self-esteem than those students in resource classrooms (Murawski, 2006).

Benefits For Teachers ~

- Teachers involved in co-teaching relationships state that this relationship resulted in increased professional satisfaction, opportunities for professional growth, personal support, and opportunities for collaboration (Walther-Thomas, 1997; Weiss & Brigham, 2000).

- Special education teachers gain insight into the realities of the general classroom while general educators learn valuable lessons in planning, accommodating, and instructing students with learning or behavioral difficulties (Friend & Cook, 2007; Salend et al., 1997).

- Teachers working together leads by extension to increased friendships, which can in turn increase both morale and student performance (Salend et al., 1997; Weiss & Brigham, 2000).

- Having two teachers in one room allows for experimentation with new teaching methodologies (Giangreco, Baumgart, & Doyle, 1995; Murawski, 2006).

- Co-teaching makes it easier to conduct hands-on activities and provide flexible testing situations (Cross & Walker-Knight, 1997). Co-teaching enables whole group instruction to be provided while still meeting individual needs (Adams & Cessna, 1993; Murawski & Dieker, 2004).

- Co-teaching provides for more on-task time as both teachers are able to manage behavior (Cross & Walker-Knight, 1997; Gerber & Popp, 1999). In fact, co-teachers will spend significantly less time having to conduct direct behavior management than teachers instructing alone (Weichel, 2001).

- Co-teaching encourages teachers to share expertise, providing one another with valuable feedback (Cross & Walker-Knight, 1997; Hughes & Murawski, 2001).

- Co-teaching allows educators to assist one another in addressing issues related to content, accountability, and structure (Dieker & Murawski, 2003).

- Educators who had experienced co-teaching found that they were more energized and creative, were able to trust one another, and had more fun teaching (Adams & Cessna, 1993; Murawski, 2003).

- Hohenbrink, Johnston, and Westhoven (1997) reported on their own personal experiences with co-teaching and stated that it prompted self-reflection and led to significant changes in their understandings and teaching practices.

- Gately and Gately (2001) stated that as co-teachers move into the collaborative stage of interaction, "communication, humor, and a high degree of comfort punctuate the co-teaching, collaborative classroom" (p. 42).

- In a survey of special and general education teachers engaged in co-teaching, special education teachers reported increased job satisfaction, while general and special educators alike noted that co-teaching increased both teaching and learning potential (Bauwens et al., 1989).

- Research studies on co-teaching have found that the value added by having a special education teacher in the room to co-teach resulted in more individual attention for students, more on-task student behavior, and more interaction with teachers (Murawski, 2006; Zigmond et al., 2003).

A true benefit to co-teaching? Having a partner to help with all the silliness!

Barriers to Co-Teaching

Naturally, any time there are benefits to an educational initiative, there are always going to be some barriers as well; nothing of value comes easily. Here are the most commonly identified barriers in the literature on co-teaching. Although each one has its own complexities, I am simplifying them here just as a way to recognize they exist and to note them early on. Some are definitely more serious than others, but each one can cause individuals or schools interested in implementing co-teaching to pause and reconsider. I don't want to minimize the impact each of these barriers can have, but at the same time, I don't want to dwell on issues. Each of these barriers will be addressed in this text so if you read on and implement the guidelines suggested throughout the text, you will find that these barriers are eliminated or at least greatly diminished.

Common Barriers to Effective Co-Teaching

Barrier	Description of Issue
Lack of training or professional development	Teachers with little to no actual training on what co-teaching should or should not look like are frequently told to co-teach with someone. This lack of professional development has led many teachers to have a negative experience with co-teaching. In addition, those teachers who have managed to make their relationship work reported that they often spent way more time trying to figure out for themselves what co-teaching should entail than they would have needed to had some upfront training been provided to them.
Personality or philosophical clashes	Personalities matter. Just like any relationship, if two people are put together for a significant time, especially if they are asked to make joint decisions regarding the education of children, it is helpful if they can compromise, collaborate, and communicate. If their personalities are so different that they struggle to connect with one another and genuinely do not enjoy being together, the students pick up on the negative vibes and the results are generally not positive—for students or for teachers.
Limited resources	Resources are always a big issue in schools and co-teaching can impact those resources. Resources might be human (e.g., not enough teachers to co-teach in all the desired classes) or material (e.g., not enough desks, tables, or teacher's guides); regardless of the issue, resource concerns can cause friction between teachers and with administrators.
Scheduling issues	Scheduling is a major concern, especially with a paradigm shift as large as inclusive education can be. For schools that already include children with special needs, this may not be as big a difficulty; for those that are just now increasing their inclusiveness, this may be a huge headache.
Reluctance to lose control	Control is hard to give up, especially when for teachers who are used to having control—of their class, students, caseload, schedule, or content. Sharing that control with another individual, particularly someone who has a different area of expertise, is difficult at best.

Barrier	Description of Issue
Lack of time	Having sufficient time to plan with one's co-teacher has been identified as the number one factor for ensuring success, or conversely the number one barrier to success when it is absent. While some teachers find ways to make time to plan and collaborate, others lament the lack of time and resort to simply providing in-class support or other options. I have never heard of a teacher who feels that he has sufficient time to do all the things he is asked to do as an educator. The good news is that, after a while, co-teaching can actually help teachers find time.
Lack of administrative support	There is a big reason I chose to include a Matchmaker, Matchmaker: The Role of the Administrator section in each of the four parts of this text. It's simple; look at each item mentioned above. Administrators play a key role in (a) providing teachers with professional development related to any new educational initiative, (b) determining partnerships between co-teachers, (c) obtaining and doling out resources among faculty and staff, (d) creating the master schedule, (e) enabling teachers to feel free to try new things and *lose* a little control, and (f) finding or creating time for teachers to plan, share, and collaborate. Obviously, the support of the administrative staff at a school is critical. When administrators support in name only, teachers know it. This will translate to minimum time and effort on the faculty's part as well. Administrators set the tone for the success—or failure—of inclusive practices, such as co-teaching.

THE DO'S AND DON'TS OF CO-TEACHING ■

While the Co-Teaching Components Checklist (Figure 2.2 on page 27) delineates the characteristics required for effective co-teaching to occur, the Do's and Don'ts of Co-Teaching (Figure 2.3 on page 41) provided in the EZ Reference format clarifies even more the difference between what we often see in the classroom and what should be occurring for true co-teaching. This EZ Reference format makes it simple for you to copy and disseminate this form to other educators (or parents or other related stakeholders) if you have the job of clarifying what co-teaching should look like—and what it shouldn't. Too often, I hear teachers who are looking at this form say, "Oops! That's us—over there on the *don'ts* side." If that is true of your former co-teaching relationships, however, give yourself a break. Maybe you didn't know. Now that you do, though, there should be no excuses. That said, keep in mind that I am a huge proponent of baby steps. If you and your partner read this list and realize that you are not ready to jump into all aspects of co-teaching, identify which parts you feel comfortable with right now, which ones you think you will be able to implement relatively soon, and which ones you will need to wait for a while to fully embrace. I'm not giving you a full pass here, though; when I say, "Wait for a while," we are not talking about a year, or two, or five. Take your baby steps and in time you will walk confidently. Soon you'll be running. Just decide here and now that you will not return to crawling.

Allow me to clarify each of these guidelines for co-teaching.

◄ Guideline 1 ►	
Co-teaching is	**Co-teaching is *not***
two or more co-equal (preferably credentialed) faculty working together.	a teacher and an assistant, teacher's aide, or paraprofessional.

Why does it matter if co-teachers are equal? Parity between educators is critical in establishing a shared classroom. If one teacher feels it is her classroom or that the students are hers, that teacher is less likely to be willing to share ownership, planning, instruction, and assessing. I have frequently had teachers tell me, "I understand that we are equals and that we are supposed to share, but I am the teacher of record and I am the one who has the ultimate responsibility so really I need to have the final say." *No!* That's just not accurate. In the co-taught classroom, both teachers are equally responsible for the outcomes—be they fabulous or awful. Just as the general education teacher should treat all the students as equals in the class, the special education teacher should also feel as responsible for general education students as he does for the students with special needs. Teachers must be able to sense from each other that they are truly sharing the responsibility for all students.

If students do not achieve satisfactorily, I would expect the administrators to talk to both teachers about why that happened, not just one. If students achieve above what was expected, again I would expect that both teachers would be lauded, not just one. Having a "teacher of record" in the classroom is merely a way to demonstrate for legal (i.e., NCLB) purposes that one of the teachers in the room is highly qualified in the subject area content. It does not mean that teacher is the *main, real, primary,* or *lead* teacher—at least not if both teachers are equally qualified otherwise. It merely identifies the content area expert; the other teacher should be seen as the pedagogical expert (e.g., expert in teaching strategies). Certainly, many special educators are indeed highly qualified in finding ways to help struggling students succeed; that is equally as important as knowing subject matter. It should also be noted at the elementary level that many special educators also possess their multiple subject credentials; thus, they too are subject matter experts.

Many teachers, especially special educators, have taught classes with a paraprofessional's assistance and, in so doing, have found that some paraprofessionals are very capable of quality instruction. While this may be so, there are multiple reasons why a class should not be considered *co-taught* if both educators are not equally trained and credentialed. First of all, paraprofessionals have not had the level of training that credentialed teachers have. Too often, general education teachers are unaware that there is such a disparity between special education teachers and special education paraprofessionals. More than once, when I have asked a classroom teacher who I know works with a special educator, if the person who comes in his room daily is a special education teacher or paraprofessional. The response is often, "I don't know. Is there a difference?" There certainly is. First, Giangreco and Broer (2005) report that paraprofessionals often have the least amount of training and education and are asked to work with the students who need the most amount of assistance. Second, the job description of a paraprofessional or teachers' assistant does not typically include planning or assessing students. Work outside of the school day is the responsibility of a teacher, not a paraeducator. A particular paraprofesssional may be fantastic at helping run stations in the classroom or at helping provide modifications to individual students, but she or he will generally not be involved in sharing all three aspects of the teaching: planning, instructing, and assessing. Third, ultimately, parity in classroom decision making does not exist between teachers and those who are not credentialed teachers (e.g., paraeducators, parents, adult volunteers). If these two individuals disagree, the teacher determines the outcome (whether the teacher's opinion is right or not). This can create a situation wherein the students quickly realize who the "real" teacher is and then tend to play on that dynamic.

In a co-taught class with two equals, on the other hand, there is no "mine" or "yours." This should be true of any marriage or parenting partnership too—be it the first, second, or third marriage. Special and general educators alike need to be careful not to refer to students as "my kids" or "your kids." Neither should trump the other in terms of power. If two credentialed teachers disagree about something in the classroom, they need to communicate and collaborate effectively to come up with a decision in private, away from the students. Occasionally, they may need to agree to disagree. At times, a decision is required and the two teachers may not be able to agree. What do you do then? One option is to defer to the general education teacher for any content or curricular decisions and to defer to the special services provider for any differentiation, modification, strategies, or accommodation decisions.

⦿ Guideline 2 ⦿	
Co-teaching is	**Co-teaching is *not***
conducted in the same classroom at the same time.	when a few students are pulled out of the classroom on a regular basis to work with the special educator. It is also not job sharing, where teachers teach different days.

Why does it matter if co-teachers are in the same classroom at the same time? In staying with the marriage analogy, it isn't cohabitation if both partners are living in separate houses. Weiss and Lloyd (2002) pointed out in their research that many teachers have been put into what are called *co-taught* classes but are not engaging in what the literature supports as co-teaching, that is, two teachers teaching as a team. Instead, I frequently hear teachers talk about the kids who "can't make it" so those students are pulled out of the class for instruction or assessment. When this is done on a regular basis, it simply defeats the purpose of collaborative instruction and what we are seeing is essentially a return to the old, comfortable—but ineffective—method of "pullout." In fact, this might even be worse than the traditional pullout. Consider how very stigmatizing it is when the student is in a general education class and is regularly asked to leave with the special educator during instruction or for testing. That is like putting a neon sign over that student's head that says, "Make fun of me at recess. I'm in Special Ed." Don't think that pulling two

Want More on This Topic?

Get a myriad of strategies for instructing all students jointly in Part IV: The Marriage, especially Chapter 13, Working Together to Wrangle the Li'l Rascals.

students who are at risk in addition to the four students with IEPs is a tricky way to argue that it is a heterogeneous group. If you are always pulling the same students to go with the same teacher, the kids figure this out pretty quickly. All six of those students will become targets of ridicule, regardless of their labels. Instead, be cognizant of who is being pulled, by whom, for what, and how often. In addition, what we find out is that, as students are pulled out during instruction because they don't know the content, they end up falling further and further behind. By the way, pulling those same six kids to the kidney-shaped table at the back of the room everyday to work with the special educator or Title I teacher is equivalent to pulling them out of the room. I address how to work with students who are falling behind later. There *is* a way to do it without stigmatizing these students. Check out Guideline 3 to see why tracking in the classroom is not a good idea either.

⟪ Guideline 3 ⟫	
Co-teaching is	**Co-teaching is *not***
conducted with heterogeneous groups.	pulling a group of students with disabilities to the back of the general education classroom.

Why does it matter if groups are heterogeneous? As mentioned previously, pulling the same group of students regularly results in the very stigma and segregation that inclusive education is trying to avoid. In addition, the research has been very supportive of heterogeneous and flexible grouping. Cooperative groups have been demonstrated to raise student assessment results when groups are formed heterogeneously, randomly, and with proper group size (Barley et al., 2002; Bouris, Creel, & Stortz, 1998; Cohen, Raudenbush, & Ball, 2003). O'Rourke (2007, pp. 18–19) writes,

> In a synthesis of recent research practices, Barley and colleagues (2002) determined that cooperative groups are a successful instructional strategy for "at risk students." Additionally, these researchers determined that cooperative groups should be formed in a heterogeneous fashion to include varying skill levels, abilities, and needs within groupings. After reviewing ten studies of heterogeneous cooperative groups, positive assessment results were identified for all of the low-achieving and at-risk students (Barley et al., 2002). Ability groupings, or forming cooperative groups based on similar abilities, have not demonstrated improved student assessment results and in fact may adversely affect student morale. A recent meta-analysis demonstrates that ability groups have not helped students with or without learning disabilities increase their understanding of content. "Using pretest and posttest scores, the study showed that ability grouping did not influence the achievement of low- or high-ability students" (Barley et al., 2002). Ability groupings may in fact adversely affect student and assessment results by creating

low self-esteem, lowering expectations of students and separating abilities. (Rea, McLaughlin, & Walther-Thomas, 2002)

It's amazing to me that, even though the current practice of whole group instruction within inclusive courses has proven ineffective (Bottge, Heinrichs, Mehta, & Hung, 2002; Calhoon & Fuchs, 2003), we still continue to see teachers resorting daily to large class, whole-group instruction, even with the knowledge that there are individuals with special needs in the class. Having heterogeneous groups is helpful to all students, not just those with disabilities, which is important for teachers and family members to know. Fortune 500 companies report that their number one desired characteristic for employees is teamwork; they want individuals who can work collaboratively with others. We need to start that skill building early in their academic careers. In addition, O'Rourke (2007) reminds us that "when students work in groups, they receive the benefit of peer assistance, exposure to differing opinions, and the ability to talk through concepts to solidify their knowledge" (p. 15). How are students going to get that if all students with learning needs are pulled together constantly? The research conducted by Gaines (2006) and O'Rourke (2007) found that flexible grouping in co-taught settings resulted in students with learning disabilities participating and succeeding in even the most challenging of math groups. Other research by Garrison (2004) and Siegel (2004) found that classrooms that used student-based learning, brainstorming ideas, debates, and learning from one another resulted in increased academic achievement. Let's also not forget the social benefits of heterogeneous groups. Membership in peer groups is important at the elementary level, as students are beginning to develop affinities and common interests. As teachers, we have the ability to positively facilitate those social interactions. Sure, we have to teach the younger students how to work together, sit still, share, and play nicely . . . but wasn't that in the job description for an elementary school teacher?

◖ Guideline 4 ◗	
Co-teaching is	**Co-teaching is *not***
when both teachers plan for instruction together. The general education teacher (GET) is the content specialist while the special education teacher (SET) or special service provider (SSP) is the expert on individualizing and delivery to various learning modalities.	when the GET plans all lessons and the SET walks in to the room and says, "What are we doing today and what would you like me to do?"

Why does it matter if educators are co-planning or not? I have already reviewed why parity is so important between educators and that is definitely part of the rationale for this component. However, co-planning is more than just establishing parity. It is actually the *key* to effective co-teaching.

Both educators need to feel that they are important to this relationship. There needs to be a reason each person is present. When one partner feels that she is superfluous (or not necessary) in a relationship, a few things may happen: (1) she may begin to badmouth the relationship to others; (2) he may begin to spend time elsewhere, doing things that feel valued or more important; (3) she

Want More on This Topic?

In Part III: The Wedding, there is much more on the intricacies of co-planning.

may begin to spend time with others who appreciate her skills; or (4) he may simply continue with the status quo, doing far less than he is able to do and feeling underutilized and underappreciated but powerless to change. Do any of these situations sound positive to you? No. This is a recipe for divorce. Similar to real marriages, the research on co-teaching has supported that these things happen in co-teaching as well. Special service providers often note that they feel like "glorified aides" and so they may describe co-teaching as ineffective, their partners as uncollaborative, or the situations as unproductive. In lieu of showing up and just walking around for proximity control, special service providers may instead resort to pulling students out, staying in their own classrooms or offices to do paperwork, or going to work in other classrooms with teachers who empower them. General educators who feel superfluous may ignore the students with disabilities, let the other educator "take care of those kids," or may leave the room to do other work when it is the special educator's turn to present information or strategies.

On the other hand, if co-teachers plan jointly, they are both able to actively participate and, in doing so, utilize their areas of expertise. Both will feel valued and will be able to see the outcomes of their participation in the success of the students. In Chapter 11 on co-planning, I provide co-teachers with multiple tips for how to use co-planning time wisely and how to ensure that your lessons incorporate both of your strengths. The level of differentiation that can occur when two professionals with different areas of expertise co-plan is impressive; since almost all classes today are inclusive in nature, and certainly are heterogeneous in nature, why wouldn't you want to have that type of input in your lesson planning?

Co-planning is a key aspect of successful co-teaching.

◖◌ **Guideline 5** ◌◗	
Co-teaching is	**Co-teaching is *not***
when both teachers provide substantive instruction together—having planned together, the SET can grade homework, teach content, facilitate activities, and so forth.	when the SET walks around the room all period or just sits and takes notes as the GET teaches the content.

Why does it matter if both teachers are engaged in substantive instruction? We have already established the importance of co-planning to ensure that both teachers are actively engaged in determining what will be taught in the inclusive classroom. This component focuses on the actual instruction conducted during the school day. Just as the special service provider should be adding in his expertise during the proactive planning, so too should he be involved during the actual instruction. This serves multiple purposes.

First, we all know elementary students. If an adult is in the room, the students will want to know who he is and what his role is in the classroom. This will vary in terms of lower elementary and upper elementary. In the lower grades, I have found that students see all adults as possible helpers. A FedEx worker might walk into the room and students would yell out, "Could you come here and help me?" or "Look at this, Teacher!" There is much more acceptance of multiple adults in the room. In the upper grades, however, students tend to want to identify and test adult authority. If one teacher is always taking the lead role in direct instruction, the students will quickly pick up on that and the other teacher will find herself offering to help a student and hearing in response, "No thanks. I'll wait for the *real* teacher," or the special educator will simply get the brush-off as the student bides his time waiting for the general education teacher to be free for a question. Thus, getting "face time" in front of students is critical in establishing our shared authority in the classroom. It tells the students that both teachers are equals and respect one another as professionals.

Second, having one educator take on the burden of planning, teaching, and grading, while the other teacher merely walks around or sits and takes notes, will quickly result in a feeling of jealousy, bitterness, or resentment. Why should one work so hard while the other gets to sit back and relax? Keep in mind that part of collaboration is a matter of public relations, or PR. Most of us are aware of the responsibilities of a classroom teacher; we have all been in school for many years. Not all teachers, on the other hand, are aware of the responsibilities and daily requirements of a special educator—especially given the recent changes in job requirements based on IDEIA 2004 and NCLB. Don't be surprised if some general educators think that their special education counterparts are lucky to only have to teach a few students at a time and not have to know any content since all of their students are slow learners. Co-teachers need to clarify to one another what their current job responsibilities entail and what they are reasonably able to contribute when dividing the tasks of planning, instructing, and assessing the co-taught class.

Want More on This Topic?

Additional strategies are given in Chapters 5 and 13 for SETs who need to co-teach a class in which they struggle with the content.

Third, an equally important rationale for ensuring that both educators share instruction, is that it is a way to force both partners to get to know one another's roles. Too often in the past, general educators have deferred any knowledge of modifications, accommodations, differentiation, or even knowing about students' disabilities to their special education colleagues. Similarly, special educators have focused on individual needs to the exclusion of learning any particular content area in depth. For example, I might know that students are learning about the planets in fourth grade, but I don't know what the expectations are or what exactly they are learning. While it is acceptable, and indeed encouraged, for partners to have their own areas of expertise in the co-taught classroom, it is not acceptable for them not to begin to share responsibilities for content and student needs. Special service educators need to educate their partners about the kids in the class, how they learn best, what instructional strategies may be more successful, and why certain assessment techniques may be invalid given student characteristics. General educators need to educate their partners about the scope and sequence of the curriculum, what most learners know at this grade/age, and why certain big ideas are the most important for this content. Knowing that she will be responsible for helping to teach phonemic awareness, or long division, or haikus, or the 50 states, and so forth, is a major impetus for the special educator to get the text and begin to relearn that content. Depending on the content area and backgrounds of different teachers, this may be more intense and difficult for some, but it is helpful if both team members are able to stay a few steps ahead of the students content-wise. In addition to helping co-teach the class, being ahead in terms of content is also a benefit for teachers who are responsible for review classes, study skills classes, learning labs, or standardized test preparation.

◆❦ Guideline 6 ❧◆	
Co-teaching is	**Co-teaching is *not***
when both teachers assess and evaluate student progress, IEP goals are kept in mind, as are the curricular goals and standards for that grade level.	when the GET grades "his kids" and the SET grades "her kids"—or when the GET grades all the students and the SET surreptitiously changes the grades and calls it "modifying after the fact."

Why does it matter if assessment and grading is shared? As children get older, grades become more influential. Parents look to grades to see if their children are studying and learning enough, and both students and teachers are assessed based on those grades. Parents see grades as an indicator of learning, of achievement, and of whether or not they are getting their "money's worth." Grades tell parents whether their children are doing their work or slacking off. In this era of accountability, even schools are not exempt from being graded. If students don't do well, teachers are identified as poor educators; if teachers don't do well, schools are identified as weak schools. Despite the fact that expert after expert has shown that multiple measures are needed to truly assess an individual's skills in an area, grades are often seen as the major indicator of a child's mastery of the content.

In addition, teachers feel strongly about their grades and what those grades reflect about themselves as instructors. Determining how students will be assessed—and ultimately graded— remains a key point of contention between many general and special educators. Suffice it to say for now that general and special educators have different frames of reference and do tend to look at assessments very differently. For a successful collaborative relationship, co-teachers

Want More on This Topic?

Chapter 3 addresses the different frames of reference teachers may have. Chapter 15 reviews a variety of ways that teachers may choose to evaluate students.

need to decide jointly and proactively how all students will be assessed and how grades will be determined. Allowing each of you to separately assess "your own kids" simply removes the parity and sharing of responsibility that is required in a successful co-taught classroom.

⫷ Guideline 7 ⫸	
Co-teaching is	**Co-teaching is *not***
when teachers maximize the benefits of having two teachers in the room by having both teachers actively engaged with students. Examples of different co-teaching approaches include Team Teaching, Station Teaching, Parallel Teaching, Alternative Teaching, and One Teach, One Support (see Friend & Cook, 2007).	when teachers take turns being "in charge" of the class so that the other teacher can get caught up in grading photocopying, making phone calls, creating IEPs, etc.—or when students remain in the large-group setting in lecture format as teachers rotate who gets to "talk at them."

Why does it matter if a variety of instructional approaches is used? Think back to when you were in school. Do you remember your favorite teachers or classes? Your least favorite teachers or classes? Chances are the ones you enjoyed the most were the ones in which you were engaged. The ones that felt like they were interminable are usually the ones in which the teacher droned on and on while students were expected to sit, listen, take notes, and keep quiet. We know that with the increased use of technology, students are now used to multitasking and getting information rapidly, like never before. They text, e-mail, listen to iPods, go on Web quests, create YouTube videos for each other, and can even fast-forward through commercials. In fact, I'm willing to bet that in a boring lecture-based class, they are doing many of these things concurrently (and wishing they could fast-forward through the lecture). Why then would we relegate these students to the old way of teaching when (1) we know it is *not* the most effective approach to instruction and (2) we actually have the manpower to do things differently? This is not to say that direct instruction via lecture should be thrown out altogether; it has its place. Some instructors are able to present information directly in an engaging manner, and some students prefer to get their information orally. It is however important to recognize that it should not be the only, or even primary, manner by which students learn content.

As a classroom teacher, I remember learning about best practices in education and genuinely wanting to implement them. As often as not, I felt thwarted, not by a reluctance to try the new approaches, but rather by the logistics involved. I either had too many students, too small a classroom, or not enough time. I found that having a co-teacher helped me address many of the best practices I was eager to employ. For example, my university coursework taught me that having a smaller student-teacher ratio is best, that teachers are encouraged to address students' learning styles and Gardner's (2006) multiple intelligences, and that cooperative learning groups are a great way to involve a heterogeneous class. I wasn't sure how to implement these techniques, though. As a rookie teacher, I benefited from being paired with a veteran teacher who was willing to try new things. I was the "expert" in the new practices; she was the "expert" in tried-and-true techniques. This partnership resulted in a natural mentoring opportunity. It helped me as a novice teacher feel more comfortable in the classroom, but it also enabled me to implement techniques I may not otherwise have been able to implement. My partner also shared that as a veteran, she benefited from seeing the new "ivory tower techniques" that might normally have been squelched by the realities of day-to-day teaching.

We weren't the only ones who benefited from our relationship. Students were motivated to learn, and my partner and I were able to get more creative in our instruction. We found we were able to increase motivation and create a recursive loop of positive interaction between ourselves and the students. Could I have done all this alone? I don't think so. Not to the extent to which I have done it with partners. Using co-teaching time to simply divide the class and to continue to do what we have always done separately doesn't make sense to me, nor will most administrators feel compelled to support having two credentialed teachers in a room when they are not doing anything substantively different with students. So get out of your comfort zone—try something new.

Want More on This Topic?

Chapter 13, Working Together to Wrangle the Li'l Rascals, provides tons of strategies for co-instruction.

◖ Guideline 8 ◗	
Co-teaching is	**Co-teaching is _not_**
when teachers reflect on the progress and process, offering one another feedback on teaching styles, content, activities, and other items pertinent to improving the teaching situation.	when teachers get frustrated with one another and tell the rest of the faculty in the teachers' lounge or when one teacher simply tells the other teacher what to do and how to do it.

Why does it matter if teachers reflect and communicate? In this respect, co-teaching is more like a marriage than in any other respect; communication is critical. If co-teachers are not able to share with one another, the relationship is doomed. It is not important that colleagues agree on everything; in fact, diversity is a strength of the co-taught classroom, but it is important that they discuss the areas in which they disagree. If one partner is frustrated with the way the class is being handled or with an aspect of the collaborative relationship, he needs to tell his partner. Dieker's (2004) *Co-Teaching Lesson Plan Book* provides a structure for co-teachers to reflect on the progress of their relationship. Whether co-teachers

Want More on This Topic?

Chapter 5, Getting to Know Your Partner, provides additional information on the manner in which feedback can and should be given.

choose to use a regular structure or not, one of my biggest tips to you *newlyweds* is to remember that anything you have to say about the co-teaching relationship, the kids in the co-taught classroom, or your co-teaching partner, needs to be said to your partner *first*. Venting occasionally to others may seem innocuous, but you will probably find that (1) those same individuals will not want to co-teach in the future because you have given them a negative view of it, (2) your partner will eventually hear about your frustrations and the situation will get blown out of proportion, and (3) there will be no positive improvement in the situation because your partner is unaware of your feelings. The answer? Talk. A lot. Frequently. With each other.

Do's and Don'ts of Co-Teaching

Co-teaching is	Co-teaching is *not*
two or more co-equal, preferably credentialed, faculty working together.	a teacher and an assistant, teacher's aide, or paraprofessional.
conducted in the same classroom at the same time.	when a few students are pulled out of the classroom on a regular basis to work with the special educator. It is also not job sharing, where teachers teach different days.
conducted with heterogeneous groups.	pulling a group of students with disabilities to the back of the general education class.
when both teachers plan for instruction together. The general education teacher (GET) is the content specialist while the special education teacher (SET) is the expert on individualizing and delivery to various learning modalities.	when the general education teacher (GET) plans all lessons and the special education teacher (SET) walks in to the room and says, "what are we doing today and what would you like me to do?"
when both teachers provide *substantive* instruction together. Having planned together, the SET can grade homework, teach content, facilitate activities, etc.	when the SET walks around the room all period or just sits and takes notes as the GET teaches the content.
when both teachers assess and evaluate student progress. IEP goals are kept in mind, as are the curricular goals and standards for that grade level.	when the GET grades "his" kids and the SET grades "her" kids – or when the GET grades all students and the SET surreptitiously changes the grades and calls it "modifying after the fact."
when teachers maximize the benefits of having two teachers in the room by having both teachers actively engaged with students. Examples of different co-teaching models include Team Teaching, Station Teaching, Parallel Teaching, Alternative Teaching, and One Teach, One Support (see Friend & Cook, 2003).	when teachers take turns being "in charge" of the class so that the other teacher can get caught up in grading, photocopying, making phone calls, creating IEPs, etc., or when students remain in the large-group setting in lecture-format as teachers rotate who gets to "talk at them."
when teachers reflect on the progress and process, offering one another feedback on teaching styles, content, activities, and other items pertinent to improving the teaching situation.	when teachers get frustrated with one another and tell the rest of the faculty in the teachers' lounge or when one teacher simply tells the other teacher what to do and how to do it.

EZ Reference

Figure 2.3   Do's and Don'ts of Co-Teaching

SOURCE: First published in Murawski, W. W. (2002a).

3

General Educators Are From Jupiter; Special Service Providers Are From Saturn

■ RECOGNIZING DIFFERENT FRAMES OF REFERENCE

One of the most commonly cited benefits of co-teaching is the fact that two individuals with decidedly different training, experiences, education and perspectives are coming together to instruct students who are equally diverse. Yet it is for those same reasons that many educators have difficulty working collaboratively. Differing opinions, frames of reference, and viewpoints lead to increased frustration, disagreements, and even arguments. While opposites may attract, we all know that there must also be some common ground for any relationship to continue to grow and blossom. Understanding where your partner is coming from is the first step to a successful experience. While many states are moving quickly toward dual certifications so that both general and special educators are trained to work with students with and without disabilities in inclusive classes, the majority of our current workforce consists of teachers trained in programs where special and general education teachers are prepared very differently. Let's consider some of the major factors influencing potential co-teachers.

General education classroom teachers are viewed as the individuals able to "see the forest." Their training has entailed learning about students at different grade levels and developmental stages. They are aware of the standards, curriculum, and general requirements for their grade level(s) or subject area(s). They know what a typical learner should be able to do at the second-grade level in math or at the fifth-grade level in language arts. Traditionally, the focus of the general education classroom teacher is to instruct the class in a manner by which the majority of the students will be able to learn the content and move forward academically. Content specificity is a job requirement. In fact, the importance of having a teacher who has his or her multiple subject credential and thereby is highly qualified was a major component of the No Child Left Behind Act (NCLB) of 2001, for students with and without disabilities. While inclusion and differentiation are usually mentioned in general education teacher preparation programs, that information may be cursory at best. Ironically, instruction in co-teaching—in which the emphasis is on parity, communication, and collaboration—is seldom included in general education preservice programs, meaning only one partner in the potential partnership has been trained on what to expect of a co-teaching situation. My marriage analogy? I liken this to the bride knowing all the details of the upcoming wedding, whereas the groom only knows (1) when to be there and (2) not to wear jeans.

Why the Jupiter analogy for general educators? Simple. Jupiter is the largest planet. Likewise, general education classroom teachers have the largest classes. In addition, Jupiter is typified by its red storm. As the primary classroom teacher for most students, general educators are usually the ones who have to weather all new initiatives, programs, and innovations. They are the ones who teach all students. If a storm is about to blow in, it is most likely the general education teachers who will experience it first and with the most students.

Special service providers are individuals with specialized training to work with subsets of students. In co-teaching situations, they are often special education teachers, but many states are increasing the co-teaching that occurs between classroom teachers and ESL teachers, Title I teachers, speech pathologists, school psychologists, and other specialists. These special service providers may have a completely different training and frame of reference from their general education counterparts. They are generally the ones who are taught to "see the trees." As such, the formal instruction for these areas is often focused on the individual learner's needs, be they academic, emotional, behavioral or social. Special service providers may identify themselves with the students on their caseloads, more so even than students in the various classes they teach or support. Coursework at the university level regularly requires these professionals to concentrate on one student for projects related to positive behavior support, assessment, individualized education programs (IEPs), instruction, academic modifications, and planning—as opposed to looking at a large number of students, such as that of a general education class. That is not to say that special service providers are not aware of the state standards or the scope and sequence of the curriculum; most are. However, despite the ability to know what most children are doing or able to do, the focus of these educators is typically on individuals who are struggling with competency due to a variety of factors, rather than a focus on the class at large.

The frame of reference of the special service provider is also frequently colored by their close working relationship with families and the ever-looming legal threat of "due process"; both of these issues tend not to impact the frame of reference of general education teachers as often. In addition, while issues related to inclusion and collaboration are increasingly taught and discussed in the area of special education, the themes of differentiation and individualization are emphasized as critical above all else. This can result in educators very capable of working one-on-one with students who have special needs and challenges, but who are less comfortable working in the typical elementary large-class setting. So, the special educator may have been taught how to "play nicely" and collaborate with a general education colleague but (a) that general educator may never have had any training in collaboration and (b) the special educator may not be comfortable teaching all students in a co-taught general education class. In addition, while professional development in co-teaching is increasingly included in special education programs, there is no indication that it is a regular component of preservice programs in ESL, speech and language, school psychology, or similar programs.

Why the Saturn analogy for special service providers? Just as Saturn is known for its rings, special service providers are known for juggling many programs, students, and schedules. Sometimes there are simply too many rings in the air at one time. In addition, Saturn is so light that, if it were small enough to fit in an ocean, it would float. Based on the numerous recent changes in the field, many special educators report a feeling of "floating" themselves. Too often, these are the people seen running back and forth in the halls from one classroom to another, from one meeting to the next, with no set space to call home and no real anchor. Not sure if you are from Jupiter or Saturn? Check out the characteristics in Figure 3.1 and then add aspects that characterize your own situation and frame of reference. Then share these with your potential co-teaching partners.

As noted by Friend and Cook (2007), frame of reference refers to experiences, acquired attitudes and beliefs, and personal qualities, as well as past and present feelings and expectations for others. Take a look at Figure 3.2. Your frame of reference affects what and how you observe and perceive a situation, and it influences how you respond to a situation. Two colleagues of mine, Sally Spencer and Amy Hanreddy, co-taught a class at our university to preservice teachers on collaboration, communication, and co-teaching. To clarify the concept of frame of reference, Sally came up with the idea of explaining it as a suitcase that you always carry around filled with artifacts of your home life, culture, beliefs, experiences, family, and community. They asked students to consider what would be in their own suitcases. As a model, Amy and Sally shared the major items in their own suitcases that they believed influenced who they are as people, instructors, friends, and now as co-teachers. Check out their example in Figure 3.3. I love this concept and am grateful to them for sharing this idea with me, and now with you.

Are You From Jupiter or Saturn? Share Your Characteristics	
Jupiter	**Saturn**
• I am a general education teacher.	• I am a special service provider.
• My classes are typically large (over 10 students).	• My classes/groups are typically small (under 10 students).
• I am a *highly qualified* content specialist.	• I am *highly qualified* in differentiation, modifications and individualization.
• I am always very aware of the pacing, curriculum, and standardized assessments related to my academic content.	• I am always very aware of the abilities, disabilities, goals, and benchmarks related to the students on my caseload.
• I typically conduct whole-group instruction.	• I typically conduct small-group or individual instruction.
Now note some of the personal characteristics that you think would be helpful for your colleague to know about you. What has made an impact on your frame of reference?	***Now note some of the personal characteristics that you think would be helpful for your colleague to know about you. What has made an impact on your frame of reference?***

Figure 3.1   Are You From Jupiter or Saturn? Share Your Characteristics

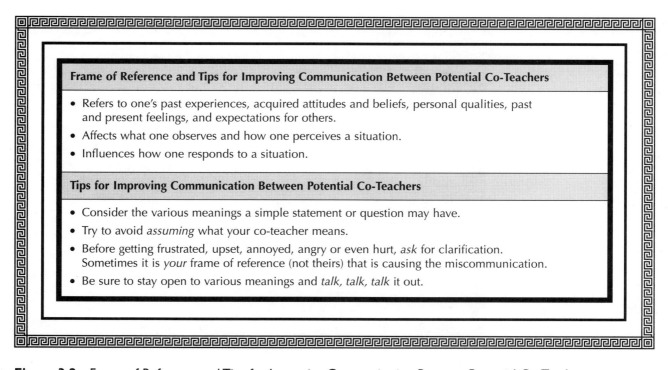

Frame of Reference and Tips for Improving Communication Between Potential Co-Teachers

- Refers to one's past experiences, acquired attitudes and beliefs, personal qualities, past and present feelings, and expectations for others.
- Affects what one observes and how one perceives a situation.
- Influences how one responds to a situation.

Tips for Improving Communication Between Potential Co-Teachers

- Consider the various meanings a simple statement or question may have.
- Try to avoid *assuming* what your co-teacher means.
- Before getting frustrated, upset, annoyed, angry or even hurt, *ask* for clarification. Sometimes it is *your* frame of reference (not theirs) that is causing the miscommunication.
- Be sure to stay open to various meanings and *talk, talk, talk* it out.

Figure 3.2   Frame of Reference and Tips for Improving Communication Between Potential Co-Teachers

Amy	Sally
Summers in Montana Thick glasses Single mom, only child Television! Theater lifestyle No religion Inclusive high school	Losing my dad Christmas and Easter Lightning bugs Playing kick the can on summer evenings Moving to England Loud family meals Sledding and snow angels Learning to read in kindergarten

Figure 3.3 Frame of Reference Suitcase Activity

SOURCE: Spencer, S. (2007).

Want More on This Topic?

The University of South Florida Clearinghouse has a multitude of realistic cases to discuss. Check them out at http://cases.coedu .usf.edu/TCases/Thats.htm.

Many thanks to Drs. Karen Colucci and Betty Epanchin for their permission to include this case as a teaching tool for this text.

Consider the upcoming case study, "I Am Solely Responsible," created from faculty and students at the University of South Florida for the Clearinghouse for Special Education Teaching Cases. Discuss with your potential co-teaching partner how you perceive this situation and what your response would be. See if you both have the same reactions. If not, why not? Is there something from your own suitcase (i.e., frame of reference) that is impacting how you are analyzing the actions, comments, or situation?

It's not always easy to agree with your co-teacher. If you have different frames of reference, remember, the key is to TALK IT OUT!

CASE STUDY: I Am Solely Responsible

Sharon Arkell, an experienced special education teacher, finds herself assigned to co-teach with another experienced teacher who refuses to relinquish any control in the classroom. The only suggestion offered to Sharon is to "be patient and don't rock the boat."

Sharon Arkell, a special educator, had been teaching in the same community of about 35,000 residents for 12 years. This year, her school district adopted a pro-inclusion policy and provided a two-day workshop for all teachers on inclusion and the collaborative teaching model. After completing the workshop, Sharon was first assigned to work with Betty, a fifth-grade teacher at her school. Betty had been teaching for 15 years and had received several teaching awards. She ran a very structured classroom and had high expectations for her students. She was known to wear a notebook around her neck the first three weeks of school, and to write down kids' names at the first infraction, so she could remember who needed to stay in from recess.

A former Title I teacher, Betty was used to having paraprofessionals in her classroom and was happy to have the extra help for students with special needs. By the end of the first week, Sharon had the impression that Betty viewed her in a similar light. Sharon felt that Betty expected her to be quiet and do what she was told. For instance, when Sharon spoke, she felt that Betty cut her off or found some reason to contradict her.

Sharon decided to talk to Betty about how she felt and asked to meet with her at the end of the day. "I wanted to talk to you about my role in the classroom," Sharon said. Betty was silent. "I have been feeling that my presence in the classroom is an annoyance to you, and I am concerned because I feel responsible for meeting the needs of the special education students within this classroom," Sharon continued.

Betty informed Sharon, in no uncertain terms, that this was her classroom. "It is fine with me that you look over the shoulders of your three students and help them keep up, but nothing else is your responsibility. It is important that the students know who the teacher is and having two adults doing the instructing will only confuse them."

"Well, I thought I was supposed to be co-teaching with you," Sharon replied.

Betty answered, "Well, for now I think it is best if I handle all of the instruction." In the weeks that followed, Sharon tried several times to talk to Betty about her discomfort with the situation. She brought in articles about inclusion and co-teaching in an attempt to enlighten Betty. When Sharon asked if she had read any of the articles, Betty responded, "I'm not sure I can handle this new approach to teaching."

Sharon took hope in those words "not sure." She went home thinking that the ambiguity contained in those words left some room for accepting the pro-inclusion and pro-collaborative teaching model. Her hopes were dashed, however, when Betty swept into the classroom the next morning saying, "I wrote this letter last night and I'm going to read it to you right now." Betty proceeded to read the letter aloud to Sharon. It included several reasons why Sharon should not be in her classroom. Betty argued that she was solely responsible for the education of her students and needed to be in control for their sake. She had a lot of content to cover and would be held accountable for the students' mastery of that content. She also felt that Sharon's presence only interfered with the efficient running of her class.

"Well, Betty, perhaps I could just work with the students out in the hall to give them some more individualized attention."

Betty responded, "You don't want them to feel different or separate from the rest of their classmates. That may embarrass them."

(Continued)

(Continued)

Sharon asked directly, "Is there any possibility of changing how things are being done?" Betty replied point-blank, "No, it will only confuse the students."

"But, Betty, they are already confused. They are not catching on to what you are teaching. They have trouble following your lecture format and completing all of the worksheets you use. I think we need to modify the instructional approach for them. I just found an article that discusses ways to meet individual students' needs by adapting things in the classroom. Cooperative learning activities, for example, are designed as activities that the whole class can take part in, but in small groups individual students' needs can be met and students can use each others' strengths for the group to be successful. I will bring it in," Sharon argued.

"My teaching methods have been successful for 15 years. I don't think that is what needs to change," Betty answered.

Sharon was exasperated and decided to share her view of the situation with the principal, Mary Allen. "I have been working with Betty since the beginning of the school year, and I feel she is not allowing me to do my job. She will not consider any of my suggestions for adapting curriculum to better meet the needs of my students and second guesses any action I take."

"Yes, I know Ms. Criner can be very controlling," Mrs. Allen responded in a soothing voice. "But, because this is your first year of collaborative teaching, why don't you just go along with her the best that you can. Maybe once you establish a relationship with her, she'll relinquish some of her authority. She is an excellent teacher, and her students always have high test scores. Don't rock the boat and see what happens."

As Sharon walked out the door she thought, "I don't know how long it will take to establish a relationship with Betty. I don't even know if it is possible. What about the kids until then? Their needs aren't being met."

Discussion and Study Questions

1. List what you learned and know about each of the characters in the case.

2. What do you think is motivating the thoughts/actions of each of the characters?

3. What are the issues and problems in the case?

Additional Questions

1. What further steps could Sharon take to resolve her difficulties regarding her role in Betty's classroom?

2. Should Sharon follow the principal's advice and give Betty some time to adapt? Do you think Betty will relinquish some authority as she and Sharon establish a relationship?

3. How can Sharon ensure that her students' needs are being met while this issue is being resolved?

4. What do you think is Betty's perception of the situation? Is it justified?

5. What more could have been done on a district level to facilitate the implementation of the pro-inclusion and collaboration policy?

6. If the boat isn't rocked, will anything change?

SOURCE: http://cases.coedu.usf.edu/TCases/Thats.htm

THE SECOND TIME AROUND: ■
GETTING OVER BAD EXPERIENCES

A negative experience with collaboration is one of the most powerful—and difficult to overcome—experiences that can influence a co-teaching relationship. Most of us have had a bad relationship at one point in our lives. While the common philosophy is that you are supposed to "brush it off and try again," that is certainly easier said than done. Getting burned once is bad enough—who would voluntarily enter a relationship knowing that the pain could happen again? And yet, in the real world, we do that again and again and again. In schools, though, a teacher might be heard telling administrators, "No thanks. I 'collaborated' once before and it didn't work. I'm not going there again." Consider how wrong that statement is on so many levels.

First of all, if it didn't *work*, I have to question how truly collaborative the relationship was. By definition, they would have been sharing resources and working toward a common goal. They would have been mutually invested in finding success, and they would have communicated about all aspects of the situation to ensure that goals were met. If the relationship didn't work, chances are some of the characteristics of collaboration were not there in the first place. Thus, it is unfair to say collaboration didn't work; what didn't work was whatever it was that was going on in that situation—clearly not a collaborative endeavor.

Second, co-teaching is a relationship and relationships involve multiple factors. People are different; situations are different; students are different; times are different. The outside forces that influenced your last relationship may not be there for this one. Perhaps you had an extraordinarily difficult class in terms of behavior issues or perhaps you were trying to complete multiple graduate courses concurrently that semester. Maybe your co-teaching partner was having personal issues or was simply not a good match to your personality type. Whatever the case, any of these factors might have negatively influenced the dynamic between you and your partner. It would be folly to judge all relationships based solely on one (or two or ten) bad experiences. If we all thought that way, our society would cease to exist.

Third, keep in mind that most "bad" experiences are usually attributed to the adults not being able to collaborate, rather than an issue due to a child's disability. Ask most teachers and they will tell you, "It's not the kids." In fact, teachers new to having students with disabilities in their classes will often report surprise that *those* kids are just like my other kids. Think about any typical elementary school classroom. At any day and time, the majority of the student body look like they have attention deficit/hyperactivity disorder (ADHD).

Finally, I have to question why a teacher may think that declining to collaborate is even an option in this day and age. Prospective employers consistently rate the ability to collaborate and communicate with others as their top desirable skills, far above the abilities to read, write, and do math. The vast majority of jobs require employees to pool resources, team up, and cooperate with one another for increased success; why would it be any different in schools? In fact, teachers need to model the behaviors we want to see in our students; if students are to learn to collaborate, they need to see collaboration in action and they need increased opportunities to work with their peers, both those with and without special needs. In one of the studies (Ward, 2003) included in the meta-synthesis on co-teaching done by Scruggs, Mastropieri, and McDuffie (2007), a teacher is cited as saying,

> There are people in my building—this really bothers me—that have the "Free from Special Ed" pass. I didn't know they [administrators] give those out, but some people in my building have one and don't have any special ed students because they exhibit qualities in the classroom that are not becoming to collaboration, so the special educator does NOT want to place students in those rooms. (p. 400)

This is often an issue in schools. Those individuals who do not want to work with others demonstrate that in their actions and are ultimately rewarded for their negativity. This needs to be addressed. In addition to being best practice, educational laws simply do not permit teachers to shut their doors on one another. Collaboration between general and special educators is mandated, as per the Individuals with Disabilities Education Improvement Act (IDEIA) of 2004 and the No Child Left Behind Act (NCLB) of 2001. Take a look at the creative professional development agenda in Figure 3.4 created by Dr. Mark Kandel and Ms. Karla Carlucci as they work with teachers and administrators in Pennsylvania. The agenda makes it clear that co-teaching helps marry the requirements of NCLB and IDEIA. Mark and Karla really emphasized the wedding theme to teachers.

Co-Teaching Staff Development

Despite the aforementioned rationale for participating in a collaborative relationship even after bad experiences, it is not suggested that administrators, teachers, or advocates unilaterally inform reluctant teachers that they have to collaborate or co-teach. That is certainly no way to garner their respect, interest, trust, or buy-in. In fact, it is helpful to go to the research on professional development and adults as learners to identify the best methods for motivating reluctant participants. Remember that providing strategies for co-teaching will fall on deaf ears if those who are shown the strategies have no inclination to participate in co-teaching. Prior to telling teachers *how* to collaborate or co-teach, it is first important that they have buy-in and understand *why* co-teaching is being recommended.

When I'm doing workshops with teachers, I find it productive to have them work together to discuss why co-teaching can be beneficial—to both them and the students! I've been amazed at the creativity of teachers. The following pictures and Figure 3.5 are a couple of examples of outcomes of staff development workshops on co-teaching. Remember, each of these activities resulted in teachers collaborating, laughing, and ultimately discussing how working together can have a positive result in the classroom.

Wedding Program

Bride: **Karla Carlucci** ~ Groom: **Mark W. Kandel**

Parents of the bride: **Mr. & Mrs. NCLB**

Parents of the groom: **Mr. & Mrs. IDEIA**

Prelude

Introductions

Agenda

Objectives

Procession

History & rationale & research

The Readings

What co-teaching is and is not

Components of successful co-teaching

Common mistakes

Who are we?

Planning for effective collaborative teaching

Homily

Designing and delivering effective instruction and collaborative teaching

Exchange of Vows

Sharing instruction & models of co-teaching

Recessional

Evaluating the effectiveness of collaborative teaching

Strategies to support co-teaching & inclusion

Figure 3.4   Co-Teaching Wedding Workshop Agenda

SOURCE: Printed with permission, M. Kandel.

To continue to gain buy-in for co-teaching and increased collaboration, share information from Changing the Minds of the Commitment-Phobic in Chapter 1. Another suggestion is to have teachers participate in activities designed to put them in each other's shoes, as well as in the shoes of their students. Disability awareness activities are easily accessible on the Web. Some

During professional development, these collaborating teachers share a laugh as they rap about the benefits of co-teaching.

A Co-Teaching Poem

I do not like to teach alone
So I call my co-teacher on the phone.

Together we can "walk the talk,"
Always sharing all the chalk.

Working together is how we thrill —
Teaching life-long learning skills.

The climate in the room is always fun
Thanks to all of the Col-lab-or-a-tion!

Showing kids how to cooperate,
Circulating the room we regulate.

All of these things we do each day.
Each in our own unique way.

An effort that we always make
Is to empty the bladder and give the brain a break!

Figure 3.5   A Co-Teaching Poem

SOURCE: By Montebello, CA, school co-teachers Jennifer Gonzalez, Mana Vera, Karen Lobos, Leyda Garcia, Vivian Paramo, Frank DelaTorre, Evelyn Guzman (October 2, 2008).

example activities that can be done with teachers (or with students) are included in Figure 3.6. An excellent resource for all educators, including faculty and staff in general and special fields, is the original F.A.T. City video by Richard Lavoie (www.shoppbs.org or www.ricklavoie.com).

A Few Resources for Learning About Various Abilities and Disabilities

- www.ricklavoie.com. Rick Lavoie has some of the best motivational videos on learning disabilities. Check out the classic F.A.T. City video, as well as other great titles such as "It's so much work to be your friend" and "Last one picked—first one picked on" and "When the chips are down." His newest book, *The Motivation Breakthrough,* is also a worthwhile read for co-teachers.

- Hallowell, E. M., & Ratey, J. J. (1995). *Driven to distraction: Recognizing and coping with attention deficit/hyperactivity disorder from childhood through adulthood.* New York: Simon & Schuster. An oldie but a goody.

- Batshaw, M. L., Pellegrino, L., & Roizen, N. J. (2007). *Children with disabilities* (6th ed.). Baltimore: Paul H. Brookes. A thorough and complete compendium of the majority of possible disabilities.

- www.allkindsofminds.org. A fantastic Web site that focuses on learning about children's abilities, strengths, and learning profiles.

Participants at a staff development on co-teaching use Wikki Stix and acrostics to share their learning.

Visual Disabilities

A visual disability affects how one sees. It might include complete blindness, partial blindness, or a loss of vision.

Activities

- Give each participant a pair of glasses smeared with Vaseline and have them pick up a pencil and write their name on paper or walk around the room.
- Have participants walk around and interact with a piece of wax paper over their eyes.
- Have participants use their hands to create binoculars around their eyes. Have them discuss how this would impact taking notes, playing games, doing typical activities, etc.
- Have participants pair up. One partner should put on a blindfold while the other acts as the sighted guide. The sighted guide leads the blindfolded partner around an obstacle course. Have partners change roles and then discuss the experiences.

Auditory Disabilities

A hearing disability affects how one hears. It might include a loss of hearing, a distortion of hearing, or complete deafness.

Activities

- Have participants put cotton balls in their ears and tie a scarf around their heads to keep the balls in place. Continue to lecture on content and expect the participants to take notes. Only repeat content when asked to do so by a participant. (This can be done with earphones also.)
- Divide participants into pairs. Have one partner communicate a message to the partner without speaking (e.g., "Please get me a glass of water" or "It's your turn to write on the board").
- Allow participants to access hearing loss simulators to hear various levels of hearing loss (e.g, http://holmessafety.org/hlsim/).

Physical Disabilities

A physical disability can affect how one moves, as well as how one speaks or writes.

Activities

- Give each participant a piece of paper and pencil. Simulate a partial loss of hand control by writing name and address with the nondominant hand.
- Have participants put socks on their hands and try shoe tying, buttoning, zipping, writing, etc.
- Have participants sit in chairs and, while seated, try to pull on sweatpants without getting up. Also have them try to wash their hands at public sinks, drink from public water fountains, and write on the front boards—all without getting out of their seats.
- Borrow some wheelchairs and have participants spend part of a day doing typical activities without getting out of the chairs.

Developmental Disabilities

A developmental disability can affect how one learns and thinks.

Activities

- Ask participants to stand in a circle and name three positions: For example, hands in air means *cat*; hands on waist means *dog*; hands on thighs means *fish*. Allow participants to practice a few times and then have them try hands on *fish*; then right hand on *fish*, left hand on *dog*. Right hand on *cat* and left hand on *dog*. Then give the directions without modeling them and add complications such as putting legs together, apart, standing on one leg, etc.

Developmental Disabilities
• Provide one partner with a lengthy and complex (12–20-step) process to read to their partner. The partner can't follow the directions until all are read. See how much the participants retain and are able to do. Discuss the experience.

Learning Disabilities
A learning disability affects how one processes information, visually, or auditorally. It can impact how one speaks, learns, reads, writes, talks, and thinks.  **Activities** • Give each participant a book and a mirror. Ask them to hold the book to the mirror and read the book by looking in the mirror. • Hold a book upside down and ask a participant to read it. • Ask participants to hold pieces of paper up to their foreheads and write their names on the papers in their nondominant hand. Then ask them to write a nonsense word on the other side (e.g., zonker). • Read a story filled with nonsense words, and then ask participants to answer questions for a quiz. • Have participants go online to experience firsthand what it is like to have visual, attentional, or auditory difficulties at the MisUnderstood Minds Web site: http://www.pbs.org/wgbh/misunderstoodminds/intro.html.

Speech and Language Disabilities
A speech disability affects how one speaks. A language disability affects how one processes language. **Activities** • Speech. Give each participant a bunch of marshmallows to put in his or her mouth. Then ask each one to tell a story to a partner. • Speech. Give participants a variety of difficult tongue twisters to try. Discuss how frustrated it was for some of them and easy for others. • Expressive Language. Ask participants to tell a story without using the letter D. Discuss how stilted and laborious their speech becomes. • Receptive Language. Begin to talk to participants in a lesser known foreign language (e.g., German). It is possible one or two students will be able to understand. Praise those students in the foreign language and look expectantly at the others. If the other participants look confused, talk at them more quickly and loudly. Discuss how they felt, being expected to do something they didn't understand.

Figure 3.6 Disability Awareness Activities

SOURCE: http://www.girlscoutsmilehi.org/content/documents/DisabilityAwarenessActivities.pdf and http://www.co.sanmateo.ca.us/smc/department/home/0,,65129_6563808_7184233,00.html

Once educators understand *why* including students with special needs is ethically and educationally valid, and once they truly understand *why* differentiating to meet those various needs is warranted, it is then time to address *why* co-teaching is a strong choice as a service delivery option. Now is the time I try to speak to teachers about why co-teaching would help them personally. This is essentially when it is important to address, "What's in it for me?" Let's face it—teachers have a lot to do on a daily basis and engaging in anything that means substantial change is not high on their list. I have found that trying to convince teachers who already have had a negative co-teaching experience to try it again based on "the law" or "because it's the right thing to do," simply doesn't cut it; on the other hand, when I tell them that I'll help them grade, that I can help with discipline and differentiating, or even that they can have a bathroom break occasionally, the attitudes become much more positive. If you are the person trying to change someone's mind about co-teaching, find out what it was about his or her experience that turned them off; then genuinely try to determine if you can provide them with a different and more fulfilling situation. If you are the person who had the negative experience, reflect on why it was negative and determine what you would need to have happen in order to consider co-teaching again. Remember that you may not be provided with the option to choose whether or not to co-teach; instead, be proactive and create the type of relationship that you want to be in. Remember that the key to any good marriage is communication. Identify your different communication and collaboration styles (Conderman, Johnston-Rodriguez, & Hartman, 2009) and then be sure to use your very best communication skills as you work with your co-teacher.

Self-Assessment 1
Are We Ready to Date?

Please recognize that even schools that embrace inclusion and purport to be inclusive may vary in their implementation of inclusive practices. Weiner (2003) suggests that inclusion may evolve in different stages. During the first level, not much inclusion is noticed on site. The typical instructional focus, which is considered Level I, tends to lend itself more toward whole-class instruction and demonstrates very little individual or differentiated instruction. In Level II schools, there is more differentiated instruction and more evidence of cooperative learning. According to Weiner, Level III schools are dynamic, responsive, engaging, and dedicated to the success of all students. What then does it take to move from a typical Level I school to that of a Level III? Use the Determining Levels of Inclusiveness chart in Figure 3.7 on page 58 to conduct a quick self-assessment of your own site. Talk to colleagues to see if there is agreement regarding your school's current level of inclusiveness.

The level chart adapted from Weiner's work is a broad glance at how a school might be moving toward inclusive practices. The worksheet provided based on Dieker's (2009) work (Figure 3.8, Expectations in Schools That Are Successful With Inclusion on pages 59–61) moves into a more specific analysis. It enables educators to examine a variety of practices at the school and classroom levels. Dieker (2009) asks educators to scrutinize the behaviors and expectations that are displayed regularly, and she provides a brief but effective rationale for why to promote certain behaviors in a school. I use this checklist when working with schools for the first time because it does not concentrate solely on individuals with disabilities. On the contrary, the checklist asks about the use of behavior management, cooperative learning, self-advocacy, literacy, and numeracy activities. Hearing teachers talk to one another about how these expectations are—or more frequently, are not—communicated to students daily is always eye-opening for me. It appears similarly enlightening for teachers when they realize that all of these behaviors and expectations can positively influence the inclusiveness of a school. Thus, I suggest that colleagues first discuss the schoolwide behaviors suggested in the chart; are they occurring on a regular basis in the school, just in pockets, or not at all? Second, teachers should consider a specific class they teach or in which they collaborate. Honesty is critical as teachers self-assess behaviors and expectations related to each component provided. Giving yourself or your colleagues the benefit of the doubt will not result in a higher grade for you or in improved instruction for your students. It is better to be honest and highly critical at this stage of the game. Our next step is to identify what we need to do to improve.

Level I	Level II	Level III
Little or no inclusion	Some students fully included	Dedicated to the success of all students
Ignores individual differences	Cooperative learning is noticed in some classes	Focus is on *how* students learn more than what they learn
Minimal efforts to accommodate diverse learners	Some student-based activities	Examines growth indicators or need for improvements
High rate of special education referrals for minority and bilingual students	Some students in special education are regarded well by some teachers	Uses self-reflection to evaluate inclusive practices
What Level Is Your School?		

Look at each row and determine which most closely represents your school site. Circle that item. Then move down to the next row and repeat your analysis. After you have analyzed all four rows, look down the columns to see which level most represents the inclusiveness at your school. In which areas was your school weak? Talk to your prospective co-teacher, faculty, and administrators at your school to determine how you can move to become a Level III inclusive school.

Currently we are mainly at Level _____

In one year, we can be at Level _____

by (what action) _____

This will require the participation and support of (whom) _____

In five years, we can be at Level _____

by (what action) _____

This will require the participation and support of (whom) _____

Figure 3.7   Determining Levels of Inclusiveness

SOURCE: Based on Weiner (2003).

This next framework emerged from the work Dr. Lisa Dieker conducted in schools across the country and specifically from work in several urban schools. These classroom and school components can often make or break the ability of students with disabilities to be included in the general education setting. This tool is designed as model for self-reflection of inclusive practices in the school and/or classroom. The first section is designed for you to reflect upon your school's overall behaviors. The second section is applicable to individual classrooms.

Questions to Frame Your Reflections

Are students with disabilities not ready for the general education setting or is the general education setting not ready for the learning and behavioral needs of students with disabilities?

Schoolwide Analysis		
School/Teacher Behavior	**Why Is This Important?**	**How Are We Doing?**
Student behavior is consistent across the school.	If students with behavioral needs are placed in inconsistent environments, their behaviors could regress with a lack of consistent intervention. A strong Positive Behavior Intervention and Supports (PBIS) program (www.pbis.org) can be very helpful.	
Makeup policies are consistent across the school.	Just as behavior should be consistent, students also benefit from classrooms where homework expectations are consistent across the school.	
Clear criteria exist for why students are in less inclusive settings.	If students are not in inclusive environments, a clear set of rules exists as to why students are in more self-contained settings so there is consistency in the way students are selected for these settings.	
Clear criteria exist as to how to move students back into more inclusive environments.	Criteria are developed that demonstrate when a student is ready to leave the special education setting to go back into the general education setting, a preparation program to assist students in the transition exists.	
Cooperative learning and/or peer tutoring are a component of every class.	Research on these two skills is strong, and in effective schools, these structures provide additional support and allow students to give back to classmates and are therefore embraced throughout the school.	
A structure exists that allows students with disabilities as many opportunities to give to others as there are to receive help.	Just as in the classroom, throughout the school should be ways for students with varying ability levels to give support in the school system to others who do not have identified disabilities.	
There are multiple ways to celebrate students with diverse learning or behavioral needs.	Schools find ways to make all students feel good, no matter their academic levels (e.g., "on a roll" list as well as an "honor roll" list).	
Literacy is incorporated in every subject area (including enrichment areas).	Research supports the need for literacy to be taught not only during reading but as much as possible; literacy instruction should be found in every class, every hour, every day.	
Math is incorporated in every subject area (including enrichment areas).	Research also supports the need for math to be taught not only during math class, but as much as possible; math applications should be taught in every class, every hour, everyday.	
Writing occurs in a meaningful way every day every hour.	Research supports the need for writing instruction to occur in more than just during language arts or English time; writing skills should be taught in every class, every hour, every day.	
Students are taught to self-advocate for their needs and know how to share their needs with their teachers.	Students with disabilities know about their strengths and the strategies to assist them with their weaknesses. All students are taught how to advocate for their own needs.	
Co-teaching and collaborative environments are at the core of the school.	Teachers are expected to work together for the success of all students. Labels have been removed from teachers and students. Teachers know that their work must be interdisciplinary for students to be successful.	

Figure 3.8 *(Continued)*

Figure 3.8 (Continued)

Classroom Analysis		
School/Teacher Behavior	**Why Is This Important?**	**How Are We doing?**
Teacher talk is less than 50 percent of the lesson and all teacher talk is paired with visuals.	Students need to be actively engaged in the lesson and brain research says that student learning needs to be chunked. Learning modality preferences include visual, auditory, kinesthetic, and tactile.	
Strategies or activities are used that promote active learning.	Student assessment must be continuous and students with attention issues need classrooms where the engagement at a low risk level is high.	
Students are taught social skills daily.	Since students with disabilities often have an IEP goal focused on social needs, then these goals should be part of the daily instruction and could be helpful to all students (e.g., using positive language).	
Physical breaks occur at least once an hour but ideally every 10–15 minutes.	Brain research indicates that a break in learning or chunking of knowledge should occur every 12–15 minutes for more effective learning. (Breaks may need to be more frequent for younger learners.)	
Knowledge is presented in chunks.	Brain research indicates that students can only remember seven things at a time so information presented should be chunked into units of seven or less for greater learning outcomes.	
Reading material used is rich and diverse and includes material embraced by info-kids.	Some children prefer reading for information instead of pleasure; therefore, the curriculum includes factual books as well as novels.	
Multiple ways exist to evaluate students beyond paper and pencil tests.	In this time of high-stakes testing, teaching skills for paper-and-pencil tests is important, but this type of assessment should not be the only way students can demonstrate their learning or else failure is inevitable for some students.	
A structure exists that allows students with disabilities as many opportunities to give to others as there are to receive help.	This area should be both a classroom and schoolwide goal. Students with disabilities need the chance to give help to others (not just receive help) to protect their self-esteem and help them grow as learners.	
Grading for students with disabilities has been addressed and is clear to staff, students, and their families before the start of the semester.	How grading in inclusive environments will occur must be determined before students are included and must be shared with the student and their family. Students who do not know how they will be graded may not be motivated to achieve their best.	
Before beginning to teach together, the learning and behavioral needs on students' IEPs are discussed, as well as the content knowledge that will be presented in the lesson for the next 9 weeks.	Just placing two people in a room together will not result in success unless prior to the start of the class both teachers clearly understand the content that will be taught and how this compares or contrasts with the needs of students with disabilities.	

After completing the school- and class-level analyses:

Where are we doing well and where are we doing poorly? _____

_____

Identify two specific actions you can take to positively address the areas in which you are not doing well *and* two specific actions you can take to nurture the areas in which you are doing well:

1. _____

2. _____

3. _____

4. _____

Figure 3.8   Expectations in Schools That Are Successful With Inclusion

SOURCE: Adapted and included with written permission from Dieker (2009). Slightly adapted for elementary.

4

Matchmaker, Matchmaker

The Role of the Administrator

■ TO MARRY THEM OR NOT TO MARRY THEM: DETERMINING WHETHER TO USE CO-TEACHING

Studies on co-teaching have found that it can be a very effective method for meeting student needs (Magiera, Smith, Zigmond, & Gebauer, 2005; Murawski, 2006; Rea, McLaughlin, & Walther-Thomas, 2002). However, administrative support is key to its implementation and, ultimately, its success or failure (Dieker, 2001; Rea, 2005; Spencer, 2005). Administrators get the ball rolling; they are the matchmakers, wedding consultants, marriage counselors, and, at times, divorce attorneys. In essence, administrators can set the tone for whether or not co-teaching as a service delivery option is implemented correctly and if teachers are set up for success. There are many things an administrator can do to demonstrate to her staff that she truly supports the co-teaching endeavor. A major part of this involves being aware of the different approaches to collaborative support in the general education classroom, providing guidance in the logistics of creating co-taught teams and their schedules, providing support for the co-instruction of students in inclusive classes, and being aware of best practices in supervising co-taught teams. I will be discussing each of these various areas as we progress through Dating, Engagement, Wedding, and Marriage phases. Each of the four parts of this text includes a Matchmaker, Matchmaker chapter on the role of the administrators; administrators are simply too important to address once and then forget. Teachers, feel free to share these specific chapters with your own administrators or read the chapters and then highlight them, providing busy administrators with the *CliffsNotes* version of the content. Do whatever works to ensure that administrators are aware of their role in supporting the inclusive, co-taught classrooms and the teachers who are teaching in them.

Are Your Teachers Ready to Marry or Should They Just "Live Together" at First?

Although having two credentialed teachers in every general education classroom appears ideal, it is clear that budgets often prohibit this from happening. Thus, administrators need to know what the possible approaches are for providing support to students with special needs in the least restrictive environment (i.e., the general education classroom). Once these various approaches are identified and understood, a more informed decision can be made based on the needs and abilities of the students, the needs and abilities of the teachers, and of course the logistics, such as resources, number of students, space, and budget. *Co-teaching* and *in-class support* are two of the primary ways general and special educators can collaborate to ensure that students with and without disabilities are having their needs met in the general education classroom. However, it is critical that all stakeholders are aware of the differences in these terms and are able to use them consistently. Miscommunication at this stage of the game can negatively impact the adoption and implementation of co-teaching. So, what are the differences then?

As previously stated, *co-teaching* is "when two professionals co-plan, co-instruct, and co-assess a diverse group of students in the same general education classroom" (Murawski, 2002b, p. 10). Both teachers are equals in the classroom, and both provide substantive instruction to all students (Friend & Cook, 2007). Co-teaching requires a commitment—from teachers as well as administrators—recognizing that *both* teachers are integral to the instruction. This means that the general education teacher is not seen as the *real* teacher for the class, while the special educator is relegated to the role of paraprofessional (Spencer, 2005). It also means both teachers are committed to all aspects of teaching the class (i.e., planning, instructing, assessing), so neither should be pulled from the class for out-of-class activities (e.g., individualized education program meetings, behavior incidents, parent phone calls) during the scheduled teaching time. Administrators must demonstrate a healthy respect for this collaborative and co-equal relationship if they want to ensure that both teachers and students value it as well.

How Does In-Class Support Differ From Co-Teaching?

In most schools, there are not enough special education teachers to enable all classes to be co-taught. Special educators are often spread thin in order to monitor the growing caseloads and cannot afford to be in one class for a committed period of time every day. In that case, in-class support may be warranted. *In-class support* varies from *co-teaching* in that the co-planning and co-assessing components are absent, or at least are not as strong as they are during co-teaching. (Murawski, 2008b, p. 27, emphasis added)

During *in-class support*, the role of the special education teacher is often to provide on-the-spot modifications and accommodations, behavioral supports and proximity control, and other academic and social assistance as needed.

Naturally, these techniques may not be as effective with students as they would be through co-teaching because the proactive planning component is missing. This is somewhat akin to teachers "living together" as opposed to being in a marriage. They are in the same room and they are getting to know one another, but the level of commitment, goal setting, and shared decision making is lacking. They may be friends, but they are not two partners sharing equally in the collaboration required by two individuals committed to raising children together. (For those of you who are opposed to individuals living together, or to those of you who are living together as a committed couple though you are not married, please remember—this is an analogy only.) As a baby step to co-teaching (Murawski, 2005b) or as one type of collaborative in-class activity, in-class supports are certainly better than no supports at all, as previous mainstreaming efforts indicate. However, for students to gain the benefit of ongoing, consistent, and structured support from a special education–general education collaborative, co-teaching is the preferred option.

Using the Correct Terminology

Administrators need to know how to recognize true co-teaching from the plethora of activities that are currently being called *co-teaching*. Weiss and Lloyd (2003) among others have found that the majority of teachers who are working in the same classroom are solely engaged in "one teach, one support." In the majority of these situations, teachers are not even truly co-teaching; the general education teacher is acting as the *real* teacher for the majority of the instruction and the special service provider ends up functioning as more of a classroom aide.

Administrators should review the terms provided in Chapter 1 with faculty and staff. Educators should discuss what is currently going on at their school sites and what they would like to see happen. In many cases, if teachers and administrators are honest with each other, they will admit that there is still often more *mainstreaming* going on than *inclusion*, more *consultation* going on than *collaboration*, and more *in-class support* going on than *co-teaching*. Administrators need to have a clear and strong understanding of where they currently are in terms of inclusive practices before they can determine a realistic and measurable goal for the near future.

As a true believer in taking "baby steps," I wrote an article in 2005 in the *Kappa Delta Pi Record* stating that schools shouldn't try to move too quickly in the pursuit of co-teaching. To do so is almost a guarantee of failure. Administrators need to work with the school stakeholders (teachers, parents, staff, community, and students) to make realistic choices for the inclusion of youngsters and to include the use of co-teaching. For major school change to be successful, there must be commitment from the administration. For example, research has demonstrated that when administrators fully accept the idea of inclusion (and support it with money and staff development), staff acceptance is better facilitated (Sindelar, Shearer, Yendol-Hoppey, & Liebert, 2006). Clearly then, for a co-teaching program to become a reality, administrators are an integral component. As we continue our relationship analogy, at this stage of Dating, the administrator may even be the critical father or mother figure—standing at the door as you leave with your date, letting you know that he or she is watching and that there had better not be any missteps.

If you've managed to get past the dating stage, you and your co-teacher will now need to determine if you are ready to get engaged. Just as each couple has its own personality, schools also have their own cultures related to inclusive practices (McLeskey & Waldron, 2002). Co-teaching pairs will develop their own preferences. Despite these individual differences, there are strategies for setting up a quality co-teaching program that can provide a structure for those interested in moving forward.

Working collaboratively, co-teachers can demonstrate multiple methods of teaching standards-based content.

Part II

The Engagement

Finding the right partner can make the difference between those who have a great classroom "marriage" and those who do not.

5

Getting to Know Your Partner

■ DRINKING OUT OF THE CARTON (AND OTHER PET PEEVES)

The difference between co-teaching and intermittent in-class support is the difference between being married and dating. When you are just dating, even over a relatively long period, you can hide your flaws. No one who is just dating neglects to put the top on the toothpaste, drinks directly out of the milk carton, or forgets to make the bed, and they never, ever have gas. At least, that is what we lead the person we are dating to believe. On the other hand, when you marry someone, those idiosyncrasies come out. Not all at once. Drip by drip at first and with apologies. But eventually they come pouring out, full force. When teachers are spending that much time together on a daily basis, they are bound to learn things about each other that touch on each other's nerves, and sometimes it is much more than just merely touching on nerves—it's more like treating those nerves as a trampoline. While this is undesirable in a relationship, it is flat out unacceptable in the classroom. So what can be done to make sure that co-teachers do not start to get on each other's nerves?

One of the first suggestions is simple: Share your pet peeves. Be honest and share with one another what you like and don't like to occur in the classroom (Murawski & Dieker, 2004). Have an open conversation about how you like to grade, what noise level you think is acceptable in the class, and your typical policies related to issues like tardiness, pencil sharpening, question asking, late work, and the like. Inform your partner about personal preferences related to giving and receiving feedback, communicating during and outside class times, the use of humor, technology, activities, textbooks, field trips, and so forth. The more you and your co-teaching partner share information proactively, the less likely a situation will come up that will surprise you or put you in an uncomfortable position.

Two co-teachers told me about a situation that occurred with them in the first week of co-teaching. I'd like to share it.

> **Sue:** "The first week of school, we had the kids working on an activity in small groups. They had their books out and were supposed to be working collaboratively. As Renée and I circulated around the room, checking that the students were working, I noticed that a lot of them were chewing gum. I walked around, quietly telling them to put the gum away. Personally, I hate gum chewing, and I made a mental note that we needed to tell the kids at the beginning of class the next day that gum chewing was not permitted. I was surprised we had forgotten to do so before then. After a while, when I noticed more and more kids chewing gum, I finally asked, 'Where is this gum coming from?' And then I saw Renée, quietly walking around to students on the other side of the room, giving out gum, and saying things such as, 'I really like how you are working together,' and 'I appreciate that you had your book here today.' What a surprise!"
>
> **Renée:** "Yeah, I thought it was a simple and effective way to provide positive behavior support to students. Imagine my surprise when I realized I was the one empowering students to engage in one of Sue's biggest pet peeves."
>
> Sue and Renée discussed their situation after class, laughed about it, and came to a compromise. They would both engage in similar activities to promote positive behavior support, but they wouldn't use gum to do it.

Rather than finding yourselves in a situation like Sue and Renée did, in which you realize one of your partner's pet peeves only when she announces in the middle of class, "Hey, please don't do that!" it is recommended that co-teachers have these conversations early in their relationship. I developed the S.H.A.R.E. worksheet (Figure 5.1) to help partners have these kinds of discussions. I recommend that you and your co-teacher sit down and complete the worksheet independently. That will encourage you to be honest in your responses. Don't try to tailor your responses to what you think your co-teacher will prefer; it is better to admit your preferences now as well as your strengths and weaknesses, rather than having your partner uncover them herself. For example, if you are a procrastinator, go ahead and write that down. If you prefer that children sit and remain quiet, admit it. If you don't, be prepared to live with a daily headache. Your partner is not a mind reader; neither are you.

The front page of the S.H.A.R.E. worksheet asks teachers to *Share* the *Hopes* they have regarding co-teaching, the *Attitudes* they harbor regarding inclusion, and the *Responsibilities* they will *Expect* to have and divide in a co-teaching relationship. Respond honestly. Many co-teachers have found that a truthful and open discussion about their concerns, expectations, and philosophies has led to a productive conversation with their future partner. In fact, Kelli H., a special education coordinator, told me that using the S.H.A.R.E. worksheet schoolwide made an enormous difference in the success of co-teaching between one year and the next at her school site. Why? Simple. This kind of conversation builds rapport, establishes an honest exchange of ideas, and opens the door for future communication. In essence, this is your premarriage counseling. It is perfectly reasonable for teachers to agree to disagree on certain issues, provided they know and are respectful of one another's opinions. It is also acceptable to admit concerns. Veronica admitted to me that she was afraid co-teaching would be more work for her: hence, she really didn't want to do it. That comment led me to work even harder to ensure that she was pleased with the parity between us. At the end of the first semester, she was overheard telling other general education teachers that co-teaching actually led to less work since I was really helping plan, teach, and even grade. I was even more driven to pull my weight in the relationship because of her early comment, and this paid off.

Once you have both independently completed the worksheet—taking the time needed to really think about your answers, get together to discuss the responses. The great thing about this activity is that teachers find it actually saves them time in the long run. By discussing these issues prior to co-teaching, teachers find that they can make decisions about how they will jointly run the class. Responses that are similar in nature (e.g., both teachers state that they think students should be responsible for bringing in their own materials but that they are okay with having pencils and paper available for purchase) will never again need to be discussed. Teachers will be on the same page from day one. On the other hand, responses that are different (e.g., one teacher thinks that students should be allowed to turn in late homework, whereas the other does not want to accept any work that is late) will need to be discussed until a consensus is reached. This allows teachers to discuss their discrepant opinions before the students can figure out how to "play Mom against Dad." Also, once teachers have spent time making decisions, those decisions will not need to be revisited during the school year, ultimately saving time. For example, if in the discussion of responsibilities, the general educator states that he prefers to be in charge of taking roll and collecting homework, the special service provider may volunteer to be responsible for the warm-up activity daily. Thus, this proactive conversation results in both teachers identifying their role for the first 5 to 10 minutes of class every day; they no longer have to have that conversation. Each day, they know what their roles are and the activities for which they should be responsible.

Want more on this topic?

Curious about roles and responsibilities in the co-taught classroom? Read the section called Who'll Do the Laundry.

■ ENSURING PARITY

We want 50/50 in this marriage—not a 1950s-style marriage where one spouse gets to do all the decision making! However, even in situations where teachers like and respect one another, sharing all classroom roles and responsibilities can be problematic. Oftentimes, teachers may feel at a loss to determine *who* should do *what*, even after determining the various activities in the classroom. As previously mentioned, giving up control of various aspects of the classroom is one of the major barriers to successful co-teaching. Sometimes the things we do in the classroom are so ingrained that we have a hard time even conceptualizing how to let go and let someone else do that activity, especially if it means

S.H.A.R.E.

Sharing Hopes, Attitudes, Responsibilities, and Expectations

Directions: Take a few minutes to individually complete this worksheet. After completing it individually, share the responses with your co-teaching partner by taking turns reading the responses. Do not use this time to comment on your partner's responses, merely read. After reading through the responses, take a moment or two to jot down any thoughts you have regarding what your partner has said. Then, come back together and begin to share reactions to the responses. Your goal is to either (a) agree, (b) compromise, or (c) agree to disagree.

1. Right now, the main HOPE I have regarding this co-teaching situation is

   _____

2. My ATTITUDE or philosophy regarding teaching students with disabilities in a general education classroom is

   _____

3. I expect to have the following RESPONSIBILITIES in a co-taught classroom:

   _____

4. I expect my co-teacher to have the following RESPONSIBILITIES:

   _____

5. I have the following EXPECTATIONS in a classroom, with regard to
   (a) Discipline _____
   (b) Classwork _____
   (c) Materials _____
   (d) Homework _____
   (e) Planning _____
   (f) Modifications for individual students _____
   (g) Grading _____
   (h) Noise level _____
   (i) Cooperative learning _____
   (j) Giving and receiving feedback _____
   (k) Other _____

Figure 5.1 S.H.A.R.E. Worksheet

SOURCE: Murawski, W. W. (2008a). Also published in Murawski, W. W., & Dieker, L. A. (2004). Tips and strategies for co-teaching at the secondary level. *Teaching Exceptional Children, 36*(5), 52–58.

they might do it differently than what we are used to. In addition to the difficulties of giving up control, the issues related to varying frames of reference I mentioned earlier also come into play. We tend to think about the class and our role in the class differently. The Teacher Actions form in Figure 5.2 is one

I created many years ago when I was working with a pair of co-teachers who truly wanted to improve but were having a hard time even identifying what the special educator could do in the class. The general education teacher said that she was just not used to doing anything but direct instruction, and the special educator said that he was not used to doing anything in the general education class but circulating and helping with behavior management. While both were eager to embrace a more collaborative, equal, and dynamic partnership, they simply found it hard to conceptualize. In addition, when it came to planning, they had so little time that they ended up merely identifying the content coming up and resorting to the "same old, same old" in terms of classroom roles. When I created this table as an example for them, they told me it really helped them see how they might vary their roles on a regular basis. Since then, I've shared this with many teachers, always with positive feedback. You and your co-teacher can print it out, refer to it frequently, or even adapt it to create your own table of Teacher Actions. I've added some additional suggestions for you to consider in Figure 5.3, Ensuring Parity or Avoiding "Glorified Aide" Status. Take time to discuss which of these activities are ones you and your co-teacher may use often and which you may want to substitute with other more frequently used activities. Sometimes just going through the action of discussing what you will be doing in the classroom and what options there are for both of you will help make your daily interactions more comfortable and natural.

Co-teaching allows teachers to work side by side in making sure all students have access to general education curriculum.

If One of You Is Doing This	The Other Can Do This
Lecturing	Modeling note taking on the board or overhead
Taking roll	Collecting or reviewing last night's homework
Passing out papers	Reviewing directions
Giving instructions orally	Writing down instructions on the board
Checking for understanding with large heterogeneous group of students	Checking for understanding with small heterogeneous group of students
Circulating, providing one-on-one support as needed	Providing direct instruction to the whole class
Prepping half of the class for one side of a debate	Prepping the other half of the class for the opposing side of the debate
Facilitating a silent activity	Circulating, checking for comprehension
Providing large-group instruction	Circulating, using proximity control for behavior management
Running last-minute copies or errands	Reviewing homework
Reteaching or preteaching with a small group	Monitoring the large group as they work on practice materials
Facilitating sustained silent reading	Reading aloud quietly with a small group; previewing upcoming information
Reading a test aloud to a group of students	Proctoring a test silently with a group of students
Creating basic lesson plans for standards, objective, and content curriculum	Providing suggestions for modifications, accommodations, and activities for diverse learners
Facilitating stations or groups	Also facilitating stations or groups
Explaining a new concept	Conducting role play or modeling concept
Considering modification needs	Considering enrichment opportunities

EZ Reference

Figure 5.2   Teacher Actions During Co-Teaching

SOURCE: Murawski, W. W. (2008a).

If One of You Is Doing This	The Other Can Do This
Lectures	
Writes on board	
Reviews timelines or dates	
Assigns homework	
Reviews for a test	
Gives new vocabulary	
Gives a test	
Teaches complex information	
Takes roll	
Reviews homework	
Disciplines a student	
Circulates around the class	
Leaves to copy materials	
Reads aloud	
Checks fluency or comprehension	
Creates cooperative learning groups	
Creates rotating stations	
Assigns differentiated work	
Gives directions	
Identifies standard to address	
Works with small group	
Writes on overhead	
Collects classwork	
Leads calendar time	

Three things that we will do to ensure parity in the classroom are

1. _____

2. _____

3. _____

Figure 5.3   Ensuring Parity or Avoiding "Glorified Aide" Status

The key to true parity is to make sure students think of you both as the *real* teachers.

WHO'LL DO THE LAUNDRY? SETTING ■ ROLES AND RESPONSIBILITIES

Now that you have completed the S.H.A.R.E. worksheet and discussed the various actions you might take when teaching, you and your partner know where you agree and where you disagree. Your next step is to have a conversation about any areas of disagreement, working to achieve agreement, consensus, or compromise. The following step is to determine what regular classroom activities can be delegated in advance. Research has shown that, on average, a large percentage of class time is spent on nonacademic engaged activities, such as behavior management, paperwork, and giving directions. However, in a study involving co-teaching and other approaches, only co-teachers spent less than 2 percent of their time providing direct behavior management. The teachers in other approaches spent significantly more time having to do so (Weichel, 2001). Others have also found that co-teaching can increase time spent on instruction. So how can you and your co-teacher increase academic engaged time and reduce noninstructional time?

Determine the activities that are typical in your class. For instance, most classes have regular attendance and warm-up activities. You might like to give students new vocabulary on Mondays, a quiz on Wednesdays, and a brainteaser

These teachers use parallel groups and technology to actively engage students.

Defining Roles and Responsibilities

1. Make sure to clarify the difference between *co-teaching*, *in-class support* from a teacher, and *paraprofessional assistance* as forms of collaborative support in the classroom for all participants. Select the support appropriate for this class.

   In this class, we will be using _____

2. Identify the roles or actions that will need to be taken by the adults in the classroom.

3. Identify which adult will take which role or action (recognizing that roles can be switched, if necessary).

4. Look over the roles or actions. Do they clearly match with the type of collaborative support that was chosen in #1? (For example, if co-teaching was selected, do the roles demonstrate parity between participants?)

Roles or Actions	Who Will Be Responsible?

Figure 5.4 Defining Roles and Responsibilities

SOURCE: Murawski, W. W. (2008a).

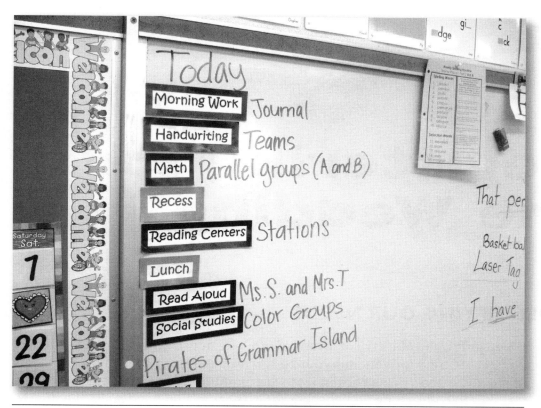

A regular agenda provides structure and demonstrates parity.

on Fridays. By identifying these regular activities, you can discuss them with your co-teacher and, in essence, divide and conquer. A special service provider who is feeling uncomfortable with content related to science or math may feel completely at ease with the responsibilities of designing daily warm-up activities, modifying already existent quizzes, and sharing interesting weekly brainteasers. In fact, if she knows in advance what the new vocabulary words are, she might also take on the responsibility of developing mnemonics, visuals, or other strategies for helping students learn the new words—even if they are related to math and science. Not only will these set roles help save co-teachers' time, they will also provide a structure for students. As students begin to learn daily, weekly, and monthly routines, they will be more comfortable with the class and more accepting of both teachers' instructional roles. The Defining Roles worksheet provided in Figure 5.4 will help you establish your preferred roles and responsibilities.

A pair of co-teachers gave me permission to share this picture of their daily agenda. Having both names (Ms. S and Ms. T) within the agenda clearly displays their shared commitment to the class. A regular posted agenda enables co-teachers to determine who will do what, without having to meet excessively to make those decisions. The students were also helped by having a structure they could expect each day. *How* the co-teachers would teach each section (e.g., "Today we'll use parallel groups during reading, but tomorrow we'll keep them together as a large group") can change, but the structure remains the same. Remember, by deciding who will do what when, you will save time and ensure that you are both equals in this relationship.

6

Registering for the Wedding

■ IDENTIFYING OUR NEEDS

Whether it was voluntary or arranged, you are now *engaged*. Congratulations! Now is the time for you and your co-teaching partner to become a team and to share the good news with others. Miscommunication is a dirty word when it comes to co-teaching and collaboration. By now, you have taken the time to complete the S.H.A.R.E. (Figure 5.1), Teacher Actions (Figure 5.2), and the Defining Roles and Responsibilities (Figure 5.4) worksheets together and are starting to know one another's strengths, weaknesses, preferences and pet peeves. It is also important that you describe to one another how you prefer to receive feedback, for example in person, through e-mail, immediately after class, or at the end of the week. This will aid in your communication with one another. Being honest and open helps any relationship; a strong partnership is necessary when you are working together to educate a group of young children.

As you get to know each other and begin to discuss how you intend to teach together, you should also be able to identify the needs you have as a team. Figure 6.1 contains questions that help you identify those needs: Not all of these items may be needed in your situation, but use the Wedding Checklist as a guide. Create your own checklist together. Remember, part of the fun of being *engaged* is registering for gifts. You may not get them all, but it doesn't hurt to ask.

■ COMMUNICATING WITH STAKEHOLDERS

The last question on Figure 6.1 relates to revealing and explaining the relationship to those it impacts and who may have impact upon it. Teachers often talk to their students about character issues, admonishing them that talking about others behind their backs is not an acceptable behavior. And then they walk right into the teachers' lounge and let the gossiping begin. A major issue

Wedding Checklist		
Questions to Ask Ourselves	**Possible Items Needed**	**Check if Needed ☑**
Where will we be teaching?	Larger classroom to accommodate wheelchairs, extra kid desks	
Is our classroom accessible?	Ramp, elevator, or other items for accessibility	
Do we each have our own *space* in the classroom?	Another teacher desk An extra file cabinet An extra bookshelf	
Do we have the technology we need for adapting, modifying, and meeting needs?	LCD projector, screen, or laptop ELMO for projecting papers Dynavox or other AT Computers with voice recognition software Small in-class photocopier Accessible class Web site	
Do we have sufficient time and means to meet and plan?	Common planning time in schedule Stipend for additional time spent Co-teaching planning books Co-teaching software Co-Teaching Solutions Systems [CTSS]	
Do we know about the students we will be sharing?	Copies of IEPs and cumulative folders Time to meet with other service providers Surveys on learning styles and multiple intelligences to give students first week of school	
Do we have all the teaching materials we will need in order to differentiate?	Two copies of teacher's guide Enough books for all students Adapted versions of materials for students with special needs Carbon paper for note taking Tape recorders for activities	
Are we both familiar with options for assessing and grading students?	Example portfolios Copies of standardized assessments from previous years Grading rubrics for common assignments	
Do we both feel comfortable with the content?	Professional development on content area (e.g., attend math conference)	

EZ Reference

Figure 6.1 *(Continued)*

Figure 6.1 (Continued)

EZ Reference

Wedding Checklist		
Questions to Ask Ourselves	**Possible Items Needed**	**Check if Needed ☑**
Do we both feel comfortable with differentiating and modifying and addressing IEP goals?	Professional development on differentiating and accommodating (e.g., attend special education conference)	
Are there any students with specific disability or ability areas on which we need more information?	Professional development on specific topic (e.g., attend a conference on autism or gifted education)	
For optimum support and to minimize miscommunication, have we communicated our situation to • Our administrators?	Letters and meetings with administrators to ensure understanding of co-teaching and needs	
• The other teachers in our school?	Faculty meeting to ensure an understanding of co-teaching	
• Paraprofessionals and other support staff?	Meeting time with paras and staff Staff development for paraprofessionals	
• The students?	Time to discuss the situation	
• The families of our students?	Letters home to families and parents	
• Other stakeholders?	Newsletters, e-mails, and invitations to visit the class or support in other ways	

Figure 6.1   Wedding Checklist

with co-teaching is that it is a paradigm shift, one with which many people are not familiar. Two adults in the classroom are frequently assumed to be simply *the teacher and an aide*. Thus, the idea of having two qualified, fully credentialed professionals sharing space, materials, responsibility for instruction, and students—even for only part of the day—is a foreign concept to many. Avoid miscommunications by addressing the following groups when starting a co-teaching program: (1) administrators, (2) other educators, (3) paraprofessionals and support staff, (4) students, (5) families, and (6) other stakeholders.

Administrators

The role of administrative support is crucial. That is why each of the four parts to this book has a chapter titled Matchmaker, Matchmaker: The Role of the Administrator. Obviously, administrators help to set the stage for the types of initiatives that teachers engage in during the school year. While some may support in name only, those administrators who are truly committed to change show their support in a variety of ways, such as allowing for more autonomy as teachers select their co-teaching partners, providing stipends or preferential scheduling and planning times, or ensuring that sufficient professional development is available for participating teachers. As a teacher, I felt that my administrators at times were lacking in their support of initiatives that were important in my area of special education. When I began my graduate coursework in educational administration and was surrounded by vice principals, principals, district supervisors, and even superintendents, I was surprised to learn how few of them had any special education background. Usually, a course in special education law was required, but other than that, the majority did not know much about special education. This led me to an epiphany; it wasn't that my previous administrators failed to support, condone, or appreciate my efforts to engage in cutting-edge work in our school, it was simply that they did not know enough about what I was doing or why. Therefore, bashing them for not providing what I considered necessary was simply not fair. I discovered that it was better to tell them what I wanted, why I thought it was beneficial to students and the school, and specifically what I required from them to make my efforts successful. We cannot assume that our school leaders are knowledgeable about everything related to education. The field is too vast. It is our job to educate those in administrative positions on what we now know about co-teaching, what their role is in supporting our efforts, and what they can do to help us be the most effective co-teachers we can be.

It is also incumbent upon us to do this without condescension. In the perfect world, we could simply state what we want and get it. This is the real world, and here, egos are fragile. Remember that your administrators want to save face as much as your teenagers do and as much as you do; so for now, keep wearing kid gloves. Couching conversations with administrators in terms of providing the research, literature, and the potential impact on student learning is typically the key to getting their attention. They will also typically prefer time to think about your requests so that they can be considered in the context of the bigger school picture, and putting requests in writing is also helpful. An example letter that you and your co-teacher might use to gain the support and attention from your administrator is provided in Figure 6.2. Remember, it will be a much more powerful message if it comes from both of you, rather than just one of you.

Other Educators

In the very recent past, teachers were expected to go to their own classrooms, shut their doors, and work miracles. The unspoken, but generally acknowledged,

May 8

Dear Dr. Incharge:

We are interested in co-teaching next year and wanted to run our proposal by you for approval. Co-teaching is when a general education teacher, such as Mrs. Hutchinson, and a special education teacher, such as Ms. Weichel, jointly deliver substantive instruction to a heterogeneous group of students in a single physical space. Co-teaching has become a very popular service delivery model for ensuring inclusive practices of students with disabilities. We would like to co-teach a group of students with and without disabilities in our second-grade class. **We are seeking your cooperation because the research very clearly states that administrative support is crucial to the success of co-teaching.**

Our proposal involves identifying students in special education who can benefit from a general education second-grade class, with supports and services provided in the classroom. Currently, Mrs. Hutchinson's classes average 22 students. We propose that these numbers remain the same, but that seven of the students will be identified as having disabilities. This can be done through the master schedule and Ms. Weichel can work with the counselor to identify appropriate students. Ms. Weichel would be able to come in and co-teach on a regular basis during language arts and math time. When students are receiving instruction in social sciences, science, or related arts, Ms. Weichel would use that time to go monitor and support students in Grades 1 through 3 in other classes. Her paraprofessional would work collaboratively with Ms. Weichel to support kids in Mrs. Hutchinson's and other classes.

In order for us to effectively collaborate and co-plan for these students, it is important that we be provided with common planning time. We would appreciate it if we could talk to you about either providing us with time during lunch, related arts time, or even through a regular sub or a stipend for outside time. Scheduled common planning time would allow us to communicate on a regular basis to make sure we can meet students' diverse needs. The value of having a regular scheduled time to co-plan and communicate has also been well documented in the literature on co-teaching and we hope we will have your support with this.

As you are well aware, the movement toward more inclusive education continues. We believe that our proposal to co-teach and serve students with disabilities in the general education classroom as the least restrictive environment will be viewed favorably by the district and parents alike. Certainly it will help to address the initiatives put forth in both the *2004 Individuals with Disabilities Education Act*, as well as *No Child Left Behind*. We would very much like to set up an appointment with you to review our proposal and to discuss how your administrative support of our efforts will help to ensure our success.

Sincerely,

Ms. Wendy Weichel
Special Education Teacher

Mrs. Linda Hutchinson
Second-Grade Teacher

Figure 6.2 Letter of Support: Administrator Form
SOURCE: Murawski, W. W. (2008a).

perspective was that if others were hearing about your class and your students, you probably were not doing a very good job. That time has passed. In this era of collaboration, teaming, cooperative learning, and interdisciplinary teaching, educators are expected to throw open their doors and welcome the input of others. This can be difficult. While many are embracing the notion that collaboration makes sense, for some, the concept of co-teaching can be either alien or completely anathema. Yet, as professional educators in special education, Title I,

Grade level teams can communicate about co-teaching successes and difficulties.

English as a second language, technology, and various types of designated instruction services, such as physical therapy, occupational therapy, speech/language, and psychological services, continue to grow in number and move toward providing their supports in inclusive environments, the possibility that co-teaching will be happening in your school increases as well. Consequently, if you and a peer have decided—or have been told—to co-teach, it is strongly suggested that you share this information with other colleagues in your grade level. Too often, teachers will hear that a colleague is co-teaching and will respond with, "What's that?" "Why does she get an aide? I want one too" "Oh, good. So I won't have any of *those* kids in my class then," or even "Huh? Why on earth would she agree to do that?" In any case, explaining what co-teaching is and what it is not is a must. Co-teaching is now part of the school culture. It is not a fad. Other members of the school family can no more afford to ignore it than they can afford to ignore special education, or kindergarten for that matter. Consider yourself an ambassador to positive change.

The best scenario is one in which the school and district administrators provide professional development for *all* teachers regarding what co-teaching entails, its benefits, and information regarding *when*, *where*, or *how much* co-teaching will be occurring at each school site. That way, all teachers are informed equally and there is less likelihood of miscommunications. "According to research, no single ingredient has greater impact on student achievement than the quality of the teacher in the classroom" (Haycock,

1998, as cited by Hirsch, 2005). If the adults in the classroom have such power over closing the achievement gap with students, they need to be on the same page in terms of their vision, behaviors, and philosophies (Weiner & Murawski, 2005). As the executive director of Education Trust, Haycock was interviewed in 2000 and stated that, unless teachers believe their hard work will produce better results for students, they are typically not interested in new approaches that seem merely to be more work for them. However, Haycock also said,

> If you create strong support structures for teachers, instruction in the school will inch upward because, even in the lowest performing schools, you typically find a few teachers who are quite good. If you create a vehicle for them to help their colleagues, you will see improvement over time. (as cited in Sparks, 2000, p. 38)

Although Haycock was referring to professional development in general, co-teaching certainly meets her criteria for faculty improvement. It is a wonderful approach by which teachers can collaborate to learn from one another and see the improvement in students.

For an entire staff to embrace a new approach to student instruction, there needs to be quality professional development, not merely a one-shot, "dog and pony" type seminar that is never again addressed. Educators need to identify their goals as a staff and work together to achieve them. Hirsch (2005) affirmed that "when beliefs are in alignment, change in behavior accelerates" (p. 39). Communicating with other educators requires the sharing of information and resources. In addition to this text, Figure 6.3 and 6.4 contain additional video, Web, and software resources available for staff development in co-teaching.

Professional Development Resources on Co-Teaching
All of the following videos and DVDs are available through National Professional Resources at http://www.nprinc.com/co-teach/index.htm.
Title: *Collaborative Teaching: The Co-Teaching Model*
By Richard Villa   Available through www.nprinc.com
Format: VHS/DVD, 35 minutes   Released 2002
Description: Describes the value of collaborative planning and the five essential components to an effective collaborative teaming process.
Title: *The Power of 2 (2nd ed.)*
By Marilyn Friend   Available through www.nprinc.com
Format: VHS, 65 minutes; DVD, 173 minutes   Released 2005
Description: This training video provides a comprehensive look at co-teaching as part of the foundation of an inclusive and collaborative school.

Professional Development Resources on Co-Teaching
Title: *How to Co-teach to Meet Diverse Student Needs*   By ASCD   Format: VHS, 15 minutes Released 2006   Description: Explore the qualities of effective co-teachers, see how co-teaching works in one classroom, and understand the planning and support that ensure co-teaching works.
Title: *Teacher Collaboration: Opening the Door Between Classrooms*   By The Master Teacher Available through www.nprinc.com   Format: DVD Released 2007   Description: Provides information to make co-planning and co-teaching successful realities in a school district.
Title: *Collaborative Planning and Collaborative Teaching Videos: 2 video set*   By Richard Villa Available through: www.nprinc.com   Format: DVDs, 35 minutes each Released 2007   Description: Provides information on collaborative planning for differentiation as well as an overview of Villa's four models of co-teaching.

Figure 6.3 Co-Teaching Videos

Professional Development Resources on Co-Teaching
Title: **Co-Teaching Solutions Systems**   Available through http://www.co-teachsolutions.com   Description: Software for administrators and teachers designed to monitor and support effective co-teaching. Observation System provides a checklist for administrative observations and walkthroughs that is able to generate multiple reports to ensure evidence-based practice. Co-Teachers' Toolbox enables co-teachers to co-plan, co-instruct, and co-assess easily by providing everything they will need to collaborate and save time, including learning styles grouping, rubric making, curriculum mapping for groups and individuals, and pages of strategies in addition to a comprehensive lesson planning software.
Title: **The Council for Exceptional Children (CEC)**   Available through www.cec.sped.org   Description: A Web site that offers journal articles, professional development opportunities and resources, and other relevant information on special education to support teachers, administrators, paraprofessionals, parents, and related support providers.
Title: **Special Connections**   Available through http://www.specialconnections.ku.edu/cgi-bin/cgiwrap/specconn/index.php   Description: Provides teacher support and tools in the area of instruction, assessment, behavior, plan, and collaboration.

Figure 6.4 *(Continued)*

Figure 6.4 (Continued)

Title: *2 Teach LLC Web site*

Available through www.2TeachLLC.com

Description: My Web site offers staff development opportunities related to collaboration and co-teaching for schools, districts, states and conferences. The Co-Teaching Lesson Plan database (2007) is a free resource for co-teachers to download lessons that were created by other co-teachers and to upload their own lessons to share with colleagues. In addition, I created the *Co-Teaching 101* staff development module to provide schools and districts with a binder, complete with PowerPoint, facilitator's scripted guide, research article, and participant handouts, that can be used to facilitate staff development for individuals who need to learn about co-teaching, what it should be and what it should not be.

Figure 6.4   Internet Resources for Co-Teachers

Support Staff

In order to facilitate inclusive practices, many schools have hired paraprofessionals to support students with disabilities in the general education classroom (Giangreco, 2003). There are numerous terms used to describe the individuals who assist teachers and students in the classroom; these include paraeducator, paraprofessional, instructional assistant, teacher aide, and inclusion aide. The 2004 amendments to the Individuals with Disabilities Education Improvement Act (IDEIA) define these employees "as persons who work directly under the supervision of licensed professionals and who often deliver instructional and direct services to students and their parents" and refer to them as "paraprofessionals."

Support staff, such as paraprofessionals, are extremely valuable in the process of collaborating in the inclusive classroom (Giangreco, Edelman, & Broer, 2003; Sherman, 2007). While, by definition, parity is not present when someone in a supervisory or professional position is working with someone in a subordinate role, paraprofessionals and other support personnel have a critical role in the inclusive efforts of a school. Paraprofessionals are often expected to provide academic, behavioral, and social supports to students in the general education classroom when special education teachers or other professionals are unable to do so (Carroll, 2001; Giangreco et al., 2003; Sherman, 2007). Unfortunately, however, teachers and support staff may be equally unclear as to the role the paraprofessional should play in the inclusive classroom; while some paraprofessionals are expected to serve as the primary instructor for students with disabilities (frequently with little or no training), others are expected to merely maintain clerical duties (Werts, Harris, Tillery, & Roark, 2004). Pickett and Gerlach (2003) found that some paraprofessionals were additionally asked to "assist with functional assessment activities; carry out behavior management and disciplinary programs developed by teachers; [and] document learner behavior and performance" (p. 24). Despite this wide array of expectations, most paraprofessionals report feeling thrown into the position without support or training (Chopra et al., 2004). J. Downing, Ryndak, and

Clark (2000) found that many paraprofessionals said they had to simply figure out the job for themselves by observing others, reading and recalling their own experiences in school. How can we possibly expect schools to be *cutting edge* and use *best practices* if we are using status quo and experience as our models? Yet, that is exactly what is happening in the case of paraprofessionals. Thus, providing both initial and ongoing staff development on effective instructional strategies to all individuals involved in collaborative teaching, including support staff who may be involved directly or tangentially, is the smart thing to do (Hourcade & Bauwens, 2001).

> In several studies (e.g., Carroll, 2001; Chopra et al., 2004; Giangreco & Broer, 2005; Giangreco & Doyle, 2002; Griffin-Shirley & Matlock, 2004; Trautman, 2004), paraprofessionals reported having an undefined job description and a lack of information regarding their duties. Paraprofessionals may receive a "few handouts" or "a brief introduction to special education" (Carroll, 2001, p. 60) prior to working with students. Without a defined job description, paraprofessionals must decide for themselves what their role should be. Paraprofessionals have "reported perceptions that their roles included: (a) not being a 'bother' to the classroom teacher, (b) being primarily responsible to provide 'on the spot' curricular modifications, and (c) being expected to be the 'expert' for the student" (Giangreco & Doyle, 2002, p. 3). Chopra et al. (2004) found that paraprofessionals may be assigned tasks that are inappropriate, such as serving as substitute teachers, doing secretarial work, serving as members on district committees, and assessing students. Often paraprofessionals are the "key service delivery support" (Giangreco et al., 2003, p. 63); and therefore, defining their role in educating students with disabilities is critical. (Murawski & Sherman, 2007)

What does all this mean related to the co-taught classroom? It means three things: (1) Paraprofessionals are frequently being asked to do many things that are beyond their training and job responsibilities, including co-teaching. While co-instructing is a possibility, paraeducators should not be expected to co-plan, co-instruct, and co-assess to the extent that teachers are expected to do so. (2) Paraprofessionals play a key role in the inclusive classroom and this necessitates collaboration and communication with the general and special educators with whom they work. There should be a regular method of communication between these entities. (3) As an integral part of the inclusive classroom, paraprofessionals should be expected to work with all students and teachers as opposed to just isolating and focusing on one student (Giangreco et al., 2003; Villa & Thousand, 2003). There are many training options for identifying the role of the paraprofessional in the inclusive classroom. The resources provided in Figure 6.5 will be an excellent start to ensuring that paraprofessionals understand their roles in the inclusive classroom. However, it is important to again recognize the difference between inclusion, collaboration, in-class support, and co-teaching, especially as they relate to the role of the paraeducator.

Web site:	http://www.nrcpara.org
Sponsor:	National Resource Center for Paraprofessionals
Web site:	http://www.paratrainingresources.com
Sponsor:	Paraeducator Training Resources, Inc.
Book title:	*The Paraprofessional's Guide to the Inclusive Classroom: Working as a Team*
Author:	Mary Beth Doyle
ISBN:	1557663122
Publisher:	Brookes Publishing Company
Book title:	*Inclusion: An Essential Guide for the Paraprofessional: A Practical Reference Tool for All Paraprofessionals Working in Inclusive Settings*
Author:	Peggy A. Hammeken
ISBN:	9781890455347
Publisher:	Corwin
Title:	*The Paraprofessional's Role in the Inclusive Classroom* (staff development module)
Author:	Wendy Murawski, PhD, & Beverly Sherman, MA
Publisher:	2 Teach LLC
Web Site:	www.2TeachLLC.com/products/

Figure 6.5   Paraprofessional Training Resources

Remember that the inclusive classroom is, ideally, any classroom. It is one in which there are students with a variety of needs. Specifically, it is one in which there are students with identified disabilities. "Collaboration is often used incorrectly as a replacement term for co-teaching or inclusion" (Murawski & Sherman, 2007, p. 37), despite the fact that collaboration is not a *thing* but rather a way in which individuals can interact. Co-teaching, on the other hand, involves the co-planning, co-instructing, and co-assessing of students by two or more co-equal parties (Murawski, 2003). Since most paraprofessionals or other support staff have not had the training to plan, instruct, or assess students—nor are they paid to do this type of extra work—it is unreasonable to ask them to assume the same job responsibilities as a trained teacher (Sherman, 2007). On the other hand, they may very well be expected to collaborate, or possibly even co-instruct, in the inclusive classroom.

Villa, Thousand, and Nevin (2007) provide examples of how paraprofessionals can co-instruct, but these should be employed carefully. Given their background, unique experiences, and willingness, paraprofessionals may be more or less able to take more active and substantive roles in the classroom. Giangreco and Doyle (2002) stressed that the instructional and noninstructional tasks the paraprofessional is assigned should augment, not replace, the work of general and special educators. Frequently, the instructional techniques that paraprofessionals know have been gleaned by observing teachers, as well as through trial and error (Chopra et al., 2004), as opposed to having any formal training.

Paraprofessionals need to be made aware of what co-teaching is, and what it is not. They need to be assured that they will not be asked to take a lead role in a class in which they are not comfortable. However, they also need to recognize their potential usefulness in assisting with co-instruction, through the facilitation of small groups (such as for Station Teaching, Parallel Teaching, or Alternative Teaching), working with individual students (such as in One Teach, One Support), or in modeling desired behaviors (such as through Team Teaching).

When paraprofessionals are provided with strategies and instructional training, they are more capable of working in a collaborative manner with teachers in the classroom. This increased role in the classroom—*again*, provided there is prior communication and that the paraprofessional feels comfortable in that role—can help the paraprofessional engage with the whole class and help avoid the "hovering" around students with disabilities that can otherwise occur (Giangreco, Edelman, Luiselli, & MacFarland, 1997).

Want More on This Topic?

Each of the co-instructional approaches will be described in detail in Part IV: The Marriage.

Thus, despite the lack of co-planning necessary for true co-teaching, there are several aspects for co-teaching in the inclusive setting that would work with a paraprofessional and general educator (Murawski, 2006). For example, when the general education teacher introduces new material to the class, the paraprofessional can assist with student questions, conduct warm-ups, or monitor student behavior (Hourcade & Bauwens, 2001). If co-teaching is going to be provided as an option in a school, it is clear that all support staff need to be educated as to what their role will (and will not) include so that they can be eager and prepared participants. "When teachers and paraprofessionals work well together, the students benefit from being fully involved with all class activities" (Murawski & Sherman, 2007, p. 38).

Remember, "effective professional development that will close the achievement gap will deepen participant understanding, transform beliefs and assumptions, and create a stream of continuous actions that change habits and affect practice" (Hirsch, 2005, p. 39). We want all individuals in our school to change their understanding, habits, and practices so that inclusive education can become a reality. So, don't forget to include your paraprofessionals and other support staff as you work to establish your co-teaching partnership. You may find that they will be the last-minute guest invited to the wedding who ends up being invaluable in helping make sure the wedding is a complete success.

Students

Why do students need to be aware of what co-teaching is? Won't they just figure it out when they see that they have two teachers in the room? Perhaps.

When done well, paraprofessional support can make the inclusive classroom successful for all students.

However, as co-teaching is increasingly used as a service delivery option for students, more students will be impacted by this arrangement. Students need to understand why there are two teachers in their classroom—or why they sometimes have two teachers and other times only have one. Let's take a moment to reflect on elementary learners. Students who are in upper elementary have already had a few years to experience the typical classroom. They are used to the "stand and deliver" approach many teachers use, essentially having students sit quietly in individual chairs as the one adult in the room talks *at* them. They have also had a few years to hear about things like *special education*, *learning disabilities*, and *developmental delays*. While younger students may not know the terminology, they still know which students are *different* from them. We can change programs, adopt more politically correct terminology, and attempt to provide surreptitious service to individuals who are different, but let's face it—kids are clever. They figure it out eventually.

That said, then, it is a good idea to let students know up front that there will be two teachers in the classroom from day one. In fact, this is a major tip for ensuring success; make certain that you both can be present on day one—on time and for the whole time you intend to co-teach (e.g., for the whole language arts time). Too often, the first week or two of school is when the special service providers are still figuring out their schedules and caseloads and therefore do not make it to classes until later. Unfortunately that loss of immediate "bonding" or establishing yourself as an authority figure in the class can work against you later. Students will automatically see the general educator who has been there every day as the *real* teacher.

How might you introduce yourselves to the students then? Here is a script you can use or tweak to meet your own needs.

First Day of Class: Introduction Script for Co-Teachers

S: Welcome to third grade. My name is Mrs. Smidlap.

D: And I'm Mr. Dingus. We will both be your teachers for this class during math time.

S: Have any of you had two teachers for a class before? Please raise your hand.

D: If you have, I hope what you found was that having two teachers can help you in a variety of ways. With two of us, we are able to keep the classroom running more efficiently, which means we can answer questions more quickly for you and answer more individual questions. We are both willing and able to help you so feel free to ask either one of us if you need assistance.

S: Yes, we're a team. But that also means there will be times when we have to check with each other to see if we're on the same page or to see if we both agree on something. Also, one of the reasons I love to teach with another adult is that we both have different areas of expertise. I personally am pretty great at coming up with strategies for remembering information and for finding neat new ways to teach different content. Math wasn't my favorite subject in school, but I'm excited about coming up with fun ways to make it more interesting for you guys.

D: On the other hand, math is definitely my thing. I majored in it in college. I'm looking forward to this year, however, because it's my first time teaching the class with another teacher. Ms. Smidlap and I already have some great ideas for how to do this class differently than I have done the past five years of teaching third grade.

S: You will see that most of our handouts say "Dingus and Smidlap" but occasionally we will use forms that we've used in the past that might just have one of our names on them. We are trying to change all of our handouts to have both names but if we miss one, no big deal. You know that there are two teachers for math time.

D: Right. Also, while I will always be here, I will sometimes have other people teaching with me also. Miss Veronica will be here during some of our science and social studies time; Mr. Johnson is called a Title I teacher, and he will be here so you can have two teachers during language arts, and sometimes we'll have other adults coming in to teach different lessons with me. You guys are really lucky to have so many teachers, and I'm lucky to have so many people I can work with to make sure third grade is the best grade!

S: Anyway, welcome to third grade and to our math time. Let us tell you a bit about ourselves and then we're going to ask you to tell us two or three things about yourselves. Mr. Dingus, should I go or do you want to start?

D: Oh, by all means, Ms. Smidlap. You go ahead.

Once students are aware that you both will be sharing the responsibility for the class, they will be less likely to try to play "Mom against Dad." Please note the word *less* in the previous sentence. This means that you and your co-teacher should create systems that allow you to check with one another. Some co-teachers I know have a check-off system; they keep a form on a front podium that has students' names and reasons for leaving the class. If a student asks one of them to go to the bathroom, the locker, or the nurse's office, they merely check off that student's name and the reason for leaving. That way the other educator can easily see who left, where they went, and why. Other co-teachers may use an initialing system. If a student requests a modification or accommodation, it is the student's responsibility to get each teacher to initial it. If one teacher questions the accommodation requested, he will tell the student that he needs to talk to his colleague before he'll initial the request. This allows both teachers to communicate when needed on some requests and to simply and quickly initial requests that don't require any communication. In either case, however, both co-teachers demonstrate their parity by being part of the approval process and both teachers are aware of any accommodations that may be provided to a student.

Families

Parents report wanting more and better communication with individuals at their children's school (Murawski, in press). Jackson and Turnbull (2004) found that parents and guardians wanted home-school communication that is "tactful but honest and open, with no hidden information or candy-coating of bad news" (p. 17). Not knowing that there are two teachers sharing the responsibility for a classroom can cause concern and confusion among parents. Family members will want to understand how Mrs. Brown can call one night and say she's Johnny's fifth-grade teacher, and then Mr. Smith can call another night and also introduce himself as one of Johnny's fifth-grade teachers.

If co-teachers proactively explain the inclusive classroom and what collaborative teaching entails, they are also more able to avoid misperceptions that may occur. For example, parents of nondisabled children may hear that their child is in an inclusive classroom and may misinterpret that to mean he is in a slower class, special education class, or class with a watered-down curriculum. They may be concerned that their child will not receive proper attention or instruction because the teachers' time will be focused on those students with special needs. Parents of students with disabilities may be worried that their children will not receive individualized instruction or have their IEP goals addressed or that the teachers will teach to the middle of the class and neglect to provide necessary accommodations. In each of these cases, parental concern can be minimized with a proactive and communicative approach by the co-teachers. I have included a prototype of a letter in Figure 6.6 that a co-teacher and I sent home to parents. Feel free to revise and tweak it to suit your needs. However, keep in mind the tips in Figure 6.7 as you write your letter.

September 8

Dear Parents,

We will be co-teaching your child's first-grade class this year and want to introduce ourselves. Co-teaching is when two professionals teach the same class together in the same room. Co-teaching has become a very popular way of teaching to address the wide variety of needs we have in our classes these days.

We believe that, together, we can better meet the needs of all of our students in this first-grade class. We each possess different areas of expertise, and we will be collaborating to ensure that the students benefit from this situation. We share a common planning time and we will be planning together on a regular basis.

In addition to co-planning, we will also be co-instructing. This can take a variety of forms. Sometimes we will both be in front of the class, while at other times, one of us will take the lead while the other will be circulating and helping with discipline, modifications, and individual needs. We will take turns doing this to ensure that the students understand that we are *both* their teachers. This will also allow us to personalize and individualize our instruction as needed.

Finally, we will also be working together to assess the progress of each student and the class as a whole. We will share grading, and we will discuss any individual modifications or accommodations necessary for students with special needs. We will work to really challenge all students, including those students who are high-achieving or exceptionally motivated.

We are very excited about working together to ensure that the students in this English class meet, and even exceed, their potential. We love first grade, and we hope to instill a love for language, reading, writing, math, science, social studies and school with your son or daughter.

Please feel free to contact us if you have any questions or concerns, or if you want to share helpful information related to your child's needs. We can be reached at 888-754-2499 ext. 211 or by e-mail at *awesomeco-teachers@bes.k12.va.us*. The best time to reach us at school is during lunch, between 11:30–12:30, or leave us a message and we'll get back to you as soon as we can. For meetings and parent-teacher conferences, you may occasionally only meet with one of us due to time constraints, but be assured that we are both actively concerned with all aspects of your child's education and that we will be collaborating and communicating with one another to ensure the success of our students.

We look forward to a successful year and working with you and your child.

Sincerely,

Ms. Wendy Weichel   Mrs. Linda Hutchinson

Figure 6.6   Letter of Support: Parent Form

SOURCE: Murawski, W. W. (2008a).

Co-Authoring a Parent Letter? Read These Tips!

- Introduce yourselves and your backgrounds briefly and explain that you will be co-teaching. Give the definition of co-teaching in layperson terms, for example, "We will be sharing the planning, teaching, and grading of all the students in this class." Don't go into too much detail; those parents who want to know more will come and ask you. Then feel free to talk to them at length.

- Be sure that the letter comes from both of you. Having just one person send the letter home sends the message that the teacher who sent the letter is the *real* teacher for that child.

- Avoid putting titles, such as *special educator* or *first-grade teacher* as that works against your purpose, which is to show that you are both sharing the role of teacher.

- Focus on the positive benefits to students. Parents do not need to hear that it may be more work for you or that it is the first time you've tried this.

- Be sure to repeat that you will both be supporting all of the children in the class during that period (e.g., language arts or math).

- Be sure to mention that you both bring strengths to the classroom, which you are eager to share with the students and with each other.

- Provide opportunities for parents to meet you both (e.g., back to school nights, etc). Try to both be present at those meetings to demonstrate again that you are a team.

- At the end of the letter, be sure to provide a way for parents or family members to ask questions or to communicate with you directly. Be aware that some individuals are very comfortable with technology (e.g., communicating via e-mail, videophone, or asynchronous chatting), whereas other parents will want to talk on the phone or meet face to face.

Figure 6.7 Tips for Co-Authoring a Parent Letter

Stakeholders

In addition to educators, students and their families, who else needs to know when you are taking on co-teaching as a service delivery model? Don't forget to communicate with other stakeholders as well. These people might include individuals at the district or central office (e.g., coordinators, superintendent), individuals who work in the school on noninstructional, nonclassroom based, or nonpermanent bases (e.g., secretaries, school volunteers, substitute teachers, hall monitors, cafeteria workers, librarians), and even community-based individuals (e.g., local business owners). I know, I know—you are thinking that I'm going a bit overboard, right? That it is not necessary to let all these people know about your impending collaboration? But, have you never heard the stories about people who *forgot* to include someone in their wedding plans? They always end badly. Be proactive.

Many districts are struggling to demonstrate that they are becoming more inclusive and are providing opportunities for more students with disabilities to be taught in the least restrictive environment (LRE). Co-teaching is a popular choice for doing just that. Sharing your desire to engage in co-teaching is a strong political move. Your "higher-ups" at the district or central office will be happy to know that you are prepared to co-teach as a method of meeting these students' needs. This is akin to asking for parental blessings on your engagement. Happy higher-ups lead to happier administrators, which lead to happier teachers, and so on and so forth. In fact, individuals at the central office level may also be aware of opportunities and resources that can aid you in your efforts, opportunities of which your own school administrators may not have been aware. For example, they may be able to dip into certain "pots of money" to send you both to training on co-teaching or on a particular subject matter, they may be able to connect you with other co-teachers in your district, or they may be able to obtain substitute teachers so that you two can co-plan or perhaps go and observe other co-teachers in action.

Letting noninstructional, nonclassroom-based, or nonpermanent individuals know about your co-teaching experience is also a wise move. As we try to get students to think about each other more inclusively, we need to do the same with the adults. All too often, it is the school volunteer, school security officer, or school librarian who says to a student, "You're in special education with Ms. Weichel, right?" Despite working diligently to get kids to forget about special education, about the us versus them mentality, or about the different types of classrooms that used to be more prevalent, that simple comment can undo a year's worth of work. Although the individual may not have meant anything negative by the comment, the damage is done. To avoid this, I have seen schools that truly embrace inclusive efforts make sure that all school personnel, in any capacity, truly understand the vision of the school. For example, in a district in Wyoming, I recently presented co-teaching to a group that included teachers, paraprofessionals, and a large number of substitute teachers. When I first questioned the assistant superintendent on the choice to include substitute teachers, he responded that they are at the schools on a daily basis and need to know what is going on. This was a strong and very proactive move on the part of the district; at the end of the seminar, even the substitute teachers and paraprofessionals reported a better understanding of inclusion and their potential roles in supporting a class that is co-taught. As different inclusive initiatives (such as co-teaching) are shared and discussed, everyone can get on board and send the same message: "We are in this together. There is not an *us* and a *them*. There is only *we*."

Letting community members know about your efforts to promote inclusive education through co-teaching is like letting a rich uncle know you are getting married; you just increased the likelihood of getting a great wedding present. When I first started co-teaching in Virginia, I didn't have many teacher materials, but I wanted to be able to do a variety of projects with our students. Armed with a letter from my school administrator on school letterhead that stated my co-teacher and I were collaborating to increase the ability of individuals with disabilities to receive quality instruction in the general education classroom, I went around to neighborhood businesses. I was amazed at how many businesses were willing—even eager—to support our efforts. For the school store, my colleague and I had decided to use to promote positive behavior support in our class, we received gift certificates for food items from places like McDonald's and Burger King, stationery items from Hallmark and a local bookstore, and other kid-friendly items like pens, pencils, stickers, paper, and so forth from a variety of other stores. I even received a class set of disposable cameras whose expiration date was passed (but which still worked marvelously) from our local drugstore. We ended up using those cameras for a fantastic project in our class; as the kids' motivation increased with the use of the cameras, so did the amount of reading and writing they were doing.

Having moved to Southern California, I have also been able to receive items of support from larger corporations like Disney and Universal Studios, but these tend to take much more time and require jumping through many more hoops. Other great opportunities I discovered in California were my local Chamber of Commerce (www.uschamber.com) and Junior Chamber of Commerce (www.usjaycees.org). Although they are not affiliated with one another, I found that both entities were very supportive of educational endeavors. We had some members of the Chamber of Commerce come to speak at our school's career fair and the Jaycees became an excellent resource for when one of my co-taught classes wanted to engage in a community service learning project. Finally, another co-teacher and I were fortunate enough to find an accounting business that was getting rid of its old computers to make way for newer versions. Rather than donating those computers to a different organization, they gave our classroom five new (to us) computers.

Discuss the local businesses and possible opportunities with your co-teacher. First, determine your classroom needs and prioritize them (see Figure 6.8 Possible Community Support Items: Classroom Wants and Needs). Then, consider how you can divide and conquer. It may not be necessary to go to all businesses, but I did find that I was much more successful in person than I was when I merely called or sent a letter of inquiry. In talking with your co-teacher, you may find that one of you is more willing to spend time writing the letter and identifying the businesses (see Figure 6.9), while the other is more willing to do the actual site visits once the preliminary work is completed.

How Can the Community Support Our Inclusive Classroom? Check Out Our Wants and Needs!	
Wants	**Needs**
Donations to pay for a substitute teacher during additional planning time	*Mac and PC computers*
Items for a school store	*LCD projector so we can address visual needs in the class*
Pizza party at semester's end for those who meet stated criteria	*Books on tape*

Figure 6.8 Possible Community Support Items: Classroom Wants and Needs

Community Stakeholder Contact Sheet

Name of business: _____

Name of contact: _____

Address: _____

Phone: _____

E-mail: _____

Web site: _____

Types of products or services that business might be able to donate: _____

_____

_____

Date contacted: _____ How? _____ By whom? _____

Follow-up: _____

Figure 6.9   Community Stakeholder Contact Sheet

7

Discussing
the Future

■ ESTABLISHING SCHOOLWIDE
IMPROVEMENT GOALS

Identifying needs and goals is one of the most critical elements for the creation of a successful co-teaching program in a school. Step one? Do a needs assessment. A needs assessment is a

> systematic process to acquire an accurate, thorough picture of the strengths and weaknesses of a school community that can be used in response to the academic needs of all students for improving student achievement and meeting challenging academic standards. [It is a] process that collects and examines information about schoolwide issues and then utilizes that data to determine priority goals, to develop a plan, and to allocate funds and resources. Students, parents, teachers, administrators, and other community members should be included in gathering data. (http://www.dpi.state.nd.us/grants/needs.pdf, p. 1)

Needs assessments will vary based on school makeup, climate, culture, and history. Work with the faculty, staff, administrators, families, students, and other stakeholders to determine what the needs of your school are as they relate to inclusive education. Topics you may want to ask them about include their

- philosophy regarding including students with disabilities in the general education class,
- desire for professional development as it relates to inclusive education,
- current level of collaboration with other faculty and staff,
- comfort using environmental strategies to help establish an inclusive school,
- comprehension of the different collaborative structures available and what each entails (e.g., in-class support, consultation, collaboration, co-teaching),

- understanding of how to differentiate or adapt curriculum in the inclusive classroom,
- facility to use technology to meet the needs of diverse learners,
- integration of social skills curriculum into the general education classroom,
- understanding and comfort level related to alternative assessment strategies, and
- willingness to co-plan, co-instruct, and co-assess with another adult in an inclusive class.

Be sure to provide room for participants to share their own concerns or related interests. The information gleaned from a needs assessment should lead directly to the establishment of goals. For example, if the results of the needs assessment indicates that school members are unaware of the different collaborative structures available to facilitate inclusive education, that would lead to the development of a goal to do professional development in that area. If, on the other hand, the needs assessment results indicate that most educators feel comfortable with the different collaborative structures, but do not feel adequately prepared to differentiate in the inclusive classroom, time should be spent creating a shared goal related to differentiation and not on collaborative structures.

The attached figures included in this chapter provide a way for school facilitators to have educators and staff create shared goals—long term or short term. Dr. Lisa Dieker developed a strong structure for identifying goals during her work with teachers through the Urban Collaborative Leadership Institute. With Dr. Dieker's permission, I am including an example of her template in Figures 7.1 and 7.2. The first box asks for the goal (which is the area of focus), while the second box asks for a measurable objective. Special educators should be *very* familiar with this lingo; it is similar to that created on an individualized education program (IEP). Objectives should be written in such a way as to *see* if the goal was attained or not. The third box asks for the data to be collected. This is the permanent product information that can be used to demonstrate if the goal was achieved or not. The fourth box asks, "What if . . ." Educators tend to have the most difficult time with this part. This is asking for your "Plan B." For example, perhaps your goal is to increase inclusive practices at your school and your objective is to have two more co-taught classes than last year. The data you are going to collect is simply the number of co-taught classes of the past year versus the number of the current year. The what-if scenario prompts a response, for example, "What if we do not have the personnel to have two more co-taught classes?" Our Plan B then would have to find a way to try to meet our goal, even given a difficult barrier. In this case, I might say, "Then we will identify the number of children with IEPs who were included in general education in the past year and compare it to the number of the current year to make sure more children are included overall." This box enables you and your team to proactively consider what you would do if your first choice of action does not come to fruition. Finally, the last box addresses your role or commitment, asking each person on the team to establish what he or she personally will do to ensure that the goal is attained. Having each participant identify his or her own role helps encourage shared participation, shared responsibility, and shared leadership. Possible areas to consider for goal statements include the following:

- Inclusive climate
- Collaboration among staff
- Collaborative structures
- Curricular planning
- Positive mind-sets
- Environmental strategies
- Learning styles and profiles
- Integration of social skills
- Families and community
- Differentiation strategies
- Use of technology
- Grading and assessing
- Other

Goal	Measurable Objective	Data to Be Collected	What if . . .	Your Role or Commitment
Inclusion. All staff will clearly understand the philosophy of inclusion	Staff will write their philosophies and we will come up with a common statement for our staff	Individual and collective goal statements	They will not agree on a goal or write a goal? Then I will give them a set of statements that they will or will not agree with in their teaching	To get the staff to write a statement or to identify a statement they can agree upon for our school
Collaboration. My team will agree to do at least one observation of each other for 10 minutes to assist with behavioral issues	Observations will occur for all team members for a minimum of 10 minutes	Observations made and the decisions that we made as a team to assist with the behavioral issues identified in our observations	Someone does not agree to the observation or it cannot occur? Then the team will spend at least 10 minutes talking about any behavioral issues that occurred in the classrooms	To set up the observations and gather data

Figure 7.1   Goals Worksheet: Examples

SOURCE: Included with written permission: Dieker, L. (2008). *Urban collaboration leadership institute*. Newton, MA: Education Development Center. Unpublished paper.

Dr. Lisa Dieker and I worked for five years in a Baldwin County, Alabama, program known as Classrooms for Excellence. During that time, we worked most closely with the director of special education, Ms. Carpenter, and the director of curriculum and instruction, Ms. Marshall. It was so empowering to have administrators in both general and special education lead this type of ongoing professional development related to collaboration, inclusion, and co-teaching. Can you imagine how much support the co-teaching teams in the district felt, knowing that their directors in both general and special education were able to play nicely and model the collaboration they were trying to inspire in their teachers? My hat goes off to leaders like Ms. Carpenter and Ms. Marshall.

Ms. Carpenter and Ms. Marshall are true models of collaboration in action!

A major aspect of what we did with that county was to facilitate having faculty and administrators reflect and act upon the goals we worked with them to develop in year one (Dieker & Murawski, 2005). We used worksheets similar to those provided in Figures 7.2 and 7.3 to get the input of teachers and administrators at school and central office levels as we determined the realistic short- and long-term goals for that county's inclusion project.

In addition to asking school personnel to work collaboratively to create goals, they can all share and support, it is also helpful for faculty and staff to reflect on specific questions (see Figure 7.4). These can be done prior to or even after completing goal sheets. Reflective questions encourage school members to think about their own responses and commit them to paper. After writing them down, team members should be asked to share their answers with their colleagues. Following a small-group sharing, one member of each group can be asked to act as a *reporter* for the group, revealing to the large group the consensus response or various responses from that group.

1. How will others who visit your district know that you are a strong inclusive co-taught school or district?

2. What will they see and hear that demonstrates your philosophy?

3. What do you want your school or district to look like in 10 years?

4. What is a goal related to your philosophy of inclusion for year one? For year three? For year five? Be sure to consider what you will need to happen in order to reach your 10-year goal.

5. How will you ensure accountability for the plan you have created?

Figure 7.2   Questions for Reflection and Discussion to Aid in Goal Setting

SOURCE: Dieker & Murawski (2005).

Questions to Guide Goal Setting

Session 1: Veteran and Novice Co-Teachers and Administrators

1. Novice co-teachers and administrators: Share your biggest concerns with veteran co-teachers and administrators.

2. Veteran co-teachers and administrators: Consider your first year of implementation and share your greatest learning or success with novice co-teachers and administrators.

3. Get into small groups that include both veteran and novice co-teachers and administrators. Be sure to identify a "Recorder" to write down your responses and a "Reporter" to share those responses with the large group. Use the Think/Pair/Share approach to address the following question:

How will you ensure effective co-teaching?

Identify at least three things you will do.

Session 2: Novice Co-Teachers Only

Discuss the following questions with your partner. Use the handbooks and resources provided for you to incorporate into your responses. Be prepared to share your responses aloud. We will be walking around to help you work through some of your questions. As you discuss the questions below, be sure to consider the types of major pitfalls you and your partner may foresee and identify what you will do to avoid those major pitfalls.

1. What are some technological tools you can use that can assist with student learning?

2. What are your current issues related to planning together?

3. What are your current issues related to instructing together?

4. What are your current issues related to grading together?

5. What goals can you identify for yourselves that will help you work through some of the issues you identified above?

Figure 7.3   Questions to Guide Goal Setting

SOURCE: Dieker & Murawski (2005).

ESTABLISHING INDIVIDUAL ■ TEAM IMPROVEMENT GOALS

In Part I: The Dating Scene, I highlighted how important it is for potential co-teachers to share with one another their frames of reference and experiences. The focus was more superficial in nature, with an emphasis on the past, just as the "getting to know you" phase can be when dating. This helps colleagues determine if they are compatible partners. As we move into the *engagement* phase, co-teachers should be deepening their knowledge of one another and focusing more on the present and future. We're getting to know our colleagues' preferences, what role they see themselves playing in the classroom we are about to share, and even their pet peeves. Grossman, Wineburg, and Woolworth (2001) remind us that for real collaboration to occur, it is important for educators to "share a sense of identity and common values" (p. 946). Now that we have shared our past and present, we need to discuss our goals for the future.

Shared goals are a critical characteristic of collaboration, and collaboration, as you now know, is absolutely essential for successful co-teaching to occur. Friend and Cook (2007) write, "Individuals who collaborate must share at least one goal. . . . Professionals do not have to share many or all goals in order to collaborate, just one that is specific and important enough to maintain their shared attention" (p. 8). Correa, Jones, Thomas, and Morsink (2005) state that "the two obvious goals for teaming approaches are . . . *improvement in treatment or education for a child with special needs,* and the *training of professionals in skills beyond their own areas of expertise*" (p. 53, emphasis in original). So, essentially, our goals may be for the students or they may be for us; in reality, it is a good idea to have goals for both. While we each may have our own ideas for what we want to see happen as a result of this experience, we also need to establish which of these goals we share. Ask each other the following questions:

Discussion of Goals

- *What goals do we have for the students in our co-taught class?*
  - *Academically*
  - *Behaviorally*
  - *Socially*
  - *Other*
- *What goals do we have for ourselves—individually or as a team—related to this experience?*
  - *Professionally*
  - *Personally*
  - *Other*

Having this discussion during the *engagement* phase of your relationship, as opposed to waiting until the students are there and the day-to-day chaos has begun, enables you both to again see where you share a vision and where you may disagree. Similar in nature to the S.H.A.R.E. worksheet (Figure 5.1, page 71),

Want More on This Topic?

In Part IV: The Marriage, Chapter 12 covers many different ways to effectively wrangle your own li'l rascals.

these questions prompt each of you to identify your personal desires and goals. Finding out that you share a common goal (e.g., I want students with and without disabilities to be able to work together in groups and not call each other names) strengthens your commitment to one another and helps solidify your bond. This process may help you learn that there are goals you do not share. For example, as you discuss students, one of you may share the following goal, "I want all students to take and pass the standardized test in this subject," while the other states, "I want some of the students to present a portfolio or other alternative assessment to demonstrate that they have learned some of the content by the end of the year." You will need to discuss how these goals support or conflict with one another. In addition, one co-teacher may state that her personal goal for co-teaching is, "I want to share all aspects of teaching this class." She may be surprised when her co-teacher reveals that his personal goal was, "I want to be able to use this collaborative time to catch up on grading papers." Being able to have a proactive conversation about shared or differing goals is empowering; you and your co-teacher will discuss those differences of opinion. At this time, you will hammer out an agreement, come to consensus, work out a compromise, or simply agree to disagree. If you wind up with the last option, you will then decide how best to handle the disagreement so that your students are not adversely affected and so they cannot exploit you. Disagreement does not have to mean continued conflict. Personal and sometimes humorous goals can be fun to share too. I have been known to divulge goals that include, "I want to have someone besides my husband who I can vent to on a weekly basis," "I want to work with someone who can make sure I'm not making any math errors on the front board," and "I want to experience a semester where there is another adult to help me with wrangle those li'l rascals."

On a more serious note, collaboration experts Marilyn Friend and Lynne Cook share the characteristics of effective teams in their textbook *Interactions: Collaboration Skills for School Professionals* (2007). They too emphasize the need for goal setting, stating that "the effectiveness of the team can be evaluated in terms of its goal attainment because . . . the team's purpose for existence is to achieve this goal" (p. 38). The characteristics of effective teams are that (1) the team's goals are clear, (2) the members' needs are met, (3) members have individual accountability, and (4) group processes maintain the team (Friend & Cook, 2007). You and your prospective co-teacher are a team. A large part of whether or not you become an *effective* team is up to you.

Double-check to see that you have met the following criteria:

- ***Are our goals clear?*** Do we each know what those goals are? Are they shared? Do we know how we will determine if we have actually met those goals? When are we planning to assess our goal attainment?
- ***Are our individual needs being met?*** Have we completed the S.H.A.R.E. worksheet to reveal to one another what our personal hopes and expectations are regarding this collaboration? Do we each feel that we are

necessary to the success of the students in the classroom or does one of us feel superfluous? If so, why?

- *Do we each have individual accountability?* Have we completed the Defining Roles and Responsibilities worksheet in Figure 5.4 to determine who will do what, when, and how? Are we each comfortable with our roles in the co-taught classroom? Do we feel that there is parity and that we each are sharing our areas of expertise?
- *Have we created processes to maintain our team?* Have we figured out ways to share leadership and participation in the class? Do we each have a time when we are "in charge"? Have we created schedules or other plans that keep us organized and working together smoothly (e.g., Mr. X will call parents Monday and Wednesday nights; Ms. Y will call parents Tuesday and Thursday nights; no calls home on Friday nights; weekend calls will depend on the situation and the student)?

Please note that the focus of this chapter is on establishing our short- and long-term realistic goals. That is because we may want to first identify goals that we want to achieve in the first day, first week or first month of school. I encourage you to create realistic goals; pie-in-the-sky goals are fun to create but not so much fun to look at when they have no chance of being achieved. Short-term goals might include the following:

- Obtaining an additional teacher desk so we both have a personal space in the room. One of us can ask the school secretary in charge of resources, while the other can go directly to the head janitor to see if there are extra desks.
- Going together to the administrator to ensure that no more than 30 percent of our co-taught class has identified disabilities. In the past, that has been an issue in inclusive classes, but we can create a united front by going together.
- Using each one of the five co-teaching approaches we've learned at least once each in the first two weeks of school. That way, we have a chance to see what works, what doesn't, and what we'll need to improve. It helps us avoid getting in a rut too early in the school year. It also helps set the tone at a time when it is easy to get overwhelmed and let good intentions go by the wayside.

Each of the above goals is short-term in nature and is realistic in scope. The following are long-term goals that you might consider establishing together.

- Collect data on the co-teaching approaches we use throughout the semester. We can do this by keeping lesson plans. At the end of the semester, we can discuss how we used the approaches and what impact we think they had on students' motivation and achievement.
- Have the special educator, who has never taught sixth grade math content before, not lead direct instruction for new content in the first semester but

instead plan to have her lead a lesson on new content first thing in the second semester. This will enable her to be comfortable with the students and teachers can use the holiday break to make sure she's more comfortable with the actual content at that time.

- Give students a survey at the end of the semester and again at the end of the school year to see what they liked and didn't like about co-teaching. That way we can use their responses to reflect together and to improve our collaborative efforts.
- Give parents a survey at the end of the semester and again at the end of the school year to identify their perspectives regarding what they liked most and least about co-teaching. We can also use their responses to reflect together and to improve our collaborative efforts.
- Present our experiences to other faculty at a staff meeting or on a professional development day. Other teachers can benefit from our experiences, and we can thereby increase inclusive practices at our school.

Self-Assessment 2

Are We Ready to Get Engaged?

Have we discussed our classroom preferences and pet peeves?

Did we complete the S.H.A.R.E. worksheet (Figure 5.1) separately and then compare responses?

Have we identified ways to demonstrate parity to the students and to each other?

Are we going to put both names on the board, door, report cards, and letters home? Are we going to check our egos at the door as we begin to work together?

Have we determined the roles and teacher actions we want to divide and those we want to share?

What if both of you want to do the *fun* activities and no one wants to do the grading?

Have we talked about the goals we have as a team for the short- and long-term?

What if the main goal for one of us is just to have a break from teaching? Are we able to really talk through disagreements we may have now? If not, we may be looking at a difficult relationship down the road.

My current concerns about this marriage are

8

Matchmaker, Matchmaker

The Role of the Administrator

■ AVOIDING ARRANGED MARRIAGES: THE SEARCH FOR SOUL MATES

Getting Volunteers and Building Teams

As the administrator of a school or district, you have decided that it is time for some of your teachers to take the plunge into that professional marriage known as co-teaching. You also know that "administrators who do not want their teachers to get *divorced* too soon need to recognize the importance of encouraging self-selection of partners" (Murawski, 2008b, p. 27). In the components of effective collaboration cited by Friend and Cook (2007), being *voluntary* is key. Unfortunately, however, many administrators feel the philosophical, legal, ethical, or logistical need to have co-teaching occur at their sites, and the result is a mandate for teachers to participate. Waiting for teachers to volunteer would not always be timely or result in the right combination of the people, grades, or subject areas in which co-teaching is desired. In these situations, administrators find themselves telling their staff that co-teaching will be utilized as a service delivery option. These announcements are often last minute, not providing teachers with sufficient lead time to prepare or get to know their partners. In addition, many teachers who are told they will be co-teaching have never been provided with any training in this area.

Although time or logistical constraints can negatively impact an administrator's ability to enlist volunteers to co-teach, there are strategies that can be used to increase the chances more educators will step forward to participate in this collaborative activity. It is important to remember that teachers who feel they have had some input in the process are overwhelmingly more responsive to co-teaching (Murawski, Boyer, Atwill & Melchiorre, 2009). Some of the following strategies suggested involve the provision of incentives to teachers to participate in co-teaching; others simply offer administrators various ways to introduce the concept to teachers so they will be more amenable to participating.

Strategies for Obtaining Co-Teaching Volunteers

Share the Model With General Educators

Tell general education teachers about co-teaching and why it will be beneficial to them. Special educators are more often exposed to the concept in their teacher preparation courses and professional development seminars than are their general education colleagues. Teachers who have successfully engaged in co-teaching can share their experiences with their colleagues at staff meetings and explain how having two teachers in the same room benefits both teachers and students. Emphasize benefits found in the literature, such as "sharing the workload," "more creative instruction," "more fun," and even "a chance to go to the bathroom." Letting teachers know they can self-select partners and get in "on the ground floor" before collaboration is mandated is another effective approach.

Set Up "Speed Dating" and "Mixers"

Okay, speed dating may be pushing it (or might be really fun), but providing opportunities for general and special educators to get to know one another will certainly open doors. Because of the culture at many schools, especially larger elementary schools, teachers may not know anyone outside of their own grade level. Teachers can be as bad as kids when it comes to having cliques. The idea of welcoming an unknown person into your classroom for a year is unsettling, maybe even a bit scary. Instead, administrators can set up times when teachers can get to know one another in a more social setting, like having a movie night with pizza and beverages. If specific grades or content areas have already been identified as the ones which require the most collaboration and co-teaching, only those teachers can be included (e.g., special educators and early elementary K–third grade teachers) and administrators can be very forthright in the purpose of the activity. For example, "I have brought you all here for the next hour—and provided the soda, chips, and dip—for a reason. At the end of this hour, you need to be able to identify at least one person with whom you feel you could co-teach effectively. I will be asking you to share that information with me individually later this week." This puts the onus of choosing a partner on the teachers but provides them with the opportunity to have a say in the people with whom they think they could work the best.

Provide Professional Development

Promise quality training in co-teaching techniques, approaches, and strategies *before* teachers begin co-teaching. The literature on co-teaching is replete with research citing the importance of training for successful co-teaching endeavors. Time and time again, teachers report that they need and want professional development on strategies prior to being thrown into this type of teaching arrangement. Administrators need to find a way to budget for such training, as well as for follow-up days and extra co-planning time for teachers. Doing so will help to establish that administrative support is earnest and not simply an empty promise. Additionally, providing professional development to the entire faculty demonstrates to the staff that this is not a "fly-by-night" approach that will only impact a few teachers but rather an initiative that is going to stay and will likely impact every one of them eventually. Administrators need to show their faculty that they are serious about professional development efforts. Teachers should be prepped in advance, and administrators should display enthusiasm for the upcoming training. If administrators are truly excited, teachers will be more willing to buy in.

Ensure Common Planning Times

Because co-planning is such an important part of effective co-teaching, administrators can also obtain more volunteers if they are able to promise common planning times for cooperating teachers. Common planning times are one of the most effective ways for teachers to get together to plan on a regular basis. That said, I also realize that most elementary teachers do not have any planning time built into their schedules at all. Thus, when common planning times are impossible, administrators can set aside other times for teachers to plan, such as getting a substitute teacher once a month to allow co-teachers to meet. Administrators who want to surprise their teachers with absolute dedication to co-teaching can even offer to substitute a class themselves. One administrator in Arizona who did this stated that she "not only got more respect from the teachers, but the students were shocked when they found out [she] could actually teach!"

Want More on This Topic?

Additional ways to find time for co-planning are provided in Part III: The Wedding. Planning is the most important element of co-teaching!

Set Firm Caps on Co-Taught Classes

Another incentive for teachers to volunteer for co-teaching is if administrators promise "capped" classes. In most schools, classes are capped at a certain number of students. For example, a fifth grade class may be capped at 18 students. However, as school begins and more students enroll, the cap rises and that same fifth grade class may end up with 25 students. Administrators could promise teachers who co-teach that their cap (while perhaps initially a bit higher than other classes because there are two teachers in the room) is 22 and that, because they will be engaging in this new arrangement and will be working with a diverse group of students with and without disabilities, the cap will be firm. While other classes' caps begin to rise to 22, 23, or even 28, the co-taught class numbers will never exceed 22.

Want More on This Topic?

Be sure to read Chapter 12, Matchmaker, Matchmaker: The Role of the Administrator, that discusses how to avoid having too many students with special needs in one class.

Provide Incentives

Teachers who agree to engage in the first phase of co-teaching at a school may need to be provided with some tangible incentives. The first time teachers teach together they will need to spend additional time getting to know one another, co-planning, co-assessing, and ultimately, "making their marriage work." Because other teachers do not have to spend this additional time or energy, it makes sense to provide the co-teachers with incentives that show them you appreciate their additional efforts. You can certainly remind teachers that a benefit to this type of collaboration is that "some people know things that others do not know" allowing for the collective to "exceed that of the individual" (Grossman, et al., 2001, p. 973). But, hey, sometimes that kind of incentive is just simply not as powerful as *teacher stuff!* These can include

- provision of materials to help with teaching (e.g., Teach Timer, Wikki Stix, laptop, ELMO, Smartboard, magnetic lap boards),
- provision of materials to help with planning (e.g., CTSS [Co-Teaching Solutions System] Teachers' Toolbox, co-teaching lesson plan book),
- the removal of additional duties (e.g., bus duty, lunch, recess, club supervision),
- a stipend for additional before or after school hours planning time,
- recognition in their files, in the school newsletter, or from the school board,
- or just ask what would make it worthwhile for them. It may be less than you would imagine. (I was always a sucker for an electric hole puncher.)

Send Out a Survey

Once teachers know that co-teaching is a service delivery option for meeting students' diverse needs, that many will be expected to engage in co-teaching in the upcoming year, and that there are various benefits and incentives for volunteering to co-teach before being mandated to do so, it is time to solicit their information and preferences. Disseminating a survey among the entire staff is preferable to sending it out only to those teachers who are sure to co-teach. I like to have the entire staff complete the questionnaire as it gives me data for future collaborative activities.

Surveys will need to differ from general education to special education and from faculty to staff. For example, general education teacher surveys should ask those individuals to identify the classes in which they think they could use the most support, the special education individuals with whom they think they could most easily collaborate, and their experiences and philosophies related to collaboration and co-teaching. Special service provider surveys, which include special education teachers as well as professionals such as Designated Instructional Service (DIS) personnel, need to identify the grades and subject areas in which individuals feel the most prepared to collaborate, the general education faculty with whom they think they could most easily collaborate, and their own experiences and philosophies related to collaboration and co-teaching. Finally, support staff, including paraprofessionals such as Title I, ESL, or special education assistants, also need to complete a survey. Their version would include the areas in which they feel the most prepared to support students, the students they feel most prepared to support, the faculty they feel most comfortable supervising them, and their experiences and philosophies related to collaboration and in-class support. Feel free to tweak the example surveys provided to gather the most relevant data on your own faculty and staff.

Getting faculty input proactively is helpful to ensuring success for any new initiative.

Co-Teaching and Collaboration Preparation Survey for General Education Faculty					
Name:					
Classes I typically teach:					
Grades I typically teach:					
Complete the following:	**Least**				**Most**
My experience working with students with special needs	1	2	3	4	5
My comfort level in having students w/special needs in class	1	2	3	4	5
My experience working with special educators	1	2	3	4	5
My comfort level in collaborating with special educators	1	2	3	4	5
My experience co-teaching with special educators	1	2	3	4	5
My comfort level in co-teaching with special educators	1	2	3	4	5
My willingness to co-teach this year	1	2	3	4	5
My concerns about co-teaching or having students with disabilities in my class are					
Working closely with a special educator could help me in the following ways:					
If I were to co-teach next year, I would prefer to co-teach with					
Other comments we should know:					

Figure 8.1   Co-Teaching and Collaboration Preparation Survey for General Education Faculty

Co-Teaching and Collaboration Preparation Survey *for Special Education Faculty*					
Name:					
Subjects and classes I prefer to teach:					
Grades I prefer to teach:					
Complete the following:	**Least**				**Most**
My experience working with students with special needs	1	2	3	4	5
My comfort level in having students w/special needs in GE class	1	2	3	4	5
My experience working with general educators	1	2	3	4	5
My comfort level in collaborating with general educators	1	2	3	4	5
My experience co-teaching with general educators	1	2	3	4	5
My comfort level in co-teaching with general educators	1	2	3	4	5
My willingness to co-teach this year	1	2	3	4	5
My concerns about co-teaching and collaborating with general educators are					
Working closely with a general educator could help me in the following ways:					
If I were to co-teach next year, I would prefer to co-teach with					
Other comments we should know:					

Figure 8.2   Co-Teaching and Collaboration Preparation Survey for Special Education Faculty

Co-Teaching and Collaboration Preparation Survey for Support Staff						
Name:						
Subjects I feel most comfortable supporting:						
Grades I feel most comfortable supporting:						
Students I feel most comfortable supporting (can be names of students or types of disabilities, like students with autism, students with behavioral or attentional needs, students with learning disabilities, etc.)						
Complete the following:	**Least**					**Most**
My experience working with students with special needs	1	2	3	4		5
My comfort level in supporting students w/ special needs in class	1	2	3	4		5
My concerns about supporting students with disabilities in a general education class are						
Working closely with both general and special educators could help me in the following ways:						
Other comments we should know:						

Figure 8.3   Co-Teaching and Collaboration Preparation Survey for Support Staff

Part III
The Wedding

Luckily, in a co-teaching marriage, no minister or formalwear is required.

9

For Better or Worse

Establishing Norms for Behavior and Academics

Just as most brides-to-be (yes, I'm stereotyping here) have a vision of what their wedding will look like, every teacher has his own idea of what a classroom should look like—how students should behave, how lessons should be presented, and how the everyday tasks should be managed. All teachers do not share an identical vision, any more than all brides want their colors to be "blush" and "bashful." While most of us do not envision the Hollywood cliché of the classroom, in which kids are always sitting on top of their desks, playing loud music on boom boxes, and dancing in the aisles while throwing paper airplanes, we certainly can vary in terms of our reasonable preferences. During your *engagement* phase, you completed the S.H.A.R.E. worksheet with your partner to proactively discuss your preferences (Figure 5.1, p. 71). That was a useful first step, but now that we are actually taking our vows, we get to put all of that theory into practice.

Have you ever heard the George Bernard Shaw quote, "Youth is wasted on the young"? I suggest the educational version of that phrase is, "Student teaching is wasted on new teachers." Individuals who are new to the classroom are often so overwhelmed by the general concept of teaching and managing a classroom that they are not in any position to retain the majority of the strategies, suggestions, and tips provided by their textbooks, professors, and mentor teachers. They are simply trying to stay afloat. A few years later, however, they are ready to improve, hone their skills, and seek strategies that will make their lives easier. By the time they can handle the extra information, they are getting set in their ways and may already be afraid to change what works for them or techniques with which they are now comfortable. Try and get your hands on a textbook for new teachers—you will find them full of best practices, strategies, and research-supported techniques for improving teaching. A few of the texts that I personally recommend are:

- Walther-Thomas, Korinek, McLaughlin, and Williams. (1999). *Collaboration for Inclusive Education: Developing Successful Programs.* ISBN 10: 0205273688
- Wong and Wong. (2004). *The First Days of School: How To Be An Effective Teacher.* ISBN 10: 0962936065
- Tomlinson and Eidson. (2003). *Differentiation in Practice: A Resource Guide for Differentiating Curriculum, Grades K–5.* ISBN: 0871207605
- Gregory and Kuzmich. (2005). *Differentiated Literacy Strategies for Student Growth and Achievement in Grades K–6.* ISBN: 0761988815
- Mastropieri and Scruggs. (2007). *The Inclusive Classroom: Strategies for Effective Instruction* (3rd ed.). ISBN 10: 0131540688
- Downing. (2008). *Including Students With Severe and Multiple Disabilities in Typical Classrooms: Practical Strategies for Teachers.* ISBN 10: 1557669082
- Vaughn and Bos. (2008). *Strategies for Teaching Students With Learning and Behavior Problems* (7th ed.). ISBN 10: 0205642659

As you and your co-teacher begin to determine how you will collaboratively run your co-taught classroom, there are three specific areas you should spend time proactively establishing with one another and with your students. These three areas relate to (1) *physical issues*, (2) *classroom management issues*, and (3) *instructional issues*. I share some practical strategies for putting them in place below. Be advised that while the physical issues are fairly straightforward, the sections on classroom management and instruction are more complex in nature.

PHYSICAL ISSUES ■

Physical issues involve the physical layout of the classroom. The way you and your partner set up the class will either aid or detract from your instruction. Similar to planning the seating arrangement for a wedding reception, there are many details to consider. Co-teachers should do the following when setting up their classroom:

- *Make sure both names are clearly posted on the door or in the room.* Even if teachers are only collaborating for one part of the day (e.g., during language arts time), it is helpful for both names to be prominently displayed. Without both names on the door or somewhere in the room, students get the unintended message that the class is the sole authority of the general educator whose name is displayed. It can also make the special service provider feel like a second-class citizen.

Posting both teachers' names is a simple, yet effective, way to demonstrate shared responsibility for all students.

Want More on This Topic?

Chapter 10, For Richer or Poorer, discusses the specifics of sharing space and materials.

- *Determine where each teacher's personal space will be.* Adults need to feel they have an area for their personal items, as well as for their class-related materials.
- *Determine how regrouping will occur* for the use of parallel teaching, alternative teaching, and station teaching. Once you cooperatively determine how you will best be able to use your classroom space, or additional space such as other classrooms, outside areas, and so forth, you will be able to instruct students how to move to these positions. If students know how to set up and move to stations, for example, there will be less chaos and frustration and teachers will be more likely to continue to utilize these regrouping approaches with kids.
- *Proactively consider any physical limitations of students.* If any of your students is in a wheelchair, for example, make sure your aisles are wide enough, that any regrouping into groups also takes the student with the wheelchair into account, and that materials are accessible for individuals who are height-challenged for whatever reason (beyond the obvious height challenge of most elementary children). Find out if any incoming students are blind, deaf, or otherwise impaired. Work with your co-teacher to determine if you need to set up an amplification device. If there are students who will need a quiet area for redirection or focus, is there a space in the room created for that activity (e.g., a cubicle or small area)?

Although it is not desirable for paraprofessionals assigned to assist an individual student to hover around that student, it is likely that he may need to sit near the student occasionally to help with academic or behavioral tasks; thus, has this been taken into consideration when thinking about where that student will sit? This can be a challenge for teachers, as students with disabilities should not always be relegated to the back and sides of the room, but at the same time, a seat or other space that will not distract other students may need to be provided for a paraprofessional.

Want More on This Topic?

Each of the co-teaching approaches is discussed in detail in Part IV: The Marriage.

- *Consider seating arrangements.* While you don't need to put out name cards or Jordan almonds at each seat, you do need to discuss whether you want to give students assigned seats or allow them to choose their own. There are certainly pros and cons to both. Allowing students to choose their own seats gives them autonomy and choice—important at the elementary level—but it also pretty much ensures that students will argue about who gets to sit next to whom. My personal preference is to give assigned seats (usually alphabetical) for the first two weeks of class. I let students know that it is so my co-teacher and I can learn their names. Later, we let them choose their own seats, which are naturally contingent on appropriate behavior. Whatever you decide, make sure you both have discussed it and agreed. Also, co-teachers should consider nontraditional seating layouts. Instead of uniform rows, desk clusters or semicircles may be more conducive to inclusive instruction.

CLASSROOM MANAGEMENT ISSUES ■

As I mentioned, the physical issues are fairly straightforward; as long as co-teachers consider their classroom and students, decision making in this area should not be overly difficult. Making collaborative decisions regarding the second area to proactively consider (i.e., classroom management) can be much more daunting. By classroom management, I am referring to the proactive decisions teachers make and share with students regarding rules and procedures, as well as the reactive decisions teachers make regarding student behavior. Every class has its own issues related to management; however, an inclusive class may have additional concerns. Consider the following scenario:

> ***Mr. Fisch (general education teacher):*** "Javier is really driving me crazy. He doesn't pay attention. He's always distracted. He doesn't stay in his seat and he is always moving, especially when I'm teaching new content."
>
> ***Ms. Dorra (special education teacher, feigning surprise):*** "Really? The kid with ADHD does all that?"

It's not that Mr. Fisch's concerns are not valid, but why is he surprised by these behaviors? While there are many pros and cons to labeling students—which we will not go into here—one of the benefits is that it does provide us with some information about the student and his areas of difficulty. In the case of the above scenario, Ms. Dorra is trying to let Mr. Fisch know—albeit sarcastically—that Javier's behaviors should not be much of a shocker. Knowing that there is a student with attention deficit/hyperactivity disorder in the classroom should have keyed the teachers into the fact that they will need to plan for certain behaviors in advance. In this case, perhaps Ms. Dorra could have suggested to Mr. Fisch earlier in the school year that they limit the length of oral lectures or that they give Javier (and other students) a form for guided note taking that he could complete during lectures to keep him focused. She could have worked with Mr. Fisch to come up with ways to help Javier stay on the task at hand.

Again, I'd like to highlight the myriad of reference books for teachers on the topic of classroom management. I have used or frequently find myself coming back to the following:

- Emmer, Evertson, and Worsham. (2002). *Classroom Management for Elementary Teachers* (6th ed.). ISBN 10: 0205349986
- McLeod, Fisher, and Hoover. (2003). *The Key Elements of Classroom Management: Managing Time and Space, Student Behavior, and Instructional Strategies.* ISBN 10: 087107877
- Walker, Shea, and Bauer. (2006). *Behavior Management: A Practical Approach for Educators* (9th ed.). ISBN 10: 0131710036
- Kauffman, Mostert, Trent, and Pullen. (2005). *Managing Classroom Behavior: A Reflective Case-Based Approach* (4th ed.). ISBN 10: 020544881X

While these books will provide you with direction and helpful strategies, following are some quick tips to address two major topics of immediate concern. Under the umbrella term, classroom management, are the topics *proactive procedures* and *reactive responses*.

Proactive Procedures

Veteran teachers know that the organization of everyday tasks is critical. Students need to know the general schedule for the day and the week. For example, every class starts with a warm-up and ends with a "ticket out the door" activity; quizzes are every Friday, and unit tests are every other week. The more structure there is in place, the better for both students and co-teachers. At first blush, structure seems to be about restriction. In reality, however, it is freeing and it allows teachers and students to relax. The stress of the unknown is removed. Structure need not connote absolute rigidity, but having a general routine helps everyone know what is expected, which is a benefit to both students with and without disabilities. In addition to letting students (and parents) know what to expect, structure helps co-teachers in determining their roles and responsibilities. For those individuals who are interested in engaging in future co-teaching but are currently only able to provide in-class support, it will enable them to determine when they would most be needed in the classroom. An example of daily schedules is provided in Figure 9.1.

Examples of Structured Daily Schedules	
The more consistent general education classes are, the easier it is for special educators and other professionals to provide consistent support in the classroom. Discuss your consistent schedules.	

Third Grade Language Arts Time: Mrs. Hutchinson and Miss Weichel	
Mon/Wed/Fri	**Tues/Thurs**
Warm-up: 10 min.	Warm-up: 10 min.
Vocabulary: 10 min.	Cultural Literacy: 10 min.
New Lesson: 20 min.	New Lesson: 20 min.
Independent work: 15 min.	Independent Work: 10 min.
Wrap-Up: 5 min.	Silent Reading: 10 min.

Fourth Grade Math Time: Ms. Chang and Mr. Narr	
Mon-Thurs	**Friday**
Warm-up: 10 min.	Brainbuster: 10 min.
Review: 15 min.	Homework in: 5 min.
New lesson: 20 min.	Review: 20 min.
Independnt work: 10 min.	Quiz: 20 min.
Wrap-up: 5 min.	Wrap-up: 5 min.

Fifth Grade Social Studies Time: Mr. Bell (Fridays with Miss Loveland)		
Mon/Wed	**Tues/Thurs**	**Friday**
Warm-up: 10 min.	Warm-up: 10 min.	Quiz: 15 min.
Vocabulary: 10 min.	People/Dates: 10 min.	Projects: 30 min.
New lesson: 25 min.	New lesson: 25 min.	Preview: 10 min.
Independent work: 10 min.	Independent work: 10 min.	Extra Credit
Wrap-Up: 5 min.	Wrap-Up: 5 min.	Phrase: 5 min.

Figure 9.1   Examples of Structured Daily Schedules

SOURCE: Murawski, W. W. (2008a).

In addition to scheduling, co-teachers also need to discuss how they want to coordinate daily procedures such as homework, pencil sharpening, asking for materials, bathroom or hallway passes, quizzes, and the like. It is important for co-teachers to jointly determine what they feel comfortable with and to share the classroom procedures with students. Many teachers and researchers suggest that classroom rules be created in conjunction with student input (Emmer et al., 2002; Walker et al., 2006), but the day-to-day logistics of the classroom need to be determined by the teachers and reinforced and practiced regularly in the first few weeks of school. By proactively determining the procedures for the class, co-teachers will be able to jointly share them with the class and avoid many student behaviors that arise from confusion or lack of structure.

Following are a few questions to guide you in your discussion as you work to create your classroom policies.

- *How will we take attendance?* While calling out names may be useful in the first few days of school as you are working to learn student names, it is generally not a strong use of teacher time. With co-teaching you may choose to have one teacher take attendance, while the other gets the class going. That is an instructional decision. Another choice that Ms. Palacios and Ms. Baral, two creative co-teachers in California, use is to have sentence strips with the students' names on them. In their case, they used a simple wall chart. When the kindergarten students entered class, they knew the procedure to find their name and move it quickly from "Home" to "School." That way, it was easier for the co-teachers to see at a glance who was absent or tardy. No time lost!

Creative co-teachers find ways to take daily attendance so that no instructional time is lost.

- *How will students find out about homework (i.e., where will it be posted)?* Try to have homework posted in a spot other than the crowded front board that already will have information on standards, class agenda and objectives, student names and information, and class work on it. Two excellent resources for posting homework are "cling sheets" (large dry erase sheets the size of chart paper) and colorful "wall charts" (found at most teacher supply stores). When using the wall charts, I find it helpful to laminate sentence strips and quickly post homework by topic that way. Another strategy is to create a class Web site and post this work online so students and parents have direct access.

- *How will students turn in their homework, and how will teachers check homework?* To save time and encourage student independence, organized co-teachers have baskets or file folders available for students in each period to turn in their homework as soon as they enter the room. If you will be reviewing homework, let students know only to turn in the homework when told, as opposed to when they enter the class. Either way, having a spot for homework eliminates the need for teachers to waste valuable time walking around and collecting work. Another strategy related to homework is to have one teacher walk around and check students' homework, while the other teacher reviews it orally or on the overhead. By using the One Teach, One Support approach in this manner, the supporting teacher can use two stamps to mark students' work: "Completed. Good job," which is used for those whose work is finished, and "Please finish and return," which is used to indicate if a student only completed part of the work. This is a helpful strategy as it encourages students to at least do partial work so that they will get credit for what was done on time and only the part done late will be graded down accordingly. Students with disabilities are often less likely to turn in work if it is not completed; this strategy demonstrates to them that it is better to do some work than none at all. By walking around and checking the work individually, this strategy also allows teachers to provide accommodations as needed; no one need know that Sally received a "Completed. Good job" for only doing half of the work. If that was an appropriate accommodation for her, she would be able to get full credit without teachers having to make the adaptation noticeable in class.
- *What is our materials policy?* Teachers need to determine jointly what their policy will be regarding student materials. If a student forgets his pencil, are you going to tell him it's his responsibility to find one or are you going to provide one so that he has no excuse not to do the work? Either option may be valid, but you and your co-teacher need to decide what you are going to do. I know teachers who ask a student to turn in a shoe in exchange for a pen or pencil; students certainly do not forget to return the borrowed item in order to get their shoes back. I have seen teachers who prefer to have materials available for purchase (pens, pencils, paper, etc). A strategy from Dr. Dieker is to have golf pencils available for students. Those short little pencils are inexpensive and students generally think they are dorky or difficult to write with, so they are motivated to bring their own writing utensils. Whatever policies the two of you agree upon, make sure you do so before students enter the classroom. Thereafter, staunchly maintain those policies with consistency.
- *What is our "out of seat" policy?* It is difficult to keep some students in their seats. I know, newsflash. Even if you and your co-teacher plan to ensure that students are actively engaged in kinesthetic learning

activities during instruction—in fact, even if you plan to do back hand-springs in class to keep their rapt attention—there will still be times when a student wants to go to the bathroom, sharpen his pencil, see the nurse, or just find a way to get into the hallway and out of the classroom. Given that fact, make sure that you and your partner brainstorm as many of these eventualities as you can and determine your general policy. Notice that I said "general" policy—there will always be exceptions, but you can deal with those as they occur. While there are numerous options for dealing with student out-of-seat behavior, I am a fan of providing structure early on with choice embedded in that structure. What do I mean by that? I mean that students at the elementary level like to make their own decisions and feel that they are more autonomous than perhaps they should be. Thus, I like to make sure they know that I respect their need for decision making, but at the same time, there have to be limits. Getting out of the room cannot be a free-for-all.

My co-teacher, Linda, and I decided to tell students that they had three "get out of jail free" passes per semester (see Figure 9.2). We told them that each pass was good for five minutes, no matter if it was for the bathroom, for taking time-out in the hallway (provided no one was disrupted), or for going to the nurse or office. This provided them with structure and choice. It was amazing to us how many students held on to their passes for most of the semester. They didn't want to give up their three chances at freedom too early. Some never even used their three opportunities to leave. In order to keep track of the three passes, we created cards for each student. Students' names were put on the cards and then we laminated them and kept the passes in a recipe box on the front desk. When a student wanted to go to the hall, she would simply come up to the desk, get her pass, and give it to whichever teacher wasn't actively lecturing or leading class discussion. We would hole punch the card (we recommend the hole punches that create holes that look like flowers or other shapes), and then we would give them the "hall pass timer." When five minutes were up, we would collect the card from the student and refile it. Students were told early on that if they lost their card or used up the three passes, they were done. These passes worked very well for us. You and your partner can decide jointly what negative and positive consequences you may want for students who are gone longer than five minutes or for students who do not use their passes during the semester. Obviously, this strategy can only be used for students who are old enough to walk in the hallways on their own.

Working with another co-teacher named Arleen, we took the idea for laminated cards for each student to another level. Arleen and I recognized that one of the issues our students shared was a need to develop self-advocacy. We thought that it was simply unacceptable that many of these students were

Want More on This Topic?

A variety of timers and information on their use is provided in Part IV: The Marriage.

unable to self-identify their own areas of strength and weakness and advocate for themselves. As the special educator, I want students who have an individualized education program (IEP) to know what an IEP is, what their disability is, and how to advocate for their own accommodations and modifications as they transition into middle school. Arleen and I emphasized the need for students to be independent and even role-played real-world situations that helped students see our point. These cards became our tool to teach self-advocacy and also helped us with classroom management; for example, when a student with an emotional or behavioral disability recognized that he was close to losing control, he could give one of us the card allowing him to take a personal "time-out." This eliminated many potential disruptions in class. (Obviously we oversaw the use of the cards to make sure they were not being overused or used inappropriately.) Check out the example cards in Figures 9.3 and 9.4. Feel free to make a variety of different kinds to suit your needs and those of your students.

Front of card

Back of card

Hall Pass

Mrs. Hutchinson and Ms. Weichel

4th grade

Student name: _____

(1)   (2)   (3)

Hall Pass

You may use this pass to leave the room for five minutes. You may stand outside the room, go to the bathroom, or walk up and down the hall quietly. However, if you disrupt any classes (including this one) or leave this hall, your hall pass privileges will be removed. You have three passes per semester.

Figure 9.2   Hall Pass

Self-Advocacy Card

Name: *Julian Chausse*

Grade: *2*

Area of need: ***Attention, behavior***

Areas of strength: ***Academics, creativity***

I am having a difficult time. Please allow me to take a two-minute break to help me get my attention or behavior back on track so that I do not get in trouble.

Thank you.

Figure 9.3   Self-Advocacy Card

Modification Reminder Card	Acceptable Adaptations to Ask From Teachers
Name: **Shawna Jones** Grade: **5** Area of need: **Reading, writing, math** Areas of strength: **Following directions, parent involvement, interest in horses and people**	• Extra time for processing and work • Reduction in load (in class and homework) • Adapted books when possible • Reduce amounts provided at one time • Provide tasks that let me be the teacher's helper • Sign off on school and home notebook • Incorporate horses and names of my family members when possible

Figure 9.4   Modification Reminder Card

This chapter is titled "For Better or Worse: Establishing Norms for Behavior and Academics." I mentioned the three areas that need to be discussed by co-teachers are physical, classroom management, and instructional decision making. As we continue to consider issues related to classroom management, we move beyond the proactive procedures (the "better" part) to the reactive responses (the "worse" part). This section relates to situations in which a student does not follow policy or makes a bad choice. Yet again, communication and consistency between you and your partner are key.

Reactive Responses

Regardless of how proactive you and your partner are in planning your *wedding*, there will still be the caterer who is a bit late, the guest who drinks too much, and the cousins who haven't seen each other in years who decide now is a good time to rehash an old argument. How is this similar to the classroom? Simple. Despite your efforts at setting up solid classroom procedures, there will still be tardiness, inappropriate behavior, defiance, and other behaviors that need to be addressed in order for instruction to continue. How you and your co-teacher address those behaviors will set the tone for the rest of the school year, aka *marriage*. Considering those scenarios in advance will prepare you both when they occur.

- *What will we do about tardies?* Many schools have adopted a policy that students who enter class tardy need to return to where they were, or go to the main office, to get an excuse pass to class. However, this may end up resulting in a student who enters class twenty seconds late, thereby interrupting the class once, having to leave the class to get a pass, to then return to the first class now much later to interrupt a second time. A tardy notebook, such as that in Figure 9.5, can help with this.

Date	Name	Time Arrived	Rationale	Excuse Note?
3/3	Marty Farrell	8:10	Woke up late	No
3/3	Wa-ling Yun	9:16	Dentist appointment	Yes (in recipe box)
3/3	Joachim Smith	8:05	Woke up late	No
3/4	Joachim Smith	8:26	Car trouble	Yes (in recipe box)

Figure 9.5 Tardy Notebook

SOURCE: Murawski, W. W. (2008a).

How does a tardy notebook work? Co-teachers place a notebook on a small table located near the classroom door as students enter. As one teacher begins the class, the other monitors for those students who are tardy. As a student enters the room, the co-teacher in the support role merely motions to the tardy notebook and then monitors that the student signs in appropriately. Students are requested to sign in with name, time, date, and reason they were tardy. (For students too young to do this themselves, the teacher in the support role can do it for them and then they can sign it.) If a student has a note upon entry, co-teachers have a place for those notes to go. (I use a recipe box sitting next to the tardy notebook.) If the student thinks he should be excused, but does not have a note, the student is responsible for obtaining one later in the day. Co-teachers can use the concept of the tardy notebook to create a similar homework notebook (e.g., Do you have your homework? Yes or no. If no, why not?).

This system helps makes students more aware of and accountable for their tardiness. In addition, however, it allows students into class without interrupting the opening instruction. It also provides documentation for future review; when the tardiness becomes chronic, co-teachers can determine if it is time for a student contract, a parent-teacher conference, an IEP meeting, or another intervention.

- *What will we do if kids are talking to each other or engaging in other little (but bothersome) behaviors?* As one co-teacher directs the instruction, the other co-teacher will often be in charge of classroom management. If you are both actively engaged with kids, you can share the task of overseeing behavior. A wonderful low-key strategy to helping reinforce—or redirect—student behavior is the "see me later" card, developed by a co-teacher of mine, Rebecca Mieliwocki.

Make a handful of the cards shown in Figure 9.6 (all on the same color—don't do "red for bad" and "green for good") and laminate them for frequent use. The key to this approach is preparation. If teachers were to put a card like this in front of students without explanation, they can be assured that they would hear things like, "What is this? Why did I get this? Why didn't he get one too?" Instead, co-teachers should jointly explain this approach to the class prior to using it. In explaining this approach, co-teachers announce that it is *their* turn to "pass notes." They have created these notes to let the students know that they are (1) doing something that needs to be stopped or (2) doing something that we hope they will continue. Co-teachers can say, "We don't want to have to disrupt class or embarrass you to let you know these things. Instead, we will quietly place a card on your table, and it will be your responsibility to read it. You will decide whether to continue or cease your behavior. You will not say anything when you receive it. You will simply give it back to the teacher who gave it to you at the end of class. Then and only then can we discuss it." By the way, feel free to alter the cards to match your students' levels. If your students are nonreaders, simply have cards with eyes on one side and a thumbs-up or thumbs-down on the other.

Front of card   *Back of card*

See Me Later 	I really like what you are doing. Please see me after class to discuss this. Thank you.
See Me Later 	I really don't like what you are doing. Please stop. Please see me after class to discuss this. Thank you.

Figure 9.6   See Me Later Cards
SOURCE: Murawski, W. W. (2008a).

After giving a card, we highly recommend that co-teachers move away from the student to reduce the chance that the student will want to discuss the issue. This approach is very effective with many of the little behaviors that frequently occur in classes, such as talking, getting out of seats, doodling, etc. In addition, it is a good way to quietly reinforce behaviors that do not always occur, such as students helping one another or taking notes. However, it is obviously not intended to be an approach used for the "big" behaviors, such as extremely disruptive or dangerous behaviors. Remember, this is a low-key approach that is easy to use because you have two teachers in the class and one is in a role conducive to this activity.

- *What will we do if a student is defiant, rude, or uses inappropriate language?* You don't want to simply give out a "see me later" card if someone is aggressive or calls you a curse word. However, if you know that you will have students included in your classroom who struggle with extreme emotions, behaviors, or self-control, you need to determine what some of your options will be.

Want More on This Topic?

Learn about schoolwide positive behavior support in Part IV: The Marriage.

One of the first things for co-teachers to find out is if any of the students who will be in the class have a positive behavior support (PBS) plan in place. These are plans created for students with disabilities who have identified behavioral challenges. Often, teachers and parents work with school psychologists to identify negative behaviors, determine the function of those behaviors, and create a plan to change behavior through the use of PBS. Since the general educator is typically responsible for overseeing the content of the class and bringing in all information related to curriculum, the special educator should take the lead in reviewing all IEPs and talking to counselors and administrators to gather information on specific students in the class. Once this information has been compiled, teachers can identify strategies that have been successful with these students. This is where the special educator can shine by identifying strategies for working with students with emotional or behavioral needs and introducing those strategies to the general educator. Strategies may include

- giving "time away" or "brain breaks,"
- making a cubicle or quiet area in the room,
- removing the student from the environment to talk to them,
- using a quiet voice,
- using a point system,
- sending the student to an in-school suspension (ISS),
- calling home,
- creating behavior charts,
- allowing the student to write or draw their feelings, and
- using "antiseptic bouncing" in advance of the behavior escalating.

Antiseptic bouncing is a humorous term referring to when you clean your room by "bouncing" a child to another room. This can be done when a student needs a break or when you need a break from a student. It is not intended for use as a punishment but merely as a way to provide teachers or students with a short break from one another. Simply have an index card with "AB" written on it (for antiseptic bouncing) sealed in an envelope. On the front of the envelope, have the name of a teacher who will do this strategy with you. When a student needs to be out of the room for 5 to 10 minutes, ask him to run an errand for you. Give him the card and ask him to bring it to a teacher (preferably one across the school campus). Tell him to wait for a response and then return. The other teacher should know about the strategy and ask the student to wait for a few minutes until she has time to respond. She will then sign her name to the card, return it to the envelope, seal it, and give it back to the student to return. That teacher knows she can have the favor returned anytime she needs to "bounce" someone as well. By the way, if you can get a bunch of teachers to use this strategy, it increases your options for where to send the student for short or lengthy excursions.

- *What will we do if a student says, "That's not fair," or calls another student a name?* One of the concepts that should be introduced early on in an inclusive classroom is that "fair does not mean equal." No matter how surreptitious teachers may try to be when providing accommodations or modifications, students will notice at some point. Rather than hiding those adaptations, it is in the teachers' and students' best interests for teachers to make it clear the first days of school that they will be doing different things for different students during the school year. I recommend having a poster in the room—and throughout the school if possible—that states, "Fair does not mean equal; it means that everyone gets what he or she needs."

Talk about this concept with students. Give them examples of when it is not fair to be equal. My favorite example is having students remove their glasses and telling them that either we all don't wear glasses (so we are equal) or we all wear the *same* glasses. Students will be quick to tell you that is not fair; not everyone needs glasses—and even those who do, don't need the same ones. I like to take this analogy further and mention that the glasses are a disability we can see, but what about those students who are wearing contacts? Those are what we would refer to as "invisible disabilities." You may not know the student has a need because you can't see it, but if we didn't provide the accommodation (in this case, contacts), the student would not be able to perform as well as he should be able. Let students know that each will have a time when they need something different from us as co-teachers, whether it is extra time because one is about to go on a family trip and will miss class, extra materials because another left hers at her dad's when she had to hop between divorced households, or copies of notes because yet another broke his arm. When students are aware that every individual will benefit at some point, most are less likely to cry foul.

Another good strategy for dealing with the "that's not fair" conundrum is to teach students about learning styles. Consider having students complete a learning styles inventory (there are plenty available on-line) and help them identify their primary learning modalities: auditory, visual, kinesthetic, tactile. Most students can identify them without even completing an inventory but it is fun to see the data. Another source of differentiation is the multiple intelligences theory by Howard Gardner (2006). Have students identify their own areas of strength first and encourage them to think diversely, including things such as, "I'm good at music, chess, sports, reading, writing, analyzing data, drawing, problem solving, singing, making friends, cooking, etc." Be sure to point out that each individual has things he excels at and things he is not good at. Make a point to emphasize the strengths of all students, especially those who have been singled out by their peers as less capable. Share your own areas of strength and weakness with students so that they see that their teachers aren't perfect either.

- *What will we do if a student engages in a behavior that is a danger to himself or others (e.g., makes a threat, brings a weapon)?* In a case like this, your school should have a policy in place. Naturally, you will want to find a way to alert the authorities. This is definitely one of those times it is nice to have two teachers in the room so that, if possible, one can stay with the students while the other goes to get help. Decide in advance what roles you will take if you are able to make that decision. You don't want to waste precious moments looking at each other as if to say, "Should I go? Should you? Which of us is going to stay?" Both of you need to know where the fire alarm is in case you need to pull it. Special service providers who travel from room to room often forget to find out this type of information but it is critical. If you know that you may have a student with documented aggressive behavior, I also recommend that you both take a course in nonviolent Crisis Prevention Instruction (CPI; www.crisisprevention.com). I did it myself, and though I've only needed it once, I was glad to have had the training.

- *What do we do if . . .* There will always be behavioral concerns that arise for which you and your co-teacher did not plan. However, the more you do consider individual students and situations and plan accordingly, the more likely you will be able to deal with those you considered and those you did not. One of the concerns about co-teaching that has been frequently shared with me by general educators is, "What do I do if the special educator is absent one day? I haven't been trained in dealing with *those* kids and their behaviors don't go away just because she did." While this is a valid concern, I would argue that, if co-teachers are doing their jobs, the special educator should be sharing her strategies with the general educator while the general educator is concurrently sharing his content knowledge with the special educator through actions as well as through direct instruction. We need to be communicating and preparing each other if we want to be the most successful. Rather than each of us taking our own role and not sharing it with our colleague, we need to be helping one another learn our areas of expertise. In the area of behavior management and strategies, one of the ways you can communicate and make each other more comfortable, especially in case of a teacher absence, is to create a form that proactively describes the student, his common behavioral infractions, and suggested strategies for dealing with those issues. Any substitute teacher would be grateful for such as resource as well. Figure 9.7 shows an example of such a "student behavior at a glance" chart. Keep in mind that this chart is created to help teachers think about their responses to student behaviors. You will want to modify or simplify the responses for a substitute teacher.

Student Name	Typical Behavior Issues	Function of Behavior (Attention, Escape, Tangible, Sensory, Unsure)	Suggested Responses
Jessie Lundgren	Talks out in class, disrespectful, doesn't follow directions	Attention from peers; wants to escape difficult work	Talk to her proactively outside of class about her behavior; set up times when she can lead discussion and get positive peer attention; use checklists to break down multiple step directions; create contract
Jake Weichel	Frequently distracted during class instead of listening; doesn't do work if asked to write	Tangible—will work for computer time; Escape—wants to avoid writing tasks	Create a contract allowing Jake to type assignments on computer instead of handwriting; build in more opportunities for him to use computer; sit in front of room to aid in proximity to ensure he's better
Todd Fridel	Frequently distracted; physically aggressive; gets out of seat often; poor social skills	Unsure	Provide lots of structure; Create teacher-directed brain breaks and kinesthetic activities; teach him nonviolent responses to frustration and appropriate social skills (maybe collaborate with school psych on those?); provide timers to help with focus on work; pair with students who are more patient

Figure 9.7   Student Behavior at a Glance Chart

INSTRUCTIONAL AND ASSESSMENT ISSUES ■

I have identified three areas for proactive discussion with your new co-teacher. The first was the physical space of your shared classroom, and the second was issues related to classroom management. The third area to discuss relates to instructional and assessment issues. The information provided in this section lays the framework for your co-planning, co-instruction, and co-assessment.

Instructional

An inclusive classroom, by definition, results in a class in which there are a variety of instructional levels. Doesn't sound any different from the typical classroom, does it? While every class has students with different interests, learning profiles, readiness levels and abilities, in the inclusive classroom, we enter both recognizing those challenges and are ready and willing to accept and address them. We don't plan to teach to the middle; in many cases, it is difficult to even identify a *middle*. At the same time, however, an elementary classroom may have 13 (e.g., Wyoming) to 20 (e.g., California) students as the average number in the general education elementary classroom (National Center on Education Statistics, http://nces.ed.gov, retrieved January 30, 2009). We certainly are not going to have 13 to 20 lesson plans. That may be ideal, but it is simply not an option.

Every teacher needs to make sure to address his HALO. (No—this is not the golden circle that you mentally polish before entering the principal's office.) HALO stands for "high achievers, average achievers, low achievers, and others," students who vary between levels or may have additional needs that should be considered when lesson planning. This is a great way to ensure that every lesson is differentiated, at least basically. After creating a lesson geared at typical learners, or your "average achievers," teachers then collaborate to determine how to adapt the lesson to challenge both the high achievers and the low achievers. They look at the lesson to ensure that it also addresses the needs of the "others," perhaps physical or behavioral challenges. Don't forget this simple and wonderful strategy—HALO.

Want More on This Topic?

Get many more strategies on planning in Chapter 11, Planning Quality Time Together.

Being proactive instructionally is oftentimes simpler than being proactive behaviorally. Upper elementary teachers often find that students don't always demonstrate brand-new instructional needs. Those who struggle with reading have often struggled since preschool. Students who had difficulties with organization; study skills; math; group work, homework, or classwork completion; and writing tasks typically had a trail of paperwork indicating those issues had existed since they entered formal schooling—or at least since we asked those skills of students. It is our job as educators to get as much information as we can to eliminate the difficulties and improve the skills. How do we do that, given the amount of time our students have struggled with these issues?

First of all, while there are a variety of research-based best practices available, the research is equally clear that many of those best practices are not frequently used in the classroom. Why not, if their effectiveness is supported by research? Simple. Most teachers are unable to put into place the structures required by many best practices and do not have the time to reorganize or recreate lessons they have taught for years. For example, while cooperative grouping may be supported in the research as a strong strategy for an inclusive class (Johnson & Johnson, 1999; Marzano, Pickering, & Pollock, 2001), many educators fear the extra time it would take to rearrange desks, get kids into groups, and then ensure they are working on the task provided rather than merely discussing the coolest toys. Given that elementary students are excitable and love to socialize, it is no wonder that we are loathe to get them together in the context of cooperative learning. However, if there are two of us now to facilitate the structure and to oversee the interactions, we will be more likely to engage in these best practices. In fact, Conderman, Bresnahan, and Pedersen (2008) provide a variety of examples of real-life cases and stories of co-teachers who work together to implement instructional strategies in the classroom.

Second, we need to gather information on our students that will enable us to make choices previous teachers may not have been able to make. Because there are two of us, we can divide and conquer. Think of it this way: When you are about to walk down the aisle with someone—or better yet, head off to Spain for your honeymoon—don't you talk to your prospective spouse's mother, sister, brother, or best friend to find out what she likes? What foods she eats? What his pet peeves are? These are things you have found out for yourself but by talking to other individuals, you get additional perspectives. You and your co-teacher should talk to students' counselors, parents, and former teachers whenever possible to gather information that can be used to help them in the classroom, instructionally and behaviorally. Find out what has worked and what hasn't. Due to numbers, you may want to start with the students who have been identified as having difficulties academically, but it will certainly behoove you to find out information on all students. Consider creating a survey to send home or to send to teachers at the grade preceding yours to gather pertinent information. I really like the Parent, Teacher, and Student Views offered through the All Kinds of Minds Institute (www.allkindsofminds.org).

Don't forget to look at the cumulative folders when you have a chance—they often provide a plethora of information.

Finally, once you and your partner have gathered this information, use it to complete the Figure 9.8 on instructional strategies. Similar to the behavioral chart already provided in Figure 9.7, this worksheet enables the two of you to identify a student's instructional difficulties and to document strategies to address those difficulties. Having this in place early on (and then modifying it as you learn more about what works) can be helpful for both teachers, as well as for substitute teachers and paraprofessionals.

Assessment

Student assessment. In Part IV: The Marriage, I have an entire chapter devoted to co-assessing (Chapter 15), but as we get ready to welcome our new students to the class, there are some basic decisions we need to make. The first, related to daily scheduling, has already been mentioned; it will be beneficial for co-teachers to determine patterns for giving quizzes and other assessments as

Student Name	Typical Academic Issues	Reason for Academic Issue (Disability, Ability, Language, Personal, Unsure)	Suggested Responses
JoAnne Webb	Weakness in math calculation and problem solving; loves reading and writing	Math disability but is cognitively gifted (twice exceptional)	Encourage her to write her own math problems; have her read the math problems aloud and break them down orally; provide her with a calculator and teach calculator skills; pair her with Mitch so they can support one another
Mitch Dryert	Reading two years below grade level; writing two years below grade level; strong in math calculations; musically gifted	Learning disability: visual processing primarily in reading and writing	Allow books on tape and adapted versions; use graphic organizers; use reciprocal reading technique; pair him with JoAnne; connect reading and writing with music when possible; have him create musical riffs that can be paired with content as a mnemonic device
Javier Bartolo	Difficulty with all academic skills in math, reading, writing; difficulty with English language	English language learner (ELL); Down sydrome	Collaborate with ELL teacher to identify appropriate strategies; use visuals, pictures, manipulatives, when possible; pair with another Spanish speaker when possible; spiral standards to identify what he can do related to the grade level standard
Amy Luckiss	Typically strong student but in the last three weeks has turned work in late or not at all; very emotional	Personal: Counselor reports her parents are currently divorcing	Talk to her individually; give her extra time on work; connect her with counselor or school psych

Figure 9.8   Student Academics at a Glance Chart

they consider their daily and weekly schedules. The second, related to logistics, has also been touched on. Co-teachers need to discuss their options related to the use of space. This also impacts assessments. Will students sit at group tables to take tests or do they need individual desks? Do we have alternative areas to take students if we decide to give active assessments or if we decide to allow some students to read the test aloud while others are proctored silently? Once we have had a chance to discuss the above issues, there are a few more questions related to assessment and grading we need to ask ourselves.

- What types of reviews are we comfortable with prior to quizzes or tests?
- Will students be allowed materials during testing (e.g., calculators, open books, review cards, mnemonics, laptops, and so forth)?
- Are there certain assessments that we want to use more or less often (e.g., role plays, paper-and-pencil tests, Scantron tests, group assessments, projects)?
- Are there certain days we do or do not want to give quizzes or tests?
- What percentage of the final grade do we want to devote to tests or quizzes?
- Do we share an understanding of the difference between assessment and grades?
- Are both of our names on the report card and benchmark assessments?

Adult assessment. For any new relationship to work, communication is key. As you and your co-teacher begin to share this new group of students, you will need to be open to feedback from one another. It can be very difficult to hear criticisms or evaluations of your instruction, especially from a colleague, so this is a tricky aspect to the relationship. There are a few strategies that can help. First, recognize the need to give one another regular feedback. One of the noted benefits of co-teaching is that we learn strategies from one another and are able to give feedback to one another related to what is and is not working in the class. If you don't share your observations, your partnership will not improve. Remember, this is your honeymoon period. If you don't tell your partner what you like and don't like now, you'll be stuck with those behaviors for the rest of your marriage.

An excellent reference for building communication skills is *Interactions: Collaboration Skills for School Professionals* (Friend & Cook, 2007). Readers will recognize the difference between descriptive statements, evaluative statements, and advising statements. For example, if I say, "Have you ever thought of walking around when you are teaching?" I am not really asking a question—I am trying to couch advice and suggestion in the guise of a question. That may not be an effective strategy. If I say to my co-teacher, "You really shouldn't stay standing at the front of the room the whole time you are lecturing; it's boring," I will likely offend my colleague. That is the type of evaluative statement that can cause conflict and resentment, especially if co-teachers are not yet completely comfortable with one another. On the other hand, if I use a descriptive statement, I can say, "During the 20 minutes you lectured at the front of the room about nouns and verbs, five of the students in the back row were doodling, two students on the side of the room were passing notes, and one student in the back corner was snoring. I noticed that when you were walking around in the middle of the lesson, all of the students were attentive." Now it's up to my partner to determine what might need to change or to ask me what I suggest. Once advice is solicited (Friend & Cook, 2007), it is appropriate to share my suggestions. It is important to remember, however, that not all individuals receive feedback the same way and that some areas may be more sensitive than others, so be thoughtful in your approach.

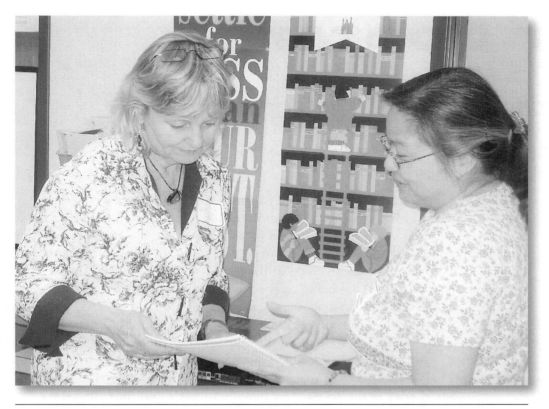

Assessment is always a tricky topic. Be sure to discuss assessment issues with one another openly and often.

10

For Richer or Poorer

Sharing Space and Materials

Think of a classroom. What do you picture? Most likely you see one teacher in front of a group of children in her own classroom. That is the past. If you grew up imagining yourself as the boss of the classroom, the king or queen of your own castle, and the sole decision maker in a shut-door environment, you may need to reconsider your choice in careers. Teaching is becoming increasingly collaborative. Doors are being opened, colleagues are being invited in, and strategies are shared daily. In many cases, teachers are not merely receiving visitors; they are realizing that theirs is to be a shared kingdom. As teachers begin to share classrooms, issues arise related to the sharing of space and materials. This chapter addresses those issues. Although teachers may feel their hands are "tied" (especially as it relates to space issues), there are definitely strategies that can make shared environments feel less like prison cells and more like forts.

Making space for yourself is vital, no matter how cramped the environment.

SHARING SPACE ■

Picture the following:

> **8:00 a.m.** School begins. Mrs. Kemmerer, the second-grade general educator, is in the classroom, welcoming students and reminding them to sit down and get started on their journal prompt.
>
> **8:04 a.m.** Miss Diamond, the special educator, arrives. She is breathing hard and looks a bit harried. She puts her purse, textbook, notebook for the class, and bag of teaching materials on the floor near the door. She takes a moment to look at the front board in order to see what students are supposed to be doing, and then she begins to circulate, providing proximity control, and offering support to those who need it.
>
> **8:13 a.m.** A student asks Miss Diamond for a piece of tape as his paper just ripped. Miss Diamond walks over to Mrs. Kemmerer to see about getting a piece of tape. Mrs. Kemmerer goes to her desk at the front of the room, opens the top drawer and gets out the tape. She brings a piece to Miss Diamond, who in turn brings it to the student.
>
> **8:32 a.m.** Another student asks Miss Diamond to write a note to his mother stating that he is doing his homework regularly. Miss Diamond walks over to Mrs. Kemmerer and asks if she may see the grade book to determine if this is true. Mrs. Kemmerer gets the book, turns to the correct page, and gives the book to Miss Diamond, who returns to the student. Miss Diamond sits at a small student desk to write the note to the parent.
>
> **8:46 a.m.** Language arts time ends. Mrs. Kemmerer and Miss Diamond help kids get in single-file line to walk to music room. The music teacher meets them and takes the students. Mrs. Kemmerer and Miss Diamond spend a few minutes debriefing on the class and talking about upcoming events.
>
> **8:52 a.m.** Miss Diamond collects her things from the floor, says good-bye to Mrs. Kemmerer, and heads off to a third grade class, although its language arts started four minutes ago.

The above scenario is not too different from what is experienced by teachers and students alike in co-taught classrooms across the country. Despite the fact that Mrs. Kemmerer and Miss Diamond may very well have an excellent rapport, may have planned some of the content together, and may be very comfortable sharing the instruction and assessment with one another, the picture that is painted above is one of inequality. When Miss Diamond comes in late and proceeds to put her materials on the floor because she has no personal space in the classroom, she gives students the impression that this is not a shared classroom—it is Mrs. Kemmerer's and Mrs. Kemmerer's alone. This may not be the impression that the co-teachers were trying to give, but it will be the one that students perceive. When Miss Diamond has to ask permission to access the grade book or Mrs. Kemmerer's desk, it is a subtle indicator to students that this is "Mrs. Kemmerer's house." Miss Diamond is only a visitor.

The sharing of space can be a major barrier for many teachers as they work together. Teachers are used to having their own classrooms and are simply unused to sharing that space with another adult. At times, this is a control issue. Anne Beninghof (2008), a presenter on co-teaching with the Bureau of Education and Research, shared that "tightening the corset" is one of the five most common mistakes in co-teaching. This means that teachers become less flexible, rather than more flexible. They hang on to the way they have taught and they react to the loss of their space by establishing control however possible. Because teachers may not have had a say in the fact that a special service provider was coming into the room to "co-teach" with them, they may react by using other ways to confirm their authority. This may be evidenced in their reluctance to change their teaching methodology, or it may be evidenced by their reluctance to give up their physical territory.

Sharing space and materials results in a class that is "ours," not "yours" or "mine."

Not all teachers are reluctant to share. Some may simply not realize the impact this can have on the special educator and, later on, the students. When a general education classroom teacher has been established in a class for a while, it may simply not occur to him or her that getting a second desk is something to consider. Even special educators may be so used to hauling their own materials from class to class they don't realize they should talk to their general education counterpart about finding some regular space for them. The benefits of doing this are multifold.

- Physically, lugging materials from class to class can be arduous for teachers. Thus, a benefit can be the physical and emotional well-being of the special educator.
- It is frequently difficult for special educators to bring all their requisite materials to each class. Thus, they end up going back to their own classroom or other space in order to get their materials between classes, which often results in them coming to class late. Also, time is lost as the special

educator works with multiple general educators and may have to vary the materials needed in each class.

- On-the-spot modifications are one of the benefits of co-teaching with a special educator, but if she does not have access to her materials in the classroom, she may not be able to implement a modification that would be appropriate. Having her own space in the classroom to store items that may be used often would increase the likelihood that those adaptations can be made when needed. This way she can have material specific to the modifications needed in this specific classroom and with these specific students. The more tailored instruction can be to students, the better.

- Parity is a necessary characteristic of co-teaching. When students enter a room that has "Mr. Mariner" on the door, then see a sign on the wall that says "Mariner's Mustangs," right above a teacher's desk with a "Mr. Mariner" nameplate and pictures of Mr. M with his family, they are likely to assume (correctly) that it is Mr. Mariner's room. When Miss Heinz tries to establish her role in the room, she will be working at a disadvantage—especially if she is coming in a few minutes late and putting her stuff in a corner. On the other hand, if there is also a desk with Miss Heinz's name and pictures, students are more likely to accept that the class will be shared. The following photos illustrate different ways co-teachers in successful relationships have demonstrated to their students that they are truly sharing the classroom. Note that even though these teachers do not co-teach together all day long, the way both names are prominently displayed ensures that the special service provider will be welcomed as part of the class much more easily.

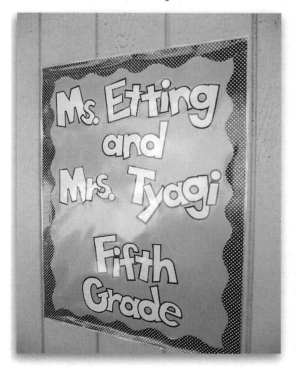

There are many ways to display both teacher names, but the end result is that students recognize this is a shared class.

- Many districts are adopting a collaborative, inclusive, and co-teaching model in an effort to save space. Special educators may no longer have their own rooms and may be sharing with other special educators or may even be required to keep their materials on a rolling cart. Thus, even though a special educator may collaborate or even co-teach with multiple partners, having one place to call "home" is important for teachers' morale and efficiency. If a co-teacher can help by providing an oasis for such a nomad, that would help the relationship and the students. Remember, we all need a home of our own—or at least a place that feels like home!

IN THE MARRIAGE OF GENERAL AND
SPECIAL EDUCATION, BOTH PARTIES AGREE
TO LEAVE THEIR BAGGAGE AT THE DOOR.

SOURCE: Reprinted with permission. M. Giangreco (2007).

■ SHARING MATERIALS

Each teacher will enter the relationship with his or her own materials, just as newlyweds enter with their own furniture. We have to decide together what materials we want to share, what we want to keep, and what we can discard. I discussed the need to share space first because that will often dictate the sharing of materials as well. If all of a teacher's materials are elsewhere or inaccessible, it is unlikely that he will offer them, even if they would improve the lesson. On the other hand, if teachers have shared space, one can show the other the various materials he has at their disposal to add to instruction. These may include manipulatives, books on tape, highlighter tape, or graphic organizers.

Too often, special service providers who are in a general education teacher's classroom simply rely on the traditional textbook and materials or wait until after the lesson has bombed to consider alternative materials that could aid student understanding.

Materials can also be shared with classes other than the co-taught one. Special education teachers often co-teach with multiple partners. I often hear the complaint that there is limited time for planning and co-planning. I discuss this issue later in Chapter 11: Planning Quality Time Together, but one of the benefits that can be addressed here is that the materials that are created or adapted for the co-taught class can be used multiple times. For example, if two kindergarten co-teachers create a game to help review number strategies or a visual to help students remember their introduction to certain sight words, those materials can be shared with all of the kindergarten teachers. Thus, more students will benefit from the adaptations and input of the special educator. This is one of the reasons many people say that special education often involves "just good teaching." While special education should also entail instruction specifically tailored for the needs of students with specific disabilities (Zigmond, 2006), many of the strategies that special educators espouse are ones that will benefit the majority of students in a class. In a truly collaborative school, if co-teachers create a particularly clever strategy for a science lesson, they will share it with all other grade-level teachers who teach that science concept as well as all special educators and paraprofessionals. If it has broader applications, the co-teachers will also share the strategy with teachers across the various disciplines.

Successful co-teachers are creative with their use of space and materials.

Do we each have our own desk? If not, what space will the special service provider use to put personal items and professional materials?

During the time we co-teach, what other spaces are available to us (other classrooms, library, office rooms, etc.)?

What materials do we each have that we can bring to this relationship (computers, manipulatives, Web sites, adapted books, textbooks, lab materials, etc.)?

Are there any materials or spaces in the classroom that we do *not* care to share or provide one another with access? (We all need our own "private" area for important things, like chocolate.)

Thanks to Christien M. for this helpful tip: If you happen to have a little fridge in your classroom, keep it stocked with drinks your partner likes or at least leave space for him to keep his own food and drinks. Not only is this a kind thing to do, it can provide nourishment for co-planning times!

Figure 10.1 Questions to Guide Our Space and Materials Issues

11

Planning Quality Time Together

Why, When, and How to Plan

WHY SHOULD WE CO-PLAN? ■

The Rationale

Let's start the conversation on co-planning by establishing this fact: Walking into the room two minutes before class and saying, "So, what are we going to do today?" does *not* constitute co-planning. Prior planning is vital to delivering services in an inclusive classroom. When a special educator walks into a room without planning in advance with her general educator counterpart, this has a negative impact on both teachers and students. By now, I have established that co-teaching does not entail the special service provider only monitoring those students with special needs while the general educator delivers all the daily instruction. The role of the special educator is not that of paraprofessional in the classroom. When that happens, there is a real concern that special educators will burn out or ask to return to their self-contained classes so that they can actually teach and not just be a glorified assistant.

A major role of the special service provider in a co-teaching arrangement is to co-plan with the general education teacher *prior* to delivering instruction to all students in the inclusive classroom. This will require significant communication between teachers. It is definitely helpful if teachers share common educational philosophies when co-teaching. Numerous experts (e.g., Dieker, 2001; Fennick, 2001; Friend & Cook, 2007; Gately & Gately, 2001; Murawski & Dieker, 2004; Murawski, 2006; Trent et al., 2003; Villa, Thousand, & Nevin 2007) emphasize that teachers need time to co-plan before beginning to work together. Furthermore, when teachers co-plan before working together on a daily basis, it allows them to discuss their different educational values, styles, expertise, challenges, classroom pet peeves, classroom discipline philosophies, and interests (Murawski & Dieker, 2004). It also helps them adapt. Most

147

Mental Exercise

Imagine spending a day as an aide to another faculty member or, better yet, as an aide to a teacher in a subject area you cannot imagine being able to teach. As a third-grade general education teacher, how would you be useful in a self-contained class of students with autism? What might the other teacher do to help you feel more comfortable and be successful in that class? What would you like her to do that would recognize your own areas of expertise?

Putting yourself in your partner's shoes is a good way to understand why it is helpful to ensure that each of you is valuable and needs to be a part of the planning for your shared class.

important, co-planning differentiated instruction and different approaches of delivering instruction is crucial to the learning of diverse students in an inclusive classroom. Special and general education teachers, administrators, students, parents, and other service deliverers all must engage in co-planning prior to the implementation of an adequate co-teaching program. Co-planning is an essential service delivery component in the process of collaborating and co-teaching (Dieker & Barnett, 1996; Jitendra, Edwards, Choatka, & Treadway, 2002; Trent et al., 2003). It is this activity that ensures there is differentiation, individualization, strategies, and other pedagogical techniques that make the lesson specific to that particular group of students so that each can access the general education curriculum more effectively.

Speaking of the general education curriculum, be aware that special service providers may hesitate to co-teach in a specific area if they do not feel they have the adequate knowledge to teach a specific topic. This is especially a problem at the upper elementary level as the content gets more complex. For example, a special educator who is not strong in science might be intimidated at the prospect of co-teaching with a general education teacher who is strong in this field. Nevertheless, while the special educator might not be strong in the area of science content, he or she is certainly capable of evaluating a lesson plan and suggesting appropriate strategies, accommodations, and modifications to better deliver the lesson to a group of diverse learners. Furthermore, the different frames of reference teachers bring to co-planning are a benefit because the special educator, who is typically not a specific subject area expert, is more likely to ask questions on the topic of instruction. By providing the special education teacher with the information first, this allows for both co-teachers to evaluate how to instruct the topic to students for a better understanding by all. The general educator may be the expert on the fifth-grade science concepts, but the special educator is frequently the expert on the pedagogy—or rather, the content of instruction.

Gately and Gately (2001) identify common planning as a critical component in effective collaboration between co-teachers. Allocated time to collaborate and cooperatively plan cohesive and productive instruction ensures that the needs of all students are being met. When general and special education teachers co-plan, they should be sharing equally in the decision making about the needs of students and the delivery of instruction in the classroom, regardless of who is the "subject area expert" and who is the "strategy expert"; parity means that neither teacher trumps the other in decision making.

One of the major reasons we need to co-plan is that we must make decisions proactively. Co-teaching is not about merely having an extra person to monitor the students; it is about making decisions as a team. Although a general educator may already have a lesson plan in mind, it is important that both co-teachers discuss the lesson plan and allow for the special service provider to use his or her expertise in the area of incorporating accommodations, modifications, and strategies to better deliver the lesson. This way students do not need to be pulled out to review or to relearn information they didn't understand the first time; teachers can use proactive planning to ensure that the way the content is presented initially allows for student understanding, engagement, motivation, and ultimately learning (Murawski & Flores, 2007). This is the essence of differentiation and universally designed instruction.

Want More on This Topic?

Learn more about differentiation and universal design for learning (UDL) in Part IV: The Marriage.

Co-planning may also be necessary in situations that are collaborative, but not necessarily co-taught. Some special service providers may find themselves working to establish relationships with general educators as a precursor to co-teaching; in these situations, acting as a consultant to provide indirect strategies through co-planning and problem solving is a strong option. General educators may also ask special educators to co-plan a single unit or lesson with them as a method by which the two can see if they will be compatible for future collaborative efforts (Huber, 2005). In addition, because many individuals with special needs are supported in the general education class by instructional assistants or paraprofessionals, we need to take a moment to discuss co-planning with those individuals as well.

Indirect Support Through Co-Planning

In some instances, special service providers provide consultative and indirect support to their general education colleagues as baby steps to eventual co-teaching (Murawski, 2005b). This is an excellent way to establish rapport, parity, communication, and confidence. Ongoing co-planning enables open communication, facilitates team problem solving and promotes equity in co-teaching (Fennick, 2001). The act of consulting in co-planning is an important factor in maintaining productive communication between co-teachers. As part of the consultation process, teachers may assist one another by bringing in their expertise to a particular area and by helping one another problem solve. When teachers share ideas, it allows them to respect and value each other's strengths and challenges. Moreover, during co-planning general and special educators may consult on a particular problem, develop instructional interventions, and evaluate placement interventions in order to improve on meeting students' educational needs. There are times when a special educator cannot personally attend a general education class, but instead will send a paraprofessional to the class instead. In that case, it is necessary to plan for—and with—the paraeducator.

Planning With Paraeducators

In addition to collaborating with teachers on the co-teaching team, it is vital to develop a good rapport with paraprofessionals. Giangreco and Doyle (2002) suggest that teachers should collaborate closely with paraprofessionals for clarification of roles and responsibilities. French (2002) reiterates the need for involving paraprofessionals in the learning of students with diverse needs. Teachers need to become familiar with the paraprofessional's work-style preference. Providing constructive feedback helps to maintain a proactive and collaborative relationship between the paraprofessional and co-teachers. Furthermore, special educators should collaborate and consult with general educators to determine the areas in which paraprofessionals should be involved (French, 2002).

Benefits of Co-Planning

According to the literature and research, co-planning is invaluable in gathering information to create a more active and productive learning atmosphere for students with and without disabilities. One of the advantages in co-planning is that teachers bring in an array of expertise to instructional planning for a diversity of students (Murawski, 2005a). When the expert in a specific subject area (i.e., the general educator) and the expert in designing adaptations and modifying curriculum (i.e., the special educator) co-plan for a heterogeneous group, the instructional plan is more uniform and can be differentiated to meet the needs of all students in an inclusive setting (Fennick & Liddy, 2001; Murawski & Dieker, 2004). In addition, Murata's (2002) findings indicate that co-teachers viewed each others' strengths as enhancements to instructional planning and personal growth.

Co-planning helps teachers establish and clarify their collaborative goals, which helps to decrease the risk of hidden agendas during instruction (Thousand et al., 2006). Furthermore, due to the increase of interaction and communication involved in co-planning, co-teachers are more likely to develop trust and respect. Similarly, co-teachers get the opportunity to problem solve, debrief and evaluate the instructional plan and their personal achievements (Murawski, 2004; Thousand et al., 2006b). When teachers engage in co-planning, their roles and responsibilities can be disseminated equally. In addition, co-teachers are more likely to invest equal time preparing, monitoring student progress, and delivering instruction. Most important, co-planning provides the opportunity for co-teachers to consider the social, academic, behavioral, and other needs of all students as they proactively plan for students' success (Fennick, 2001; Murawski, 2004).

Time spent co-planning will always be time well spent.

Barriers to Co-Planning

Despite the obvious benefits of co-planning, many teachers report that they do not actually plan together (Austin, 2001; Murawski, Boyer, Melchiorre, & Atwill, 2009; Weiss, 2004). The most common issue? Time. No surprise here. Scheduling time for co-planning is challenging for teachers, largely due to teachers' instructional schedules and the fact that most elementary teachers do not have scheduled planning time in the day. Lack of time to plan leads to unclear roles and responsibilities in the co-teaching partnership, overwhelming the individuals (Cook & Friend, 1995; Murawski & Dieker, 2004; Trent, 1998; Trent et al., 2003). Insufficient time for co-planning often reveals a lack of administrative support (Mastropieri et al., 2005). When co-teachers are not provided with sufficient time to plan, it may lead to a lack of parity.

In many cases, *co*-planning is not the primary issue. The issue is planning in and of itself. The dirty secret is that many teachers, especially those who have taught for a while, do not plan even their solo lessons. While Madeline Hunter's Seven-Step Lesson Plan is required of many student and novice teachers, we may be lucky to see a seven *word* lesson plan from many veteran teachers. Over the years, they have gotten by without preplanning lessons, or they think they have. Some veteran teachers resort to what they have done year after year because it takes less time and effort. Here are my three thoughts about that. (1) Most of the time, this is not working as well as they think it is. The kids can tell they are coasting. (2) This won't fly in the co-taught classroom.

The diverse needs of the students require individualized, specific instruction that needs to be co-planned and *requires* the expertise of both the general and special educator. (3) Learning to plan again can be liberating. Structure equals freedom. As teachers work together to plan instruction, even veteran teachers report learning new and exciting techniques that invigorate them and re-interest them in the art of teaching.

Want More on This Topic?

I discuss the issue of teacher schedules in Chapter 12: Matchmaker, Matchmaker.

Another issue special service providers face when trying to find time to co-plan relates to the scheduling issue created by being assigned to multiple classrooms (Cook & Friend, 1995). According to Dieker and Murawski (2003), even if teachers are excited to co-teach, the issue of using time adequately and productively continues to be a problem when teachers are spread too thin and are not able to focus on what they need to teach.

The literature explains that frequently the focus of many co-planning sessions is to discuss specific students' needs and not to discuss curricula, social aspects, behavioral aspects, and assessments (Dieker & Murawski, 2003; Thousand et al., 2006b). This takes away from co-teachers being able to see the *big* picture (Murawski, 2005b).

Co-teacher compatibility and lack of a common frame of reference are other issues that impede an effective co-planning experience. Teachers in a co-taught environment must share common goals, be able to positively collaborate, and equally put effort in the lesson preparation and planning; otherwise, disagreements between co-teachers might arise (Fennick & Liddy, 2001; Mastropieri et al., 2005). The S.H.A.R.E. worksheet (Figure 5.1) described and provided in Part II: The Engagement, Chapter 5, is designed to help proactively assist co-teachers in developing necessary compatibility and open communication. In essence, effective co-planning reflects a dynamic co-teaching relationship in a classroom; therefore, it is crucial for teachers to be proactive about cooperative planning (Gately & Gately, 2001).

■ WHEN SHOULD WE CO-PLAN?

Creating Time to Co-Plan

Do you have a child? A few children? A pet? A needy parent, sibling, or friend? If you have any of these, you know how difficult it can be at times to find time for yourself. Now imagine trying to carve out quality time with someone else when you have 10 children—or 15, or 20. It can be nigh impossible. Yet, that time is crucial for teachers to be able to plan their future actions and be effective. Schools successfully employing co-teaching as a service delivery option have become *creative* in finding time for co-planning to occur. Schools should work toward providing co-teachers with common time if they want to maximize the effectiveness of every co-teaching interaction. Administrative support continues to be an important factor in ensuring co-teaching success as administrators are frequently responsible for finding ways to enable partners to have common planning time and for supporting any extra efforts co-teachers may be making.

Following are some tips for carving out co-planning time (Murawski & Flores, 2007; Murawski, 2008):

Want More on This Topic?

Then read on! I'll provide some strategies later in this very chapter on how to use your co-planning time more effectively.

- *Common planning times are the best strategy when possible.* With administrator facilitation, teachers are provided a common time to plan. This may be built into the schedule before or after school or may occur when students are attending enrichment activities like music, physical education, or art. Teachers working with upper elementary classes using class periods may be assigned common planning periods. While helpful, creating common planning periods in a master schedule is not a simple task; administrators will be loathe to do the extra work if they frequently see co-teachers using that time to simply catch up on their own work and not use the time effectively with their partners. If teachers plan to meet for two or three days a week and solo plan on the other days, administrators should be told the strategy so that they do not think teachers are slacking or not using their time effectively.

- *Banked times given at the school district level provide a routine time for planning and staff development training.* By "banking" instructional minutes, schools can ensure a weekly time for teachers to collaborate and communicate, rather than waiting for a future staff development day that might be filled with other formal trainings. For example, a particular school district may schedule Tuesdays as the time when all students are dismissed two hours early and co-teachers may use this time to co-plan. Interested school districts can find the answers to many frequently asked questions about banked time at www.mtea.org/Resources/MTEALeader/BankingTimeVote/BankingTimein200809.nws.

- *Scheduled meetings are the most common strategy for co-planning among co-teachers.* Basically, co-teachers schedule a time that accommodates them and meet to co-plan. This might be before school, during lunch, after school, or even on the phone or on weekends. Co-teachers are reminded to make this a regular time and to hold it at least once weekly. Let me warn you from experience—if you try to find time each week as it comes, you will never find the time. Make sure you establish a set schedule and hold to it. A note to administrators—if you pay teachers for this extra time, they will be more likely to value and honor it. Providing stipends for extra work shows teachers you respect them and their time.

- *There are a variety of ways to ensure class coverage for additional planning.* Some schools provide a specific substitute assigned on a daily or weekly basis (funded by school site) to cover classes during co-planning times. Administrators may also cover classes themselves to allocate time for co-planning. Recall my anecdote in Chapter 8 about the vice principal in Arizona who did this and experienced real success. In addition, teachers can arrange to cover for each other. For example, two third-grade teachers who co-teach with the same special educator can arrange so that each week they will put the classes together for a short time so that one general educator can oversee the large-group activity while the other co-plans with the special educator. Later in the week, the other general educator will reciprocate the favor.

- *Student activities, such as watching a short video or working on an independent or group project, keep students engaged so teachers may use that time to co-plan in the classroom.* While concurrently keeping an eye on the students, teachers can grab a few extra minutes of planning time. Even short chunks of time can be used effectively if co-teachers are focused and purposeful in their planning. In addition, co-teachers may utilize enrichment time (e.g., music, art, or physical time) when possible, to co-plan.

- *In and out boxes can work well for special educators who are supporting multiple general education teachers.* This entails simply having a box where the special education teacher may drop in questions or suggestions throughout the day without interrupting instruction. General educators can use the same box to communicate with their special education counterparts. School mailboxes or cubbies are not very effective, as teachers may not visit them regularly; e-mail is an excellent option *if* both teachers are able to check it throughout the day.

- *School assemblies, such as pep rallies, plays, or school spirit activities, which do not require teachers to be present, are an excellent time for co-planning.* With administrative support, other faculty or staff at the school can supervise the class of students so that co-teachers can use the time to stay in their classroom and plan together.

- *Research projects by universities conducting research on inclusion or co-teaching may involve grants that allocate time for co-teachers who are taking part in the research to receive co-planning time.* Pilot programs can seek out these grants. In addition, teachers are encouraged to write their own grants for additional funding that will support additional planning time; there are many funding opportunities for educators willing to seek them out.

- **The Co-Teaching Lesson Plan Book** *(Dieker, 2004) is another helpful tool, especially for those who are not very technologically savvy.* This co-planning book includes sections where the general education teachers write down anything regarding content and special education teachers write their individualized information regarding how to teach the content. This planner also provides suggestions and strategies to aid co-planning throughout; it is an excellent resource and is available at www.NPRinc.com.

- *Using basic technology requires that both teachers have basic computer skills.* Co-teachers may communicate via e-mail, phone, instant message (IM), or even text message to provide each other with ideas, feedback, and suggestions on co-planned lessons.

- *Co-teachers can also use advanced technology, such as the Co-Teaching Solutions Systems (CTSS), which enables co-teachers to create their lesson plan simultaneously or asynchronously on the lesson planning software (Murawski & Lochner, 2007).* The lesson planning worksheet allows teachers to identify state-specific content standards, automatically spiral those standards to address lower level students, and identify the approaches and roles for co-instruction. In addition to lesson planning, the software has features to group students by learning style, to provide pages of academic strategies, to map curriculum, and to create differentiated rubrics. Lessons can be archived and even e-mailed back and forth. This is an efficient and effective device that is designed to save co-teachers' time. Figure 11.1 describes additional features of the CTSS (Co-Teaching Solutions Systems) toolbox and observation systems. A trial version of this software is available for those interested at www.coteachsolutions.com.

Co-teachers learn how to use the CTSS software at a training seminar.

Figure 11.2 is an EZ reference for you to review to see which ways may be possibilities for you and your co-teacher to find time to plan. Now that you have carved out time for yourselves, how should you use it? Co-teachers need to conduct long-range planning as well as short-range planning. They also need to know how to use their time most effectively. After reviewing the components involved in long- and short-range planning, I will share tips for using co-planning time most efficiently.

Co-Teaching Solutions System: A Software Option to Aid in Co-Planning
www.coteachsolutions.com

Co-Teachers' Toolbox

- Provides co-teachers with pages of staff development training strategies
- Allows co-teachers to easily identify and group students by learning styles
- Enables co-teachers to do curriculum mapping at the beginning of the year with a whole class and individual students
- Presents co-teachers with a rubric maker that aids in differentiated co-assessment
- Furnishes co-teachers with a revolutionary 21st-century collaborative lesson planning tool that
  - o Gives teachers a pull-down menu of state standards (*Even spirals them!*)
  - o Encourages co-teachers to identify each teacher's role for the lessons
  - o Lets co-teachers import, export, update, and archive co-planned lessons
  - o Interfaces with the curriculum mapping tool to document standards-based lessons
  - o Reminds co-teachers of individual student considerations and needed adaptations, including the need to address different RTI levels

Observation System

- Allows administrators to observe co-teaching in the classroom and can be easily loaded onto desktop, laptop, or PDA
- Helps observers know what to look for, listen for, and ask for to determine co-teaching effectiveness
- Enables administrators to have co-teachers conduct a self-survey on their own effectiveness and compare it to the observer's report—a great way to start a conversation with co-teachers on how they can improve
- Assists observers in collecting clear data on what is and what is not going on in the co-taught class so that correlations can be made related to student outcomes
- Creates numerous reports that include
  - o Effectiveness by teacher, grade, subject area, or even entire school
  - o Effectiveness over time (historical and trend data)
- Directly links to the co-teachers' toolbox, enabling administrators to provide strategies according to co-teachers' observed strengths and weaknesses

Figure 11.1 Co-Teaching Solutions System (CTSS): A Software Option to Aid in Co-Planning

Long-Range Co-Planning

Obviously, we have to figure out as a team *what* is going to be taught and *how* it is going to be taught. Special educators are in the co-teaching engagement to add to the pedagogy (*how* to teach), while the general education teacher typically is adding the specific content (*what* to teach). However, teachers are individuals and as such will have their own preferred style for instructing. It is important that teachers respect this fact, so that both are comfortable with their plan related to *what* will be taught as well as *how* it will be taught. For long-range decision making, *curriculum mapping,* wherein teachers sit down together to figure out where

Creative Ways to Create Co-Planning Time

- Common *planning times*
- *Banked time* on a weekly basis
- Weekly *lunch meetings*
- *Before or after* school meetings
- *Co-sponsoring* a school activity or group
- One floating *full-time substitute* to cover teachers
- Scheduling *cooperative learning* groups, peer tutoring, or independent student work
- *Monitoring* by support staff or paraprofessionals
- Strategic *video clips*
- *In and out* boxes for ongoing communication
- *Vary co-teaching schedules* with floating planning periods
- *Administrative coverage* on a monthly basis
- Collaborative planning time on *staff development days*
- Friday fun days or *happy hours*
- Strategic *brain breaks* for checkup planning
- *Swapping coverage* during other teachers' planning periods
- Participating in *co-teaching research projects* that provide extra time or support
- Regularly scheduled *assemblies* staffed by parents, paraprofessionals, volunteers, and school staff
- *Release time* monthly for planning as perk to co-teaching
- *Breakfast* or *Starbucks' meetings*
- *Journaling notebook* back and forth
- Write a *grant* for extra co-planning time or funding
- *Co-Teaching Lesson Plan book* (Dieker, 2004)
- E-mail, scanned documents, phone calls, IM, video phone—*using technology* to help make time
- *Co-Teaching Solutions System* software (www.coteachsolutions.com)

Discuss these with your partner to see which ones are viable options for you.

> In its "Prisoners of Time" report in 1994, the Subcommittee on Education, Arts and Humanities, concluded that "American students will have their best chance at success when they are no longer serving time but when time is serving them."

> **The same is true for co-teachers.**

EZ Reference

Figure 11.2   Creative Ways to Create Co-Planning Time

SOURCE: Murawski, W. W. (2008a).

they are going in the long term, is an excellent strategy for co-teachers in planning. Koppang (2004) suggests curriculum mapping as a tool to enhance the collaboration among co-teachers in the instructional process (i.e., curriculum, skills, and assessment). Curriculum mapping is a tool used to collect data in reference to what is being taught in schools and how to improve the delivery of instruction. The focus of curriculum mapping is on facilitation planning, preparation and, communication between participants in a co-teaching team. Consequently, as general and special education teachers become more knowledgeable and skilled in the curriculum standards, they begin to better communicate what instructional tools they need to adequately meet the needs of diverse students.

Backwards planning is another important concept for quality long-range planning. G. Wiggins and McTighe (2005) refer to this as Understanding by Design (UbD). Teachers need to discuss what they want to accomplish prior to determining how and even what they are going to teach. In UbD, the three stages of planning are

- Stage 1: Identify desired results
- Stage 2: Determine acceptable evidence
- Stage 3: Plan learning experiences

This concept is akin to that of the individualized education program (IEP). First, we need to determine our present level of performance, then we need to establish our goal, and then finally we can decide on our objectives, benchmarks, and how we are going to achieve our goal in a timely manner. Only after we know where we are going and what we want to see as a result, do we determine how we will get there. As general and special educators sit together to plan, they should break the year into manageable chunks or tasks. Using the curriculum map as a guide, teachers can then look at what they would like to accomplish by month, unit, or chapter.

Start the year by capitalizing on each other's *areas of expertise*. General educators should create a snapshot of their curriculum, in terms of where the class is going for the school year, month to month, week to week, in terms of standards, objectives, and past lesson plans. General educators should take the lead on the content pacing plan. Special service providers, on the other hand, are responsible for synthesizing all IEPs to determine student profiles, goals, objectives, and strategies for differentiating instruction. Special educators should focus their early energies on identifying students' strengths and challenges and then highlight and share any significant information needed to help the students be successful in the general education setting.

One strategy for getting a good handle on each student's key information is to create a one-page reference. Figure 11.3 is an example of a Student Profile I created for one of my students. This type of form can be shared with general educators and special service providers who work with a student on a regular basis. I created this form as a sort of *CliffsNotes* version of the IEP. The educators with whom I collaborated were delighted to have such a helpful reference. It took time to create in the beginning, but after the forms were originally designed and made for each student with an IEP on my caseload, we only had to tweak them each year as students changed.

Student Profile

Case manager: Wendy Weichel

Name: John Doe   Age: 10   Grade: 5

Parents' names: Jack & Jill Doe   Home language: English

Address: 111 Doe St., Palmdale 91111   Phone: 661-123-4567

Eligibility: Learning disability and auditory processing

Strengths:

- above average intelligence and strong verbal skills
- strongest in language arts (KTEA = grade equivalency in reading of 6.7)
- loves to read, play football, help others, and work on computer
- parents have indicated interest in working with him at home
- on the Pee-Wee football team

Concerns:

- very social in classes
- does not follow directions well (especially those given auditorally)
- weakest in math & science (KTEA = grade equivalency in math of 2.5)
- has difficulty turning in homework (prefers to play football after school)
- has attentional difficulties (possibly due to auditory processing?)
- Goals and objectives needed in areas of math application and computation, attention, transition to middle school

Appropriate modifications and accommodations:

- Be prepared to repeat directions given auditorally or have John repeat them to you
- Give important directions in both written and auditory format
- Provide manipulatives for math and science concepts
- Provide copies of lecture notes or have a good student copy notes on NCR paper
- Talk to parents (and football coach if possible) to determine a reasonable amount of homework John can be expected to accomplish even with football practice
- Send weekly schedules home to parents so that they can assist John and know what homework and assignments are coming up
- Create a reward system or contract with John that encourages homework completion and provides time on the computer (for academic games, tasks, writing) as positive reinforcement
- Seat students who are not easily distracted or distractible near John and encourage peer shaping of model behavior
- Provide opportunities for John to be social in appropriate ways (cooperative learning groups, leading discussions based on readings, etc.)

Please see me if you have any other questions or concerns about John. I will be his case manager this year and look forward to working with you on a regular basis to make sure that this year is a good year for you, me, and John. Please feel free to contact me at the following numbers:

School ext.: #111   **Home phone**: 661-555-6789   **E-mail**: wwweichel@aol.com

Thanks!

Figure 11.3 Student Profile

SOURCE: Murawski, W. W. (2008a).

Student Profile

Case manager: _____

Name: _____   Age: _____   Grade: _____

Parents' names: _____   Home language: _____

Address: _____   Phone: _____

Eligibility: _____

Strengths:

-
-
-
-
-

Concerns:

-
-
-
-
-

Appropriate modifications and accommodations:

-
-
-
-
-
-
-
-
-
-

Please see me if you have any other questions or concerns about this student. I will be his case manager this year and look forward to working with you on a regular basis to make sure that this year is a good year for all of us. Please feel free to contact me at the following numbers:

School ext.:   **Home phone**:   **E-mail**:

Thanks!

Figure 11.4 Student Profile

Short-Range Co-Planning

For short-range decision making, teachers can ask one another: What are we going to do tomorrow (or next week)? These are the type of short-range decisions that obviously need to be discussed on a regular basis when co-planning. Here are some tips to help ensure that your planning sessions are the most effective and efficient.

- *Have and keep an agenda.* By this I do not mean that you need to take excessive time to create a formal agenda for each meeting. I do however mean that you should ascertain right away what the key items are that need to be discussed during that planning time. This will help you both with time management. Jot those items down right away so that you both can see them as you plan. Some teachers find it helpful to create a template for their meetings so they can follow a similar format each time, adding to their comfort and ensuring that they are most efficient in their use of time.

- *Use your time wisely.* While it is nice to establish a rapport with your co-teacher, if you spend valuable time each session asking about family, personal projects or other noninstructional events, you will quickly find yourself dreading the planning sessions that last for an hour or two instead of the slated half hour. Be sure to set your time up front and then watch the time as you discuss class-related and nonrelated information. When the scheduled time to end comes, stop the meeting even if the two of you are not done planning. Eventually you will both realize that either (1) you need to plan more time together or (2) you need to use your time more wisely. If there is time left after planning, that is the ideal time for your rapport-building conversations and questions, such as, "How is your house project coming along?" or "Is the baby sleeping yet?"

- *Start with the "big picture" items first.* While it is second nature to want to start talking about those students who are driving you both crazy, restrain yourselves. Your time will be better spent talking with one another first about what content you are going to teach as well as when and how you both think it should be taught. This will help special service providers have time to bone up on content areas in which they might be weak and to consider the appropriate strategies, modifications, or adaptations that might need to be introduced to the lessons. Consider creating bullet points for the other things that come up that you want to discuss (e.g., specific students or situations) and then trade lists. You can deal with these things at the end of the session, in an e-mail thread, or even during a scheduled chat online later. Do treat all conversations online with discretion, of course, as this information is saved.

- *Discuss individual students second.* After determining the content, pacing, and general instruction for the upcoming week, teachers can then spend any additional time discussing the specific needs of students in their class. This is the time to vent about the fact that Javier never does his homework, that Keisha talks incessantly, and that Mason needs additional challenges or he is going to be bored.

- *Don't re-create the wheel.* Teachers spend an inordinate amount of time complaining about a lack of planning time—and then spend the small amount of time they have designing a lesson from scratch. Guess what? Teachers teach the difference between a noun and a verb in Virginia. And in Texas. And in South Dakota. And in Massachusetts. My point is that, in this day and age of technology especially, teachers need to be collaborating, communicating, and sharing even beyond their own classrooms, departments, and schools. There are a variety of lesson plans available on the Internet and in books. I developed a free lesson plan database on my own Web site (www.2TeachLLC.com) so that as I work with teachers to create co-planned, co-taught lessons, we upload them to one site to share with others. I have already uploaded many lessons and have hundreds more to come.

- *Have a regular schedule for meeting.* I cannot emphasize this enough. If you and your co-teacher do not have a regular time for meeting and planning set in stone, it will not occur. You will eventually find yourself resorting to "in-class support," wherein the special service provider just walks in and reactively assists in whatever way possible.

Co-teachers committed to a successful experience always make an effort to co-plan.

Co-Planning: What and When
Before School Starts:
• Complete S.H.A.R.E. worksheet (Chapter 5)
• Determine roles and responsibilities
• Do curriculum mapping for the year
Before School or Beginning of School:
• General educator—Know your content and share the highlights
• Special service provider—Know the kids' profiles and share the highlights
• Determine grading and assessment together
• Make sure letters to parents and other materials are developed and sent home as a team
Monthly meetings:
• Create unit or chapter overview for the month
• Complete one week's worth of full-blown lesson plans in order to stay a week ahead at all times
Weekly Meetings:
• Identify the standards that need to be addressed
• Decide how standards will be spiraled and how the content can be differentiated
• Decide how material will be taught and how the process can be differentiated
• Agree on how learning will be assessed and how products can be differentiated

EZ Reference

Figure 11.5 Co-Planning: What and When?

HOW SHOULD WE CO-PLAN? ■

Recommendations for Effective Co-Planning

Richard Villa (2006) has shared that the traditional approach to teaching involves the following steps:

Step 1: Select content

Step 2: Select teaching process

Step 3: Select assessment

Step 4: Discover a mismatch between the facts about the learner and the facts about the activity (i.e., content, process, product)

Step 5: Send the learner away (to special education, Title I, ESL, etc.)

The new approach that inclusive education espouses is quite different. In fact, if teachers are able to co-plan effectively, the new approach to teaching should instead look like this (Murawski, 2007):

Step 1: Select content

Teachers ask each other: Will the content be appropriate for all? If not, what can we do to "spiral" or "adapt?" Teachers use Tomlinson's areas of differentiation to determine students' readiness, interests, and learning profiles to guide their instructional planning.

Step 2: Select teaching process

Teachers ask each other: What can the two of us do to help all students in class access this curriculum? Do we need to regroup students to allow for cooperative learning?

Step 3: Select assessment

Teachers ask each other: What will we do to check learning? Do we need to adapt the "product" that shows students have learned the information? What do we want all, most, some to have learned?

We now know *why* it is important to plan together, *when* we should plan together, and *what* we should generally discuss when we plan together. Next, we need to know *how* to guide our planning interactions. I've developed some questions found in Figure 11.6 that are helpful in facilitating the most efficient and effective use of your planning time. I recommend copying these 10 questions onto a card and using them to help structure and guide your planning sessions.

Remember that, just as you divulged your strengths, weaknesses and preferences when you completed the S.H.A.R.E. worksheet (Figure 5.1) together, it is important to be honest with your partner. This holds true when referring to elements of lesson planning as well. For example, if you and I were going to co-teach, we'd need to share important information with each other. If you tend not to plan at all and are the "Queen of Winging It"—share that with me. I'm a Type A kind of personality, so I need to share that kind of information with you as well. If the two of us were to work together, we'd drive each other nuts—you "winging it" and me wanting to over plan—*unless* we discussed this in advance. Then I would know to let go of the need to discuss every little detail, whereas you would know that we will need to do at least the most preliminary of planning in order to keep me sane. If you are a procrastinator, tell me. If you love to grade papers, hate to do "cutesy" activities, love to have kids work on the computer, hate to facilitate group work—tell me. If you see yourself as disorganized or often forget to bring in required materials because you are more laid back, if you prefer to make copies because it is a task that requires less thinking—tell me. The more we share our planning and teaching preferences, the more we can work together peacefully and effectively.

Questions Framing Our Weekly Lesson Planning

1. *What is the standard/content/big idea/enduring understanding?*

2. *What needs to be accomplished by the end of the day (our "objective" or the students' "essential question")?*

3. *How comfortable do we both feel with the content?*

4. *What co-teaching approach makes the most sense (given the content and our comfort with it)?*

5. *If we're regrouping kids, how will we do it most effectively and efficiently?*

6. *What types of behavioral or academic adaptations might we need to make? Think about our HALO—high, average, low, other—and about the differentiation CPP—content, process, product.*

7. *How much time will we need for each part?*

8. *What will the general educator do and what will the special service provider do? Are we both actively engaged?*

9. *How will we know we are effective? (Assessment of ourselves and of the students)*

10. *What materials do we need and who will do what?*

Figure 11.6   Questions Framing Our Weekly Co-Lesson Planning

Co-Planning Roles

What does the general education teacher bring to this co-teaching relationship that should be shared during co-planning?

My Areas of Strength   *My Areas of Weakness*

What does the special education teacher or other special service provider bring to the co-teaching relationship that should be shared during co-planning?

My Areas of Strength   *My Areas of Weakness*

Step	Time	Description of Activity for Co-Teachers
1	2–3 min.	Pick your content area, grade level, and standard
2	5–7 min.	Decide what grade level instruction would look like in terms of essential questions students should be able to answer, resources that would be needed, how they would be assessed, and what instruction would logically follow
3	5–7 min.	Determine how the lesson would need to be modified for students who were at a foundational or lower level and at a higher advanced level

National Standards to Use for Practice Lesson Planning

English:	Students use the general skills and strategies of the writing process.
Mathematics:	Students use a variety of strategies in the problem-solving process.
U.S. History:	Students understand the people, events, problems, and ideas that were significant in creating the history of their state.
Science:	Students understand the nature of scientific inquiry.
Economics:	Students understand the concept of prices and the interaction of supply and demand.
Civics:	Students understand how certain character traits enhance citizens' ability to fulfill personal and civic responsibilities.
Health:	Students know how to maintain mental and emotional health.
Art:	Students understand and apply media, techniques, and processes related to the visual arts.
Music:	Students understand the relationship between music and history and culture.
Physical Education:	Students use a variety of basic and advanced movement forms.
Foreign Language:	Students use the target language to engage in conversations, express feelings and emotions, and exchange opinions and information.
Technology:	Students understand the nature and uses of different forms of technology.

Figure 11.7 Creating a 15-Minute Tiered Lesson

Lesson Planning Practice

Want to practice? Prior to creating a full-blown lesson plan with your co-teacher, consider trying this miniversion to get you working together and seeing how easy differentiation can really be. This activity should take a total of 15 minutes. First, take two to three minutes with your co-teacher to select one of the following subject areas and the related national standard in Figure 11.8 (or pick one of your own if you prefer). Next, take five to seven minutes with

Example		
Creating a Tiered Lesson *(format adapted from Fattig & Taylor, 2008)*		
Unit, Chapter, or Big Idea: *Animals, like humans, change as they grow. What are the similarities and differences between humans and butterflies?*		
Grade Level Standard: *(2nd grade) Relate observations of a butterfly's life cycle to students' growth and changes.*		
Preassessment: *Have students studied life cycles of other animals before? What do they know already about changes and growth?*		
	Grade Level	**Foundational**	**Advanced Grade Level**
Critical Questions	How is your life cycle similar to and different from that of a butterfly? Compare and contrast.	How are you like a butterfly? How are you different from a butterfly?	Compare your life cycle to that of animals other than butterflies. How is it similar or different?
Resources	Butterfly kit, Observation forms and journals, Graphic organizer, KWL, Word Wall	Butterfly kit, Modified observation forms (simplified terms) and journals (can cut and paste), Modified graphic organizer (Cloze), KWL, Word Wall (only required to do some)	Butterfly kit, Observation forms and journals, Graphic organizer (can also create own if desired), KWL (can research independently for "what I want to know"), Word Wall
Means of Assessment	Cooperative groups create slideshow of animal life cycle and model of butterfly's life; all students participate and have active roles; Rubric	Cooperative groups create slideshow of animal life cycle and model of butterfly's life; all students participate and have active roles (roles will match readiness level); modified rubric	Cooperative groups create slideshow of animal life cycle and model of butterfly's life; all students participate and have active roles (roles will be sufficiently challenging); modified rubric
Where Next	Begin to observe other animals and discuss habitats as they relate and differ from humans	Begin to observe other animals and discuss habitats as they relate and differ from humans	Begin to observe other animals and discuss habitats as they relate and differ from humans
Estimated length of activity in minutes, periods, days: Entire unit is five weeks long		

Figure 11.8 Example—Creating a Tiered Lesson

SOURCE: Fattig, M. L., & Taylor, M. T. (2008).

Creating a Tiered Lesson
(Fattig & Taylor, 2008)

Unit, Chapter, or Big Idea: _____

Grade Level Standard: _____

Preassessment: _____

	Grade Level	Foundational	Advanced Grade Level
Critical Questions			
Resources			
Means of Assessment			
Where Next			

Estimated length of activity in minutes, periods, days: _____

This is Step One.
Step Two is creating your more specific lesson plan together.

Figure 11.9   Creating a Tiered Lesson

SOURCE: Fattig, M. L., & Taylor, M. T. (2008).

your partner to consider how you might plan to teach a lesson to that standard for typical learners. Together, identify what critical questions you will want grade-level students to be able to answer following your instruction, what resources you will need to teach that content, and how you intend to assess students' learning. Once you have completed that for the students who are at grade level, take another five to seven minutes to do the same for students who have more foundational (lower) and advanced (higher) comprehension of the content. *Voila!* You've created a tiered lesson. If you have time left, try to differentiate further by working together to consider your own students. Would each of them be successful with the instruction in one of the three columns? Would additional differentiation be required for academic, behavioral, physical, attentional, or emotional reasons? Adding that additional level of individualization will only improve your lesson. By the way, another wonderful benefit of doing this type of fast planning—in addition to how quickly it can be accomplished— is that it results in a general lesson that can be used as a basis every year as you teach the same content. You and your co-teacher can break out your tiered lessons as a foundation and then "tweak" and individualize them to match the current class of student needs.

Comprehensive Lesson Planning

It is time to actually plan a lesson together. Remember when you were a student teacher and you actually created those narrative, multipage lesson plans? Unfortunately, you and your partner will have to go through a bit of those growing pains that happen anytime there is a new experience. Newlyweds need to spend more time getting to know their spouse; after a time, decision making is much quicker and more natural. So too will teachers new to co-teaching have to spend a bit more time and actually co-plan their lessons together. Remember what I said earlier though—the more you write down your lessons now and document them, the less you will have to do later.

Research on lesson planning has identified numerous components necessary for a quality lesson plan. Following are some of the components that you and your partner will need to ask yourselves as you create your co-taught lessons:

- What grade level, subject area, and content standard will you be addressing?
- What is the lesson's objective? How will you know if you met the objective?
- What are the essential questions that students should be able to answer by the end of the lesson?
- What key vocabulary will students need to know or learn for this lesson?
- What preassessment do you need to do to determine students' levels of readiness?
- What materials will you need for this lesson?
- How much time will you be taking for each part of the lesson?

- What are you going to do in the beginning of the lesson related to anticipatory set (the introduction, opening, or "hook"), warm-up, review, or modeling?
- What are you going to do in the middle of the lesson related to direct instruction, checking for understanding, and guided or independent practice?
- What are you going to do at the end of the lesson related to closing the lesson, conducting assessments, previewing upcoming information, and extending the content for those who need it?

For co-taught lessons that also address the need for differentiation, the following should be considered:

- Will you be differentiating in this lesson? If so, will it be by content, process or product?
- If regrouping, how will you group students—by readiness, learning styles, interests, or other?
- What types of considerations do you need for our diverse learners?
- Are there any IEP goals or objectives that you will need to address in this lesson?
- Are there any accommodations, modifications, or adaptations that need to be provided to students with disabilities, as per their IEPs?
- What co-teaching approaches are most appropriate for the beginning of the lesson? The middle? The end?
- What do each of you need to do or bring to prepare for this lesson?

The lesson plan format provided in Figure 11.10 is similar to that from the CTSS teachers' toolbox. In the software version, however, teachers are guided in many areas with drop-down menus as they complete parts of the lesson plan. The lesson can then be exported (e-mailed) to a co-teacher who would subsequently complete her part and e-mail it back. A free downloadable Microsoft Word version of the lesson plan format in Figure 11.10 is available at www.2TeachLLC.com.

Example
Co-Teaching Lesson Plan

Subject Area:	Math
Grade level:	3rd
Content Standard:	MA 3.1.12
Lesson Objective:	Students will be able to solve money problems
Essential Questions:	How would you spend your money if you had $10 to spend?
Key Vocabulary:	money, spending, addition
Preassessment:	Basic addition skills; Basic money-handling skills; Bill/coin identification
Materials:	Shopping catalogs for each kid; fake $5 bills, fake $1 bills

Lesson	Co-Teaching Approach (can select more than one)	Time	General Education Teacher	Special Service Provider	Considerations (may include adaptations, differentiation, accommodations, or student-specific needs)
Beginning: (may include: Opening; Warm-Up; Review; Anticipatory Set)	☑ **One Teach, One Support** ☐ **Parallel** ☐ **Alternative** ☐ **Station** ☐ **Team**	5 min	Take roll Pass out folders to tables that contain catalogs, order forms and money	Overview today's objective. Tell students that they will be spending some money as they do a little imaginary shopping from a catalog. Their goal is to spend exactly $10 without going over or under.	Give enlarged money bills and simplified catalog to Jason and Brandon. Give more complex catalog to Tiffany, along with coins.
Middle: (may include: Instruction; Modeling; Checking for Understanding; Independent or Group Practice)	☐ **One Teach, One Support** ☐ **Parallel** ☐ **Alternative** ☐ **Station** ☑ **Team**	15 min	Teacher 1 and Teacher 2 do a "Think-Aloud" as they model the assignment. Teacher 1 talks through selecting items from the catalog as Teacher 2 writes the amount on the board and cautions her friend to not exceed $10. They then model filling out the order form and adding the correct total.	After seeing teachers model the assignment, students are divided into 2 groups to begin the assignment.	Make sure Jason, Javier, and Sam are up front to observe (and to help with proximity control).
End: (may include: Closing, Assessments, Extension of the Lesson)	☐ **One Teach, One Support** ☑ **Parallel** ☐ **Alternative** ☐ **Station** ☐ **Team**	15 min	Circulate and help students in group A. When a student is finished, he needs to list the items that he selected from the catalog and to show the total purchase and how he calculated it to the teacher. If it is correct, he can become a "teacher's helper" and begin to walk around group A to see if anyone else needs assistance. When all students are done, everyone will get $1 Classroom Buck to spend in the classroom store.	Circulate and help students in group B. When a student is finished, he needs to list the items that he selected from the catalog and to show the total purchase and how he calculated it to the teacher. If it is correct, he can become a "teacher's helper" and begin to walk around group B to see if anyone else needs assistance. When all students are done, everyone will get $1 Classroom Buck to spend in the classroom store.	Jenny and Vicki will show an example to both groups of items that don't exceed $10 limit and items that (when combined) do exceed $10 limit. Tiffany is encouraged to spend her $10 by adding items that are more complex (e.g., $1.25 + 4.75 + ...) as compared to the whole numbers everyone else is doing.

Figure 11.10 Example—Co-Teaching Lesson Plan

SOURCE: Murawski, W. W. (2008a).

			Example		
			Co-Teaching Lesson Plan		

Subject Area: _____

Grade Level: _____

Content Standard: _____

Lesson Objective: _____

Essential Questions: _____

Key Vocabulary: _____

Preassessment: _____

Materials: _____

Lesson	Co-Teaching Approach (can select more than one)	Time	General Education Teacher	Special Service Provider	Considerations (may include adaptations, differentiation, accommodations, or student-specific needs)
Beginning: (may include: Opening; Warm-Up; Review; Anticipatory Set; Modeling)	☐ One Teach, One Support ☐ Parallel ☐ Alternative ☐ Station ☐ Team				
Middle: (may include: Instruction; Modeling; Checking for Understanding; Independent or Group Practice)	☐ One Teach, One Support ☐ Parallel ☐ Alternative ☐ Station ☐ Team				
End: (may include: Closing, Assessments, Extension of the Lesson)	☐ One Teach, One Support ☐ Parallel ☐ Alternative ☐ Station ☐ Team				

Figure 11.11   Co-Teaching Lesson Plan Template

SOURCE: Murawski, W. W. (2008a).

Self-Assessment 3

Are We Ready to Marry?

Are we ready to work as a team for better or worse?
What if that means dealing with students who have very bad behavior or low academics?

Are we ready to work as a team for richer or for poorer?
Are we willing to share our materials with one another on daily basis?
What if that means I might get into your chocolate stash?

Are we ready to work as a team to plan together on a regular basis?
What if it means we have to find time to actually write down and share plans that we haven't written down since our student teaching days?
Are we willing to find a consistent time to meet and plan together?

Are we ready to work as team as we talk to the administrator?
What if that means spending a few days hashing through the master schedule or working with our colleagues to help convince them how important it is that we have common planning time?

My continued concerns about working as a team are . . .

Figure 11.12   Self-Assessment: Are We Ready to Marry?

12

Matchmaker, Matchmaker

The Role of the Administrator

■ AVOIDING POLYGAMY: TOO MANY IS SIMPLY TOO MANY (WHEN SCHEDULING)

Administrators have a lot to consider when it comes to the implementation (i.e., the *wedding*) phase of a co-teaching program. One of the major issues relates to scheduling. This chapter provides you with many strategies and suggestions to make scheduling for co-teaching feasible. In addition to scheduling-related issues, other items of focus at this stage of the game include articulating with secondary schools, planning for noninstructional time, and scheduling individualized education program (IEP) meetings. Each of these areas is tackled in this chapter.

Creating Viable Schedules

For every administrator, there is a different scheduling nightmare. Finding ways to ensure students with disabilities are appropriately included in general education classes is difficult. Determining which classes will be co-taught, which will have in-class support by a special education teacher, and even which will have paraprofessional assistance or indirect support only adds to the difficulty. There are, however, things an administrator can do to increase the chances that students will be more effectively scheduled into classes and that teachers will be able to provide the necessary assistance. These include understanding the collaborative continuum, working with the master schedule, keeping appropriate proportions of students, ensuring common planning times, teaming creatively, and ensuring monogamy of teachers.

Understanding the Collaborative Continuum. For years, special education has been seen as an "all or nothing" perspective. Students were identified as *self-contained,* meaning they received all of their academic instruction in the special education classroom, or *resource* meaning that they would be in the general education class for some parts of the class and pulled out for instruction in other areas. Students with behavioral issues were often placed in self-contained classes resulting in classes that had students with strong academics and poor behavior skills with students with the lowest academics (and sometimes excellent behavioral skills). Is it any wonder that teachers of these classes felt more like babysitters or guardians than teachers? Instead of determining that a student is all in or all out of general education, administrators need to encourage their faculty to view each child as an individual. Consider the flowchart in Figure 12.1.

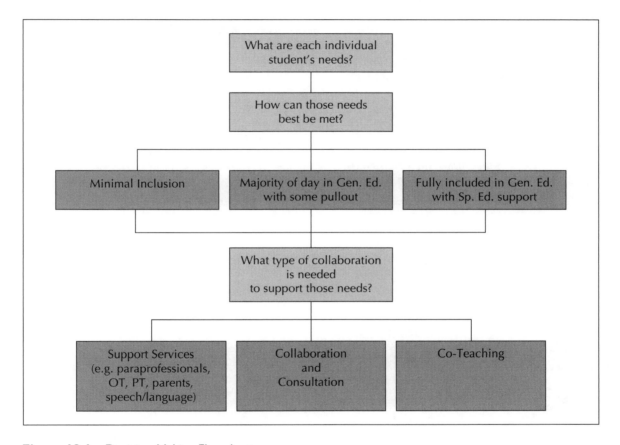

Figure 12.1   Decision Making Flowchart

SOURCE: Friedman Narr, Murawski, & Spencer (2007).

To consider the paradigm shift that moves from the "all or nothing" approach to one that is more individualized, read below the example of Quincy.

Quincy is a student with an identified disability in math; as a result, he has extremely poor math skills. As a fifth grader, Quincy struggles to do even the most basic math calculations. Quincy is only minimally helped by the use of a calculator. It is not reasonable to imagine Quincy working on division, fractions, and decimals like his fifth-grade peers, so Quincy's parents and teachers want him to master more basic and applied math skills. It is decided at the IEP meeting that Quincy will receive special education services from his special education teacher, Mrs. Cackowski, for math only. Because science contains some math, Quincy's fifth-grade teacher,

Ms. Buzzoni, is concerned about his success during that part of the class. It is decided at the IEP that Quincy would be successful in the general education during science if that part of the class is co-taught, providing Quincy with daily support from Mrs. Cackowski and Ms. Buzzoni working in tandem. Because the school is using response to intervention (RTI), Quincy will be considered Tier Three during science so that he will receive additional small-group and even one-on-one instruction when needed during that time. Having two teachers co-teach during that time makes RTI tiers and intensive instruction more doable for teachers (Murawski & Hughes, 2009).

Because Quincy's reading and language arts skills are on grade level, but he still does lack some organizational and attentional skills, he is going to need some in-class support throughout the day. A special education paraprofessional will be able to come support that class every other day to help Quincy and Ms. Buzzoni, and to act as a liaison between the general education teacher (Ms. Buzzoni) and the special education teacher who has Quincy on her caseload (Mrs. Cackowski). In addition, there is a Title I teacher who frequently comes in to co-teach lessons with Ms. Buzzoni during language arts time. This means that Quincy (who is considered Tier Two in RTI related to language arts) is also able to benefit from instructional supports and smaller student-teacher ratios during that time as well. Finally, it is decided that Quincy probably won't need additional supports during the social studies, physical education, and art or elective times because in lessons that provide more kinesthetic learning opportunities, Quincy tends to do well; thus, he is Tier One during those times.

——————— ✀ ———————

Want more on RTI and co-teaching? See Chapter 16, Co-teaching and other initiatives.

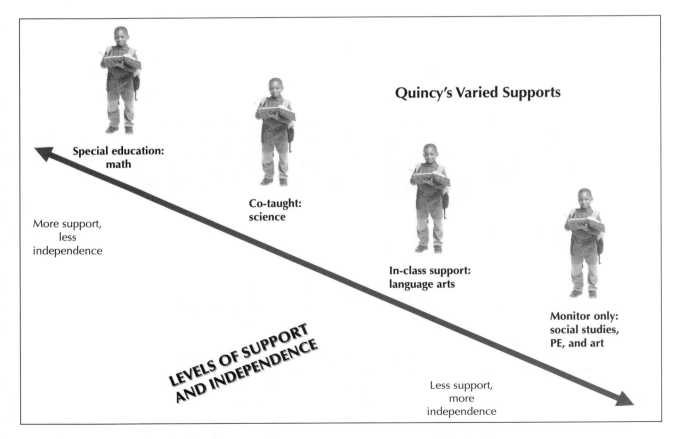

Quincy's Varied Supports

Special education: math

Co-taught: science

In-class support: language arts

Monitor only: social studies, PE, and art

More support, less independence

Less support, more independence

LEVELS OF SUPPORT AND INDEPENDENCE

Figure 12.2 Independence Increases as Support Decreases

SOURCE: Friedman Narr, Murawski, & Spencer (2007).

Quincy clearly needs a variety of supports. These supports vary along a continuum. If teachers look at students as "all or nothing" in terms of their supports, they will end up giving too much or too little. Too much support, such as what often occurs when students are placed in self-contained special education classes, limits independence and can be as detrimental to students as providing too little support, which results in student frustration and anxiety. Instead, teachers need to work with administrators to identify students' abilities and needs across the collaborative continuum. As the graphic in Figure 12.2 depicts, the goal of all supports is to provide scaffolding for students in order to increase their independence, not to give them too much or too little support (Friedman Narr et al., 2007).

Working With the Master Schedule. Although computers can easily generate random classes for the Master Schedule, this is not the best approach to take when first establishing co-teaching at a school. Until we can program computers to understand the collaborative continuum and take into account students' specific needs for support, students with disabilities should be put into the master schedule **first.** In many cases, this means hand scheduling. When classes begin getting large, teachers are often resistant and even resentful to those they think are causing the increased numbers (e.g., special education students). It is best, therefore, to schedule those students in classes first, so that as the class numbers increase, students with special needs are not perceived to be at fault. In addition, assigning students with special needs first allows special educators, Title I teachers, ESL teachers, and academic coaches to work with the administrator or those in charge of scheduling to ensure students are with the faculty who are best able to meet their individual needs.

—————————— **Putting It in Practice** ——————————

One middle school administrator in Alabama reported that hand scheduling made all the difference and that she simply had to get rid of everyone's "sacred cows" and start fresh. Many of the veteran faculty had classes they preferred to teach in the morning so their planning could be in the afternoon or right after lunch. Other sacred cows involved courses that were traditionally taught at a particular time, such as 6th period band. This administrator decided to start from scratch and not take into account "the way it has always been done." She ended up changing the schedule from six periods to eight in order to keep subjects, allow students' electives, and still ensure that teachers had both a common team planning period as well as an individual planning period. Teachers now report having little difficulty meeting to co-plan, since they know they'll also be able to have time for themselves as well. Upon praising this administrator for her willingness to think outside the box, she replied, "Well, I learned that sacred cows end up making the best barbeque!"

Keeping Appropriate Proportions. Teachers often want to know how many students with disabilities are considered *too many* for one class. While there is no set number, experts repeatedly recommend having "natural proportions" (Salend, 2008) of students with disabilities in general education classes. While the percentage of natural proportions is also vague, most agree that approximately 15 to 20 percent of the population has disabilities. Therefore, an ideal proportion of students with disabilities in a classroom to those without is 20 percent of students with disabilities to 80 percent of students without. Another recommendation is to have the proportion of students with special needs in each class mirror the proportion of students with disabilities in the school if possible (Villa, 2006). That said, most educators will find quickly that in order to schedule teachers so they are able to help the maximum number of students with IEPs, students with disabilities need to be "clustered."

My own experiences indicate that, while 20 percent may be ideal, more students with disabilities need to be in a general education class to warrant having a special education co-teacher on a regular basis. Is there a tipping point? Definitely. In order to continue to glean the research-identified benefits of a heterogeneous inclusive classroom, appropriate behaviors and academics need to be modeled. Thus, administrators need to avoid creating classes wherein more than one-third of the class has identified special needs. Although it may be convenient to cluster more students with special needs (e.g., disabilities, English language learners, slow learners) into one class (even if the students do not all have IEPs or other labels), the reported benefits of inclusion and co-teaching can be negated by this action, leading to lower academics, more behavior problems, and increased teacher frustration (Dieker & Murawski, 2003). In essence, this becomes tracking rather than the inclusive setting that is the goal. In addition, general education teachers often report feeling like they are now teaching a special education class that merely has allowed a few general education students to be in it (Murawski, 2006). Some states have even taken to adopting policy that limits the number of students with identified disabilities in the classroom (e.g., West Virginia Policy 2419, p. 79).

When clustering students, administrators need to limit the inclusion of students with special needs to approximately 30 percent of the general education class total (Murawski, 2008b). For an elementary class of 20 students, that means that no more than six of the students have identified disabilities. It is ideal, however, to strive for a smaller percentage. When determining which students should work with which pair of teachers, administrators should collaborate with the staff who know the students and their needs best. Decisions about student groupings should consider the following:

- Student grade level (the higher the grade, the more complex the content; also there tend to be more students identified with disabilities in the upper grades)
- Student academic needs
- Student behavioral needs
- Student personalities
- Student preference of teacher gender (only when significant)
- The level of support the student will require, given the above factors

One way schools have strategically clustered students is by using a weighting system. For example, a student with minor academic needs who primarily will be monitored in the general education classroom with minimum additional support might count as a "one," much like general education students. A student with moderate learning or behavioral needs might count as a "two," whereas a student with very significant needs who will require extensive time or support would count as a "three." By assigning a numerical value to each child, based on the level of support he may need (rather than just by his label), teachers can create classes that are manageable and do not result in one class overloaded with the more challenging or time-intensive students.

Want More on This Topic?

Examples of school coding charts are provided in this chapter on page 190.

Students who are not in special education (to include students who are English language learners, students on a 504 plan, gifted students, and even typical general education students) can be included in this weighting system. If the entire school subscribes to the system, administrators can work with teachers to balance classes schoolwide so that all teachers have classes with comparable weights.

Ensuring Common Planning Times. Although I already mentioned how important common planning times are, I need to address them again under scheduling. Clearly, for the scheduling of common planning times to be accomplished, administrators and teachers must decide early on who will be co-teaching with whom. While this should be ideally determined based on individual student need, you are usually able to detect a trend in which classes typically have the most students with significant needs (e.g., fifth-grade or language arts times). While most elementary teachers do not have a planning period the way their secondary counterparts do, there are ways to build in time in the schedule for co-teachers to meet daily. For example, this might entail ensuring that special and general education teachers can meet when students go for music with the music teacher, or it might mean scheduling classes for concurrent recess so that general educators can take turns monitoring students while the other teacher is meeting with a co-teacher. Insightful administrators will find a way to give prospective co-teachers time *before* the end of the school year *and* during the summer to meet and begin to proactively plan their instruction. Throwing teachers into an *arranged marriage* with no chance to get to know one another or plan how they are going to "raise their kids" is a surefire way to ensure failure.

Teaming creatively. Few teachers would willingly sign up to teach a class with children who ranged from K–fifth grade. Thus, it is a disservice to special service providers to expect them to do a quality job when asked to teach multiple subjects, grades, and disability types all at the same time. However, prior to No Child Left Behind (NCLB, 2001), many special educators were asked to teach classes for students who were unsuccessful in their general education class—despite the fact that the special educator had no content expertise in the subject at hand (see the following box). Administrators should encourage strategic grouping so that special educators do not burn themselves out having to "do it all." When possible, find ways to enable special educators to specialize. This may entail having one special educator focus on a specific grade level (e.g., third grade), or on a particular subject (e.g., math), or on a particular cluster of teachers (e.g., the early elementary PreK–second grade teachers). Some schools have special educators follow a caseload year after year, which results in teachers who really know their students, their needs, and their parents. This is called looping. While this can be very helpful, it presents the additional difficulty of having to work with new teachers and new content each year. It is an option, however. Each option has its merits and, because the dynamic of each school varies (McLesky & Waldron, 2002), it is important for administrators to work with their own teachers (both general and special) to resolve which would work best for them.

Pre-NCLB

Johnny B. has a learning disability and is failing his sixth-grade math class. Mr. Brown, who has 15 years of math teaching experience, a math teaching credential, and a love of the subject, requests that Johnny B. be removed to receive "more individualized instruction" in a "smaller class setting" so that "his needs can be met more easily." Mr. Brown truly cares about Johnny B. and doesn't want to see him overly frustrated by a negative math experience. Johnny B. is put into a special education class, taught by Ms. Smith. Ms. Smith is a caring, dedicated special educator with 10 years of teaching experience, but no expertise, credential, or particular interest in math. The class Johnny B. is put in has 15 other students with disabilities, all of whom need more individualized attention in academics and many of whom have behavioral needs as well. In addition, because of scheduling, some of the students in Ms. Smith's class are there for math, some are there for English, some are there for social studies, and still others are there for science. There are even two students there for "study skills," which was written into the schedule as an elective replacement.

Post-NCLB

With the new requirement that teachers be highly qualified in their content, Johnny B. will no longer be sent to a special education classroom for academic instruction. Instead, Ms. Smith can co-teach with Mr. Brown in the sixth-grade classroom during math. Even though Ms. Smith lacks the math background and expertise that Mr. Brown has, she has an equal role in ensuring the success of all of the students, to include Johnny B. When co-planning, she looks at the content with an eye toward those individuals who, like herself, find math a challenge. She brings in strategies for differentiation, ideas for making the lesson more accessible to different learning styles, and proactively assesses where students may find difficulties. These are not the areas in which Mr. Brown has expertise.

In the above scenario, the likelihood that Johnny will receive mathematical instruction from Ms. Smith in the special education setting that supersedes what he would have received from Mr. Brown is doubtful at best. Yet, this is the reality that many special educators faced prior to the requirement of "highly qualified content specialists" by NCLB. In post-NCLB, however, the collaboration provided through the co-teaching efforts of Mr. Brown and Ms. Smith would result in math instruction that not only meets the needs of Johnny B., but the wide range of abilities that the other students in the class exhibit as well. However, if Ms. Smith is asked to "co-teach" in math, science, social studies, language arts, and even art on the same day and for a variety of different grade levels, we can rest assured that she will not be able to do it all. Creative teaming is an important factor for ensuring that special service providers can be effective in their job.

There is another issue that comes up when considering teaming. Many elementary schools have embraced the concept of "walk throughs," wherein the administrator or a team of observers can walk through the school and see all teachers teaching the same content at the same time. Teachers at similar grades are given scripted programs and pacing plans and asked to follow these exactly. While this may be helpful to the new teacher, or for schools struggling with teachers who are not engaging in best practice instruction, it can serve to make special educators' jobs difficult at best. More often than not, special educators and other special service providers (like Title I teachers and speech and language specialists) are asked to provide in-class assistance or co-teaching during language arts and reading times. However, when all teachers are teaching language arts and reading at the same time, special service providers are unable to be maximally efficient. They end up running around to a variety of classes, poking their heads in or doing one quick station activity, and then moving on to the next class. Their mornings have them running ragged, and their afternoons are a waste. While this certainly isn't true of all schools, I have worked with enough schools across the nation to know it is a real problem. Administrators need to recognize that, for a special educator to co-teach in reading or math with two or more teachers, those teachers must have the flexibility to craft schedules that complement, rather than mirror, one another. Allowing teachers to work collaboratively to create and then share those schedules is a creative teaming option that will increase teachers' sanity, effectiveness, and gratitude—not to mention allowing them to better meet the needs of students.

Ensuring Monogamy Among Teachers. This is often more easily said than done. When scheduling for collaboration and co-teaching, administrators need to remember the rule that general educators need to be restricted to one special educator with whom they are expected to collaborate daily. I am including both in-class support and co-teaching here.

Consider this typical situation: A fourth-grade general education teacher, Mr. Ross, teaches his fourth-grade students the usual content areas: math, science, social studies, and language arts and reading. It is determined that different content areas in that class need support, either through co-teaching or in-class support, because of a large number of students with behavioral and academic needs. Thus, one special educator, Miss Nelson, comes in to help during math; a paraprofessional, Miss Katie, comes in to help during science; another special educator, Mr. Jake, comes in to help during social studies; and finally, during language arts time, Miss Nelson returns and is joined by the Title I teacher, Mrs. Jay. Poor Mr. Ross!

Instead of having a different service provider in each of those sections that requires the general educator not only to have various preps but also to try to meet and communicate with multiple people (which, let's face it, won't happen), administrators should try to ensure that the same special service provider is assigned to those classes. That way, when those two individuals meet to plan, they can meet one time and talk about all of the various content areas. For example, in this situation, Miss Nelson might be able to remain in the class with Mr. Ross for all four content areas. This will free up Miss Katie, Mr. Jake, and even Mrs. Jay to go and help in other classes. Miss Nelson can communicate and collaborate with the other special service providers to make sure she is able to provide whatever adaptations or assistance are needed to the students in that class. The likelihood that Mr. Ross and Miss Nelson will plan together and form a more perfect marriage is greatly increased, since there aren't so many other adults vying for Mr. Ross's attention.

In addition, when Mr. Ross and Miss Nelson meet to plan, Mr. Ross can bring up concerns he has about aspects of the class that occur but that are not supported directly by Miss Nelson. For example, perhaps the art teacher, Mrs. Weiner, has indicated that a few of the students in the class have been acting up during art time, or perhaps Mr. Ross has noted bullying behaviors on the playground during recess, a time that Miss Nelson is not around. Because these teachers meet and plan regularly, Mr. Ross will have Miss Nelson's expertise for all questions, even for times when she is not directly providing support to students. This approach also ensures that general educators know their "go to" person in case of questions about accommodations, IEPs, or student behaviors. Special educators would then take responsibility for following up and supporting all the students who are in that co-taught class. That might involve some additional observations or assessments, all of which are commonplace in an elementary classroom, especially as schools embrace the concept of RTI.

I would love to say that special service providers should also be *monogamous*, but the truth is that most of these individuals have no choice but to "get around." Due to staffing and students in various subjects and grades, it is usually necessary for special educators, Title I teachers, teachers of the gifted or English language learners and so forth, to support and collaborate with a wide array of teachers. While creative teaming is a great way to limit and at least focus teachers' time (as previously mentioned, by grade, subject, or case-load), special educators may still find themselves working with multiple partners. For example, while Miss Nelson may be co-teaching with Mr. Ross during the four content areas, she may also have to go and work with another fourth-grade teacher during Mr. Ross's recess, enrichment, and lunchtimes. Or she may choose to only provide in-class support to Mr. Ross during social studies every other day, thereby freeing herself up to go into another class occasionally as well. In these situations, it is highly recommended that teachers are reasonable in their expectations and that they do not set themselves up for failure.

If a special service provider needs to collaborate with 12 different teachers, do not pretend that she will be able to co-teach with each of them. Use the correct terminology to accurately portray what will be occurring. Make sure the general educators know that the special educator will be collaborating, supporting, monitoring, and consulting with 11 of these teachers. Work with the special educator to identify one teacher with whom she can co-teach daily and ask her to focus her energies there in terms of co-planning, co-instructing and co-assessing. It is important that consistency and planning are in place for true co-teaching to occur. For the other classes, ask her to do what she can to support actively in both direct and indirect methods. Teachers often tell me that they are supposed to "co-teach" in multiple classes during the same time period. That is simply not possible. If this is the situation, I recommend you talk to teachers to get their input related to what is working and not working. Then, engage in "baby steps" by finding out what can be done immediately to improve the situation and what will need to be reflected on and shelved until it is time to create next year's schedule.

Articulating With Secondary Schools

Think about how often you hear teachers complain that the IEPs written at the elementary schools do not reflect what is happening at the middle school. Or how often elementary school teachers complain that they make significant progress working with students in inclusive settings, only to have them placed in self-contained classes when they move on to secondary. If this is a common complaint, I suggest having the administrator at the elementary school invite the administrator or counselor in charge of scheduling at the middle schools and the special education department chair to take a day to come visit your elementary school so that you can work with them to hand-schedule students into classes. When I did this in Burbank, California, we found that it solved a lot of problems. In advance of your meeting, prepare a folder on each student in special education who would likely be coming up to the middle school in question. It is helpful if folders include

1. a copy of the child's current IEP,

2. a completed informal reading, writing and math assessment for them to review, and

3. the student's current grade and teacher's name.

My experience was that having this day organized, allowed the secondary school folks to meet with students and talk to them about their upcoming move to middle school, to include finding out what kinds of classes students would like and in what extracurriculars they wished to participate. In addition, we asked special and general education teachers to drop by to talk to the visitors; this way secondary educators got the "skinny" on the classes teachers really thought students would be able to be successful in, as well as any other information on student personalities, preferences, behaviors, strengths, and needs. One day with each school should enable the secondary schools to determine rather quickly how many special education content classes they would need to support students' more significant disabilities, how many co-taught classes they would need, and how many students could be in general education classes with minimal monitoring or direct support. In addition, they will obtain a lot of valuable information, including copies of IEPs, so that they won't need to wait until later in the next school year to begin meeting students' specific needs. Thus, this is a collaborative way to ensure that the work done to help students be successful at the elementary grades is communicated and carried on in secondary schools; everyone wins.

Planning for Noninstructional Time Requirements

Another frequent concern by special service providers is the need to have time built into the daily or weekly schedule for activities that do not directly relate to teaching in a classroom. Special educators and others often have to assess students on an individual basis; they have to communicate with parents regularly; they have to complete a large amount of paperwork; they have to facilitate or otherwise participate in multiple IEP, parent-teacher, and student success team meetings; they have to create adaptations, modifications, and accommodations for a variety of classes, teachers, and students; and they have to be available for consultation and observations. These are activities that simply cannot be done outside of school hours or at home. Thus, it is important for special educators to have some daily time in their schedules wherein they are not expected to be teaching students, either in a co-taught setting or in a resource or pullout setting.

Most schools have found that it is in their best interest to provide special service providers with time in the schedule to take care of these requirements. What if you have general education teachers who don't have planning or non-instructional time in their schedules and they use the "that's not fair" argument when they see their special education colleagues with "testing, consulting, collaborating" time? Hopefully you don't have to remind them that *fair is not equal.* However, you may need to remind them that the job of the special educator entails many noninstructional activities that they don't have. It is important, however, that special educators who do have these times provided use them productively. Special service providers may need to be told that rolling into a class 15 minutes late, holding a cup of coffee and a breakfast burrito, does not set the tone they want with their general education colleagues. Special educators may need to be reminded that appearances matter. Part of what needs to be done in establishing a supporting and inclusive community relates to PR (public relations). Special service providers need to be aware that how they use their noninstructional time will be watched closely, not only by administrators but by their fellow teachers as well.

Ask special service providers to create a schedule that will show where they are and what they are doing during that noninstructional time. This type of consistency in schedule is helpful to you as the administrator when you need to find the teacher, but it is also helpful for teachers because it requires them to think through how their time will be used. Special educators often feel like they are pulled in too many directions and their time is spent running all over. Example schedules, such as those offered in Figures 12.3 and 12.4 on pages 185 and 186, provide teachers with structure. Notice how, even when many things need to occur in one hour, it is well scheduled. This will also enable general educators to plan for when the special service provider will be in the room, so that his services are maximized. Remember, structure equals freedom. It will also result in more understanding from colleagues, fewer headaches, and better outcomes for students.

Want More on This Topic?

Figures 12.3 and 12.4 provide administrators with example schedules that incorporate time for the noninstructional job requirements of SSPs.

An Ideal Schedule		
	Mrs. Hutchinson, Third-Grade Teacher	**Ms. Weichel, Special Education Teacher**
8:30 a.m.–Recess	Warm-up language arts with Ms. Weichel	Co-teach third grade with Mrs. Hutchinson
Recess–11 a.m.	Language arts with Ms. Weichel	Co-teach third grade with Mrs. Hutchinson
11 a.m.–Noon	Math with Ms. Weichel	Co-teach third grade with Mrs. Hutchinson
12:30–1:30 p.m.	Social sciences	Indirect support: Planning, testing, IEPs
1:30–2:40 p.m.	Enrichment, science	Monitoring other classes; meeting with paraeducators; creating modifications

Rationale for Ideal Scheduling

- Mrs. Hutchinson can share the ideas and materials she gets from working with Ms. Weichel in language arts and math with the other third-grade teachers.
- In this ideal schedule, Ms. Weichel is only co-teaching with one general educator. This will ensure that they are able to plan together and build a rapport and consistency helpful for students.
- Working with core subjects, such as language arts and math, allows teachers to focus and makes it easier to ensure competency with standards. Ms. Weichel won't be frustrated trying to cover too many subjects at too many different grade levels, which would take away from her ability to be effective.
- Indirect support time allows flexibility for special service providers to monitor or assess students, to assist in classes, to create accommodations, to draft goals and conduct IEP meetings, as well as to provide collaborative or consultative services for a variety of teachers.
- Having time built into the schedule to attend IEPs, create modifications, and meet with paraeducators ensures that special educators are not leaving during critical instructional times.
- This also helps with a feeling by general education teachers that the special service providers with whom they work are dependable and not always pulled out of the class for other tasks.

Figure 12.3   An Ideal Schedule

SOURCE: Murawski, W. W. (2008a).

	Mrs. Greenspan	**Mr. Vola**	**Miss Delta**
8:30 a.m.–recess	**SPED:** Learning lab, resource support Grades K–3	**COT:** Math fifth grade, with Yu	**ICS:** Math sixth grade, with Jones on Mon and Wed, with Barton on Tues and Thurs
Recess–11 a.m.	**COT:** Language arts kindergarten, with Zephyr	**IDS and Plan:** *Plan with Yu on Mon; Snyder on Tues while their classes are at enrichment; testing and IEPs on Wed*	**COT:** Language arts sixth grade, with Barton
11 a.m.–Noon	**COT:** Language arts 1st grade, with Farrell	**SPED:** Learning lab, resource support math Grades 4–6	**ICS:** Science, with Barton on Mon and Fri, with Jones on Tues, Wed, Thurs
12:30–1:30 p.m.	**IDS and Plan:** *Planning, monitoring, Assessing IEPs on Mon*	**COT:** Math fourth grade, with Snyder	**ICS:** Language arts 6th grade, with Jones
1:30–2:40	**ICS:** Math, second grade with Farrell on Mon, Wed, Fri, with Chalk on Tues, Thurs	**SPED:** Learning lab, resource support Language arts Grades 4–6)	**IDS and Plan:** *Planning/ Monitoring/ Assessing IEPs on Fri*

Figure 12.4   Example Schedules for Special Service Providers

Key: SPED = Special education; COT = Co-taught class; ICS = In-class support; IDS = Indirect support (monitoring, consulting, testing, accommodating, IEP meetings); Plan = planning (team or individual)

Scheduling IEP Meetings

I am stunned by how many teachers have their co-teaching partnerships jeopardized by the frequency with which the special educator leaves the classroom. Being called out of the room to deal with a behavioral problem ("one of *your* kids is causing problems"), to talk to a parent, or to substitute another class are issues that simply need to be addressed as a paradigm shift; special educators need to hold firm that they are about to teach a class and are simply unavailable to do these other things at this time. Calling an educator out of a co-taught class to attend an IEP meeting is therefore unacceptable. A good rule of thumb: If you wouldn't call a solo teacher out of the room for it, don't call a co-teacher out of the room for it. Just because there are two does not make one expendable.

IEP meetings should be scheduled in advance to give all stakeholders plenty of time to plan, assess, reflect, and prepare. They should never take anyone by surprise—not parents, students, teachers, or administrators. One of the best ways I have seen for preparing for IEP meetings is to select one day a week (more or less depending on the size of the school) and keep a calendar (electronic or hardcopy) for teachers to sign up as IEPs come due. Teachers, or preferably, a designated coordinator, can call parents to find out what time would work for them, given the openings on the calendar. Having this system in place will eliminate many of your headaches. Teachers, school psychologists, designated administrators, counselors, and others will all know what day they need to set aside for IEP meetings. Once determined, this day is sacrosanct. In addition, special educators can make sure that they sign up to have the IEP meetings for students on their own caseload during times when they are not co-teaching. Once a month, alternatives can be made available for before or after school hours for parents who otherwise cannot attend. An example of an IEP calendaring schedule is provided in Figure 12.5.

Ready, Set, Schedule!

Think you are ready to schedule? Follow these Ten Steps for Scheduling and you should be able to navigate this treacherous territory. If there are issues, remember "baby steps." Do what you can right now and pay attention to where you are finding difficulties. Do you need to bring in alternate perspectives? Are you trying to hang on to too many sacred cows? If making co-teaching work is a priority for you and others at your school, you can do it.

Example					
IEP Scheduling Calendar					
Friday, Oct 1	**Student Name/Case Manager**	**Contact Info**	**Friday, Oct 7**	**Student Name**	**Contact Info**
8–9 a.m.	Josie Edwards/ Wendy Murawski	Mrs. Edwards – 555-868-4398	**8–9 a.m.**	Tommy Manager/ Rachel Narro	Mr. Manager – 555-994-2496
9–10 a.m.	Valerie Smith/ Douglas Rachet	Mrs. Sue Smith – 555-672-7865 ssmith99@ cox.net	**9–10 a.m.**	Jupiter Garcina/ Rachel Narro	Mrs. Io Garcina – 555-994-2939
10:15– 11:15 a.m.			**10:15– 11:15 a.m.**	Brandon Farless/ Ginger Gillyson	Mr. Martin Farless – 555-337-4581 May take up to two hours
11:15 a.m.– 12:15 p.m.	Franco Petrilli / Rachel Narro	Mr & Mrs Petrilli – 555-239-3496	**11:15 a.m.– 12:15 p.m.**		
1–2 p.m.	Claire Hoosier/ Ginger Gillyson	555-338-8105	**1–2 p.m.**	Bennett Wardell/ Wendy Murawski	Mrs. Washington- 555-8310
2–3 p.m.	Franklin Evans/ Wendy Murawski	Mr. Jakob Evans – 555-338-4567	**2–3 p.m.**	Caspian Badger/ Douglas Rachet	Mr. Badger – Bigbadger@itt .net
3–4 p.m.		May take up to two hours	**3–4 p.m.**	Christine Zycorn/ Rachel Narro	Mr. Zycorn – 555-994-8844
			4–5 p.m.	Fabian Macostas/ Douglas Rachet	Mr. and Mrs. Macostas – *they can only come after 4 p.m.* 555-672-9055

Figure 12.5   Example—IEP Scheduling Calendar

Step	10 STEPS FOR SCHEDULING
1	**Gather the key players.** Typically this will include an administrator, a counselor, and a special education teacher (often the department chair). If you know you would like to start co-teaching in just a few subjects or grades first, it will be wise to invite key general educators also. While many people may want to participate, try to keep your numbers low at first.
2	**Identify the number of special service providers** (teachers and paraprofessionals) on staff.
3	**Identify the number of students with special needs in your school.** This can include just special education if you want to start more simply, or you may choose to also consider students who are gifted, English language learners, those on 504 plans, and so forth.
4	**Review each of the students** along the provided Worksheet for Scheduling Collaboration and Co-Teaching (Figure 12.8, p. 191) and check the appropriate boxes. See the Worksheet for Scheduling Co-Teaching: Codes (Figure 12.7, p. 190) to see the key to each number.*
5	**Count the number of areas in each grade** that need to be special education (high to low), general education with support, and co-taught. This is merely a frequency count.
6	When grouping students for special education or general education classes, **consider the students' weighting**. Try to keep each class at a similar weight by dividing up students so no one class has too many students with significant behavioral or academic difficulties. Example: Class 1 = 1 + 1 + 2A + 2B (weight = 6 with 4 students); Class 2 = 1 + 1+ 1+ 3B (weight = 6 with 4 students); Class 3 = 3A + 3B (weight = 6 with 2 students)
7	**Monitor the percentages of students with special needs** in each class. In order to ensure the direct support of special educators and paraprofessionals, students with IEPs need to be clustered somewhat, but if done too much, it becomes a special education class and more akin to "reverse mainstreaming" than an inclusive class that will garner academic and behavioral benefits. Remember, too many is simply too many. Rule of Thumb: • *Cluster* for co-teaching (up to 30 percent of the class can have special needs) • *Cluster* for in-class support (try not to exceed 20 percent) • *Spread out* for monitoring (if general educators will not be getting direct support, do not overwhelm them with large numbers in each class of students with identified special needs)
8	**Limit each general educator to one special educator.** Again, too many is simply too many. Reducing the number of individuals teachers have to work with increases the chances that effective co-planning and co-teaching will occur between partners.
9	**Invite a few other stakeholders** in to view the schedule and give feedback to see if you missed anything. Remember not to kowtow to too many sacred cows. This is a paradigm shift; things *will* need to change.
10	**Work with this schedule for a year.** See what works and what doesn't. Be open to suggestions for improvement. Make sure everyone in the school knows that you are working toward improvement in inclusive and co-taught education, but that you are a big believer in "baby steps."

Figure 12.6 Ten Steps for Scheduling

*The worksheet (Figure 12.8, p. 191) is often best completed by the case manager or teacher with the most experience with the student. You can save time by giving this form to teachers at the end of the school year and asking them to complete it in advance of creating the master schedule for the next year; these teachers will know the students best and will be able to complete the form quickly. Be careful, though, that teachers all have the same frame of reference when it comes to determining if a student can be successful in a general education class or not. (Some teachers will automatically check "special education class" just based on previous placements, as opposed to really considering if the student could be successful in a general education co-taught class.) Ask teachers also to weight students in terms of their academic (A) and behavioral (B) levels of needed support. Creating a form similar to this electronically will save time and paper and will make tallying the responses much more efficient.

Teachers who get along can make the co-taught classroom a fun and learning environment for all students.

Worksheet for Scheduling Co-Teaching:

CODES

Student Name: *Name of the student receiving special education services*

Disability Type: *Reason for services*

Write school-based acronym that would provide the most information, such as RD (reading disability), LD (learning disability), ED (emotional disability), AUT (autism), ASP (Asperger syndrome), HH (hard of hearing), VI (visually impaired), ADHD (attention deficit/hyperactivity disorder), OI (orthopedically impaired), etc.

For the following subject areas, select the best support type for that student:

1 = General education class, monitor only

2 = General education class, some in-class support (para or teacher)

3 = General education class, daily in-class support (co-teaching)

4 = Special education class, but general education curriculum (higher academic level)

5 = Special education class, maximum support needed (lowest academic level; possibly alternative curriculum)

Content areas include: Language arts (can identify reading vs. writing), **math, social studies, science, and other** (can identify PE, art, music, recess, lunch, etc.)

"Weighting" Student Support helps determine who to cluster where and with whom to reduce teacher burnout and increase parity among classes

For each student in a general education class, select the amount of support needed

1 = Minimal support; similar to typical general education student

2 = Moderate support; identify whether "A" academic or "B" behavioral

3 = Strong support; identify whether "A" academic or "B" behavioral

* Try to cluster students to maximize opportunities to support effectively without overwhelming one class or teacher with too many "3s" or "Bs" in the same class.

Figure 12.7 Worksheet for Scheduling Co-Teaching

Worksheet for Scheduling Collaboration and Co-Teaching

Name of school: _____   Administrator in charge of scheduling _____

Number of general education teachers in school: _____   Number of special education teachers in school: _____

Number of paraprofessionals in school: _____   Number of other support providers in school: _____

Number of general education students: _____   Number of special education students: _____

For the following subject areas, select the best support type for that student:

1 = General education class, monitor only
2 = General education class, some in-class support (paraprofessional or teacher)
3 = General education class, daily in-class support (co-teaching)
4 = Special education class, preparing for general education
5 = Special education class, maximum support needed

Complete the following table for each grade:

Grade _____			Recommended Levels of Support					
SE Student name:	Disability type:	"Weight" (1, 2, 3) (A, B)	Language arts (1–5)	Math (1–5)	Social studies (1–5)	Science (1–5)	Other (1–5)	Other (1–5)

Figure 12.8   Worksheet for Scheduling Collaboration and Co-Teaching

Part IV
The Marriage

A partnership that works is like a marriage made in heaven.

Don't worry. These teachers are actually married in real life too!

13

Working Together to Wrangle the Li'l Rascals

■ FIVE PRACTICAL APPROACHES FOR CO-INSTRUCTION

As you will recall, co-teaching requires three things: co-planning, co-instruction, and co-assessment. In Part III: The Wedding, I told you a lot about the aspects of co-planning. I reviewed how to make time for planning, how to use your time in planning, and when you should conduct different aspects of planning. However, now that you know how and when to plan, we need to discuss *what* you are planning to do. This is when we get into the co-instruction part of co-teaching. Notice that I don't consider *instruction* the same thing as *teaching*. Indeed, it is a subset of it. That is because I believe that teachers who show up to the classroom and simply impart their knowledge without planning or assessing aren't really teaching. They are merely acting as the "sage on the stage." Presenting material without ever checking that the students are with them and ready to move on is not effective teaching. This results in adults who say they "covered the information," despite the fact that the students did not actually learn it. For teaching to occur, we need to plan what we are going to do, do it with the students, and then evaluate whether or not they learned and if we can move on—ergo, the need to plan, instruct, and assess.

In this chapter, I share five approaches to co-instruction. If you are familiar with the research on co-teaching, you may already know these approaches in theory; they are the most commonly cited approaches in the literature and they were conceptualized by Dr. Lynne Cook and Dr. Marilyn Friend. While other approaches exist, I recommend you first become fluent with these five approaches. Having a common language and vision (Weiner & Murawski,

2005) is crucial for individuals who want to collaborate. If you and your partner are both conversant with these five approaches and know how to use them in the classroom, you will be ready to plan for them and then maximize your effectiveness during instruction. This chapter provides you with a visual and a description of each approach. I also provide strategies for how to divide your roles and share the pros and cons for you both to consider when planning the use of one of the approaches.

Before jumping into the approaches, however, I need to emphasize my three keys to co-instruction.

Three Keys to Co-Instruction

1. **Demonstrate parity between teachers.**
   Remember, you are both equals in this shared class. Make sure that the special educator is not always expected to work with small groups or take the support role.

2. **Ensure parity between students.**
   Heterogeneous groups are key to inclusive education. Be sure not to always cluster or "track" your slower students in one group and your bright or gifted students in another.

3. **Use a variety of the approaches.**
   While you and your co-teacher may feel more comfortable with one or two of the approaches at first, be sure not to overly rely on the same approaches over and again. Look at your content, your comfort levels with the content, and your students to determine which approach would best work for instruction. Mix it up to keep motivation and increase learning.

SOURCE: Murawski, W. W. (2008a).

Approach 1: One Teach, One Support

What It Should Look Like

One Teach, One Support is the most frequently used approach in co-teaching. In a One Teach, One Support approach, one of the teachers may take the majority of the responsibility for planning and content instruction. The other teacher may take the primary responsibility for adaptations, classroom management, communications, charting, paperwork management, and other support as needed. *These roles should change often so that one teacher is not always relegated to the support position. To do so will result in that person being viewed as an assistant.*

As one teacher takes the lead in content instruction with students, the other teacher is actively engaged in the support role. The support role should involve more than just walking around and passively watching students or merely using proximity control. While behavior management is certainly a benefit to this approach, there is much more that the individual in the support role can do. For example, this co-teacher can be setting up materials for an upcoming activity or lab. She can be disseminating or collecting papers. She can be providing quiet accommodations to individual students, and she can remove disruptive students to the hall to help redirect and then return them to the class. She has as much authority and responsibility as any other teacher. Keep in mind that the support role should be an active one and should improve the learning in the classroom.

As with all approaches, this approach should be used in conjunction with other approaches.

Students remain as a large group, which means this is considered a "whole class" approach. It is illustrated in Figure 13.1.

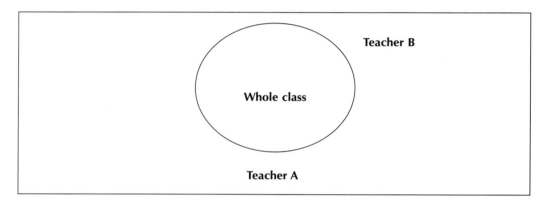

Figure 13.1   Whole Class Approach

What It Should Not Look Like

One Teach, One Support has become the fallback approach of many co-teachers. Weiss and Lloyd (2002) found that many teachers who said they were co-teaching were in fact merely having the general educator lead the class while the special educator circulated. Too often, if this becomes the case, the special educator begins to feel relegated to the role of paraprofessional or classroom assistant and will resent the role (Dieker & Murawski, 2003). In addition, there is no real benefit to the students (other than that which is reactive in nature) as the special educator has had no role in the planning of the lesson.

Another common misuse of One Teach, One Support is when co-teachers "pass the chalk" and then disappear or do their own thing when they are in the support role. For many, this has become more of a "one teach, one grade papers," "one teach, one make copies," "one teach, one check e-mail," "one teach, one text message," "one teach, one read the newspaper" or "one teach, one catch up on individualized education program (IEP) paperwork." None of these is acceptable. The individual in the support role needs to be actively engaged with students in order for there to be a clear rationale as to why co-teaching is needed in the class. If co-teachers are merely taking turns delivering instruction, it begs the question, **What is substantively different about this class as compared to that of a traditionally solo taught class?**

Finally, the amount of time One Teach, One Support is used must also be addressed. Too often, co-teachers will find themselves relying on this approach. It is certainly the one most comfortable to teachers who are used to having sole control of the classroom. It is also the approach that takes the least amount of time to co-plan. However, it is recommended that co-teachers use this approach only about 15 to 20 percent of the class time, as opposed to the 80 to 90 percent of the time it appears to be frequently used. Figure 13.2 is an in-action glimpse at how co-teachers might divide their roles using the One Teach, One Support approach, while Figure 13.3 provides a snapshot of the pros and cons of this approach.

Ask yourselves: If we are using this approach most of the time, are we really maximizing the use of both teachers? What can we do together using this approach that we could not do alone?

Mrs. Hutchinson, Lead for Today	Ms. Weichel, Support for Today
Plan lessons based on standards and grade-level curriculum	Make adaptations and modifications "on the spot" for students who need them
Deliver majority of content instruction to large group	Circulate during instruction, providing proximity control and determining who may need assistance
Evaluate majority of the classwork, with feedback from Ms. Weichel (*or* this may be done by Ms. Weichel with support from Mrs. Hutchinson)	Chart information or take notes on overhead to model good note taking
	Ask questions, repeat information, or provide an oral synopsis of what was said to provide repetition and to add, clarify, or expand on information presented
Remember, this approach should not be overused. Try to use it only 15–20 percent of the time. Consider the other approaches for regrouping students for improved student-teacher ratio and individualization.	Discreetly communicate to Mrs. Hutchinson if extra time is needed or if more explanation is required on a topic for the class as a whole
	Assist Mrs. Hutchinson in knowing how to grade modified work

Remember: This approach is *not* about having the general educator always teach and the other educator always support. Both teachers need "face time."

Figure 13.2   One Teach, One Support in Action: What Is My Role?
SOURCE: Murawski, W. W. (2008a).

EZ Reference

Pros of This Approach	Cons of This Approach
Most similar to traditional teaching	Most similar to traditional teaching, which does not always work for many students
Strong comfort level for teachers	So comfortable that teachers may not try to do new things and may resort to what has always been done—just taking turns doing it
Least amount of time to co-plan	Teachers may opt not to co-plan at all and may just divide the lesson, resulting in a lack of true collaboration.
Good for information that needs to be delivered by one voice	Some teachers feel that when they are not "on stage," they can leave or do things other than work with kids.
Supporting co-teacher can help with class management	If co-teachers haven't talked about classroom management, they may not use similar approaches, and this may be distracting during the lesson.
Can help increase instructional time as supporting co-teacher can take care of paperwork and noninstructional duties, such as taking roll, collecting homework, etc.	Too often, the special educator is relegated to this role, especially if he is not comfortable with content, and effectively becomes an assistant.
Supporting co-teacher can ensure that students receive accommodated or modified materials as needed	If the special educator is always the one providing the accommodations, students begin to associate her with special education. This role needs to be shared to avoid stigmatization.
Teachers can "pass the chalk" to ensure that both teachers get face time and both can lead the part of the lesson with which they feel most comfortable	Co-teachers can overuse this approach so it ends up becoming "your turn to speak, my turn to speak," rather than a truly collaborative endeavor designed to maximize the expertise of both educators.
The teacher in the support role can help identify which students are or are not "getting it" during the lesson and share that with the teacher in the lead role	If teachers are not yet comfortable with one another, the co-teacher in the support role may not share that information or jump in during the lesson, choosing instead to "pull" students or "reteach" later, in essence returning to a reactive, rather than proactive, method of addressing students' needs.

Figure 13.3   One Teach, One Support Snapshot

Approach 2: Parallel Teaching

What It Should Look Like

In a Parallel Teaching approach, teachers share responsibility for planning and content instruction. Teachers break the class into two heterogeneous groups and each instructs half of the class. If in the same room, it is suggested that co-teachers have the groups facing away from one another while the teachers face one another. This cuts down on noise issues and other nonverbal distractions.

I have identified three ways to use Parallel Teaching. The first is to teach *the same content in the same way.* This is the main way Parallel Teaching has been taught in the past (e.g., Friend & Cook, 2007). In this example, teachers are dividing the class in order to benefit from a smaller student-teacher ratio. They are covering the same content in the same style but may move to different parts of the room or even to different rooms, if space allows. For example, if teachers want to review lab safety with a group of students during science time, it would behoove them to divide the class in half so that the students can cluster around one teacher as she shows them the correct way to work the lab equipment.

The second option for Parallel Teaching is for co-teachers to teach *the same content in a different way.* In this case, teachers may introduce the same material to students utilizing different teaching styles to match the students' varied learning styles. For example, if teachers are trying to teach addition to students, one may introduce the skill to those students with primarily visual and auditory learning styles in a more traditional approach. That group might review problems using the white board as they watch a variety of problems written out and discussed. The other group, however, may be composed of students with primarily kinesthetic, tactile learning styles. They might be introduced to addition using manipulatives and other kinesthetic methods, such as making a human number line. After the original introduction to the skill in the students' primary learning modality, students may then change groups so that they are able to have the skill reinforced in the other method. In addition to providing students with additional reinforcement, switching groups also enables students in the first group a chance to play with the manipulatives and students in the second group to practice the more traditional approach, which, in all likelihood, will be the method by which they will be assessed. By changing groups, this may resemble Station Teaching, which I review next. but because we are in two similarly sized groups, I prefer to consider it an element of Parallel Teaching.

The third option for Parallel Teaching is for co-teachers to teach *different content.* In this case, it is important to note that I am not indicating they should have one teacher instruct reading, while the other teacher has a group of students color. However, if co-teachers want to use this approach to "divide and conquer," it is certainly appropriate. An example of this might be as co-teachers begin to start a writing or research project with students. One co-teacher could take a group of students to the library for a lesson on library research (perhaps co-taught with the school librarian, who will be thrilled that there is only half of the class coming and may be excited that her area of expertise will be valued during co-instruction). The other co-teacher might stay in the classroom with the other half of the class, teaching them how to organize their writing using a graphic organizer or thinking map. (For wonderful strategies related to graphic organizers, check out www.specialconnections.ku.edu, www.graphic.org, www.eduplace.com, and www.teachers.teach-nology.co. For more on thinking maps, see www.thinkingmaps.com.) Again, after teachers have worked with one group, they may choose to switch groups and repeat instruction so that everyone receives the same, parallel instruction.

As with all approaches, this approach should be used in conjunction with other approaches as well and the students should change groups occasionally.

In this case, students are moved out of a whole class approach into two groups. Thus, this is considered a regrouping approach. Figure 13.4 illustrates what Parallel Teaching looks like.

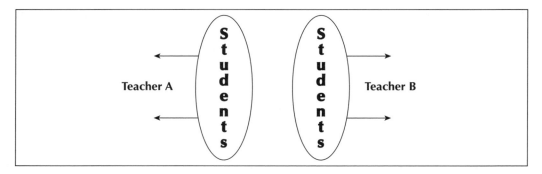

Figure 13.4

What It Should Not Look Like

Parallel Teaching sometimes enables teachers to feel that they can adopt a "separate but equal" approach. In this case, they may divide "your kids" and "my kids" and choose to keep working with "their" students on a regular basis. That is not the intent of Parallel Teaching. Teachers should not plan and teach on their own "island." As with all approaches, teachers should discuss what they'll be doing with their individual groups and collaborate on the best approaches. Students should be clustered heterogeneously, rather than having one teacher have all the "strong" kids, while the other has the "weak" ones. To do that kind of homogeneous grouping is reminiscent of tracking and the old pullout special education approach. Also, when presenting new content, the Parallel Teaching approach should only be used if *both* teachers feel similarly comfortable with the content. Figure 13.6 shows how co-teachers might divide their roles using the Parallel Teaching approach, and Figure 13.7 gives an EZ Reference snapshot of the pros and cons of this particular approach.

Ask yourselves: Are we avoiding the stigmatization of always grouping the same students? What can we do together using Parallel Teaching that we could not do alone?

Mrs. Hutchinson Takes Half the Class	Ms. Weichel Takes Half the Class
May take primary role of planning lesson based on state standards and grade level curriculum	May take primary role of reviewing IEPs, 504 plans, and behavior plans to consider possible adaptations needed
Collaborates with Ms. Weichel in planning instruction to ensure uniformity of content instruction	Collaborates with Mrs. Hutchinson in planning instruction to ensure necessary modifications, strategy instruction, and adaptations are available as needed

Figure 13.5 *(Continued)*

Mrs. Hutchinson Takes Half the Class	Ms. Weichel Takes Half the Class
Delivers content instruction to half of the large group (making accommodations as required)	Delivers content instruction to half of the large group (making accommodations as required)
Evaluates half of the large group and shares those results with Ms. Weichel during a debrief session	Evaluates half of the large group and shares those results with Mrs. Hutchinson during a debrief session

Remember: In this approach, we are ultimately teaching the same content. We may be doing it in a different way, the same way, or at different times, but all the students will eventually obtain all of the same content. This approach merely allows us to have smaller groups.

Figure 13.5 Parallel Teaching in Action: What's My Role

SOURCE: Murawski, W. W. (2008a).

Pros of This Approach	Cons of This Approach
Both teachers are actively engaged in instruction with students.	Teachers may feel they can "do their own thing" with "their" group, instead of ensuring that students in both groups are getting consistent instruction.
Both teachers get "face time" with students.	Some teachers may not be as familiar with the content and thus may be uncomfortable with this approach.
This approach provides teachers with a smaller student-teacher ratio for more individualized instruction.	Both space and noise can be a factor if groups are held in the same classroom and teachers and students are not careful.
Teachers may be encouraged to do more kinesthetic, hands-on, or otherwise engaging lessons if there are fewer students to manage.	Some teachers may not be familiar with constructivist or kinesthetic activities and would need to do additional planning or research to come up with these lessons.
Breaking into smaller groups enables teachers to "chunk" material and have students focus on one particular topic with one teacher.	Both teachers need to be familiar with the content to be taught and they need to co-plan who will do what.
Groups can stay with one teacher or can later switch so that each teacher sees both groups.	Timing is essential so that one group does not finish before the other, thereby causing additional chaos.
Each teacher can select an area with which they are the most comfortable to teach in a group.	Teachers may both want the same topic or may find it difficult to determine what or how to divide the content.
Each teacher can plan for his/her own group which lessens the need for co-planning time.	Teachers may see this as an opportunity for them to avoid co-planning and just divide and stay on their own "island."
Teachers can put students in groups by learning styles, interests, or readiness levels.	Some teachers may think that having two groups is an excuse to group special education students, which is not the intent.

EZ Reference

Figure 13.6 Parallel Teaching Snapshot

Approach 3: Station Teaching

What It Should Look Like

In a Station Teaching approach (such as that illustrated in Figure 13.7), teachers divide the responsibility for planning and content instruction. Students are rotated between three or more stations, also known as centers, which are either manned by a teacher or assistant or are *independent* stations. Teachers repeat instruction to each group that comes through the station, though content or delivery can vary based on differentiated needs. Co-teachers can structure stations so that students are able to focus on one aspect of a topic per station, essentially "chunking" information for students. For example, one station discusses the characters in a reading, while a second station identifies the plot/setting, and a third station reviews the themes in the reading. Another use of station teaching is when each station focuses on a different topic altogether. For example, one co-teacher may be working with students on fluency exercises, while another co-teacher may be working with students on phonics and decoding, while a third station has students independently answering comprehension questions after listening to the questions on a tape recorder. Teachers can work together to determine how many stations are appropriate for a given activity. For older students, multiple independent stations may be acceptable. One group of students could be watching a brief video, while another group reads their textbook and answers questions, while a third group works collaboratively on a project. The fourth and fifth groups each can be working with a co-teacher.

As with all approaches, this approach should be used in conjunction with other approaches as well and the students should change groups occasionally. Station teaching is considered a regrouping approach, since students do not stay in the traditional large group.

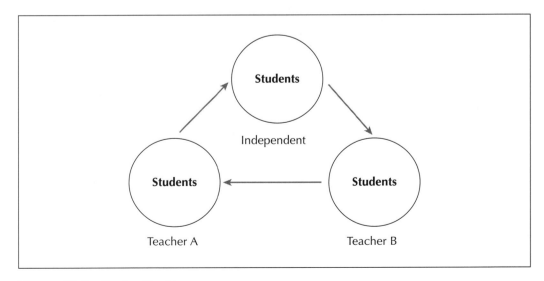

Figure 13.7   Station Teaching

What It Should Not Look Like

Stations should not be activities that are linear in nature or dependent on one another. For example, students who are learning about the writing process should not be expected to learn how to write an introductory paragraph in one station, the body of the paper in the second station, and the closing information in the third station. This won't make sense for the students who have to start in Station 3 and then rotate.

Also, Station Teaching sometimes allows teachers to think that they can—or even, should—divide students into groups by their ability. Groups are created that segregate the students who are struggling by putting them in one group that would include students in special education, English language learners, slow learners, and so forth, while the typical students would be in a second group, and the stronger students—or "gifted" students—would be in a third group. This tracking does the opposite of what inclusion intends; it stigmatizes and creates homogeneous grouping from which students do not benefit from one another. While some students may occasionally benefit from groups created by readiness level, groups should never (1) remain static so that students never change, or (2) always be based on ability level. For an in-action glimpse at how co-teachers might divide their roles using the Station Teaching approach, check out Figure 13.10. A snapshot of the pros and cons of this approach is provided in EZ Reference format in Figure 13.12.

Ask yourselves: Does our content lend itself to being chunked into stand-alone components? Would students benefit from a cooperative learning situation when learning this content? What can we do together using stations that we could not do alone?

Mrs. Hutchinson May Take a Station	Ms. Weichel May Take a Station
May take primary role of identifying needed skills instruction based on standards, grade level curriculum	May take primary role of helping to identify 3-4 appropriate station activities that would address needed instruction
Collaborate with Ms. Weichel in planning instruction for each station to ensure high quality of content instruction	Collaborate with Mrs. Hutchinson in planning instruction to ensure modifications, strategies and adaptations are available as needed
Create small heterogeneous groups of students	Teach students how to appropriately get into groups and how to quietly transition between stations
Deliver instruction at a station, or circulates to ensure stations are working smoothly	Deliver instruction at a station, or circulate to ensure stations are working smoothly
Evaluate half of the stations and share those results with Ms. Weichel during a debrief session	Evaluate half of the stations and share those results with Mrs. Hutchinson during a debrief session
Remember: Students are going to need some help with transitions, timing, and working with peers.	

Figure 13.8   Station Teaching in Action: What's My Role?

SOURCE: Murawski, W. W. (2008a).

Pros of This Approach	Cons of This Approach
This approach enables a much smaller student-to-teacher ratio for more individualized instruction.	Teachers are sometimes apt to put students with similar abilities or disabilities together.
The smaller stations or centers often provide a safer environment for students to engage in discussion or to participate more actively.	The noise factor can be an issue with any regrouping approach. Teachers need to teach students (and each other) to use "6-inch" voices.
The physical movement of students moving between stations provides a kinesthetic element and brain break that many children need.	Transitioning between stations can be chaotic and frightening for students who need structure. Co-teachers need to work with students on transitioning.
Stations help students focus on one topic for a more specific, shorter amount of time, which is very helpful for students with academic, behavioral, attentional, or social needs.	When material is broken into "chunks", students are more likely to learn and retain it, but they may still have difficulty with generalizing and making the connections.
This approach allows teachers to focus on one particular topic area for planning purposes. Each can be primarily responsible for his/her own center.	Despite the fact that teachers can take primary responsibility planning one or more stations, they still need to know what the other stations are doing.
Materials can be easily reused by each group if there are not sufficient materials for use by the whole class.	Co-teachers need to plan in advance to make sure the materials are ready and can be disseminated quickly.
Planning and presenting one topic allows co-teachers to have content with which they are familiar and are able to improve as they reteach it multiple times.	Only focusing on one aspect of the lesson may allow teachers to disengage from the other aspects. They need to communicate with each other.
Stations also provide the opportunity for co-teachers who are engaged in Response to Intervention (RTI) are able to provide intensive instruction for students in Tier 2 or 3, without "pulling out" to another classroom.	Not all teachers are aware of RTI or trained in its use. Both co-teachers would need to be trained in RTI and work together to use co-teaching strategies for the multiple tiers.

Figure 13.9   Station Teaching Snapshot

Approach 4: Alternative Teaching

What It Should Look Like

In an Alternative Teaching approach, a regrouping approach displayed in Figure 13.10, teachers can divide the responsibility for planning and content instruction. The majority of students remain in a large-group setting, while some students work in a small group for *reteaching, preteaching, enrichment,* or other *individualized instruction.*

Imagine if teachers used the small group at the beginning of the day as a preteaching technique for Bob, a student who didn't understand yesterday's lesson, Sally and Hakim, two students who were absent, and Tomas, a student who needs to be prepared for upcoming material. In addition, a small group may be pulled aside at the end of the lesson for reteaching, while others begin their independent practice. This time, Bob, Jonathan, Veronica, and Sarai may be included in the small group, because they were the ones who needed it.

One of the keys to using the Alternative Teaching approach effectively is to make sure that the large group is **not** receiving new direct instruction while the small group is pulled. If that occurs, you run the risk of having the same problems the old "pull-out" method had. While one co-teacher is pre- or re-teaching material, the large group is learning something new that the small group is missing out on and thereby falling further behind. Consider how helpful this approach can be if the majority of the class needs reteaching of some material, while a small group of students can receive enrichment from either of the co-teachers. Now the small group will receive a positive association, rather than a negative stigma.

What It Should Not Look Like

This approach is often misused, as many teachers resort to using the small group as a de facto "pullout." If students with special needs are continually being chosen for the small group and are then taught by the special education teacher, the result is a "class within a class" approach wherein the old special education technique of "pullout" has been brought back to the classroom. Too often, the same students are asked to go to the small group merely because

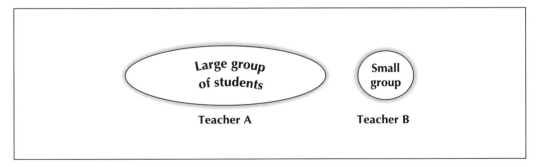

Figure 13.10 Alternative Teaching

they are in special education or have an IEP that states that the student would benefit from small groups. Researchers have found that co-teachers will often have the special educator continue to work with the special education students only, pulled to the back of the room rather than to a different resource classroom. This serves only to further stigmatize these students and is often worse than a resource setting would have been because now the student differences are made even more apparent to both students with and without disabilities. That is *not* the intent of Alternative Teaching. This increases stigmatization of students and is an ineffective technique. However, when used appropriately, Alternative Teaching can be very effective.

While this approach can certainly be beneficial for bringing some students up to speed, helping students who were absent, preteaching for students who may need the additional explanation and time, or even providing remediation for those who need it, the group makeup should be based on need and should change regularly. Co-teachers may find that Alternative Teaching is used most

ISLAND IN THE MAINSTREAM
MRS. JONES AND MRS. COOPER ARE STILL TRYING TO FIGURE OUT WHY FRED DOESN'T FEEL LIKE PART OF THE CLASS.

INSPIRED BY DOUG BIKLEN

© 2002 MICHAEL GIANGRECO, ILLUSTRATIONS KEVIN RUELLE

SOURCE: Reprinted with permission. Giangreco, M. (2007).

often when the large group is doing a warm-up, review, group activity, or guided or independent practice. In this way, students in the small group are not missing out on new content instruction. Dr. Michael Giangreco's cartoon, "Island in the Mainstream," does a nice job of pointing out the problems that can occur when small-group instruction in the general education classroom is not used appropriately. An example of a suggested division of roles in the Alternative Teaching approach is provided in Figure 13.11, and the EZ Reference pros and cons snapshot is shared in Figure 13.12.

When students are put in a small group for preteaching, reteaching or enrichment, ask yourselves: (1) Who needs this instruction? (2) Are we selecting students based on identified need, or merely on habit or label? (3) Will using this approach right now make these students miss out on new content instruction? (4) Will using this approach right now humiliate the students in a way that we are essentially putting a neon sign over their heads saying, "Make fun of us later for being different from everyone else"? (5) Are we making sure to use this approach for enrichment as well so that the

Remember: This approach is *not* about having the students with special needs, such as disabilities, ELL, at-risk, gifted, always clustered together. Address *needs*, not *labels*.

small group sometimes has a positive stigma? (6) Which one of us will work with the small group this time? Are we varying it up enough? (7) What can we do together using Alternative Teaching that we could not do alone?

Mrs. Hutchinson May Take Large or Small Group	Ms. Weichel May Take Large or Small Group
May take lead on planning a lesson to support material already covered	May help identify a small group of students who would benefit from remediation, repetition, or even enrichment
May work with large group on activities or assimilating content already given (e.g., doing projects, silent work, or book work)	May deliver content instruction to small group of students in a quiet environment, using strategies to teach to diverse learners
May evaluate majority of the classwork, with feedback from Ms. Weichel	May evaluate progress of small group and share this information with Mrs. Hutchinson to elicit her feedback
OR	
May work with one small group to check work, assist with writing or new skill building, as large group is self-facilitating or monitored by an assistant and co-teacher is working with another small group	May work with one small group to check work, assist with writing or new skill building, as large group is self-facilitating or monitored by an assistant and co-teacher is working with another small group
Remember: Using the small group for enrichment can help make sure the small group is not stigmatized as the "slow learners"	

Figure 13.11   Alternative Teaching in Action: What's My Role?

SOURCE: Murawski, W. W. (2008a).

Pros of This Approach	Cons of This Approach
This approach enables a much smaller student-to-teacher ratio for more individualized instruction.	Teachers are often apt to put students with similar abilities or disabilities together too frequently, essentially creating a "class within a class."
The smaller group often provides a safer environment for students to engage in discussion or to participate more actively.	The noise factor can be an issue with any regrouping approach. Teachers need to teach students (and each other) to use their inside voices.
This approach allows teachers to identify a specific skill that a small group of students has or needs to have and work on it specifically.	Co-teachers need to be sure that the large group is not learning a new skill or new information while the small group is reinforcing or learning an "old" one.
If the majority of the class needs to be re-taught material that they didn't understand, the large group can be re-taught while this approach enables a small group (those who "got it") to work on something that provides more depth or breadth to their curriculum and learning.	Teachers need to be prepared to do enrichment and extension activities so that students who are high achieving are not bored and are able to be in a small group for alternative teaching.
This approach allows teachers to focus on one particular topic area for planning purposes. Each can be responsible for his own group.	Despite the fact that teachers can take primary responsibility with one group, they still need to know what the other group is doing.
Warm-up, review, independent practice, and closure activities are a great time to use alternative teaching as new material is not being taught during those times.	Co-teachers need to be very aware of time so that they will both end at the same time in order to move onto new material together. The use of various timers is helpful.
This approach is the perfect time to provide the intensive instruction required for Tiers 2 and 3 in the response to intervention (RTI) model so students do not have to be pulled out of class.	Co-teachers need to be familiar with RTI, know which students are one which levels, and identify the specific research-based intensive intervention they will use during this approach.

Figure 13.12 Alternative Teaching Snapshot

Approach 5: Team Teaching

What It Should Look Like

In a Team Teaching approach, teachers share the responsibility for planning and content instruction. The students remain in a large-group setting while teachers work as a team to introduce new content instruction, work on building skills, clarifying information, and facilitating learning and classroom management. This approach typically takes the most trust and respect between teachers because it is the only approach in which co-teachers are "sharing the stage." To be comfortable enough to allow your co-teacher to jump in with comments, take notes on the board as you are talking, or ask you questions for clarification requires co-teachers to truly value one another and know that there is real parity.

There are moments in the classroom that Team Teaching is able to capitalize on which simply cannot be achieved with only one teacher. For example, during team teaching, co-teachers can role-play, model appropriate behaviors, or debate one another. They can show with their actions how adults can disagree without fighting. They can provide different viewpoints for the same information so that students can learn how to "think outside the box" and to realize that multiple responses to some answers are entirely appropriate. Team Teaching is a whole class approach depicted in Figure 13.13.

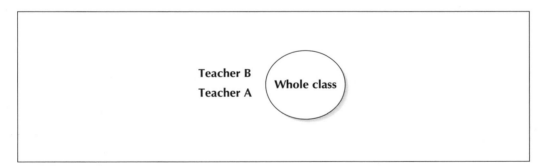

Figure 13.13   Team Teaching

What It Should Not Look Like

During the Team Teaching approach, co-teachers also have to be sure there is a reason they are using this approach. Some co-teachers seem to feel that this is the "ultimate" co-teaching approach and that once they feel comfortable enough to team teach, they should use this approach constantly. That is not the case; as with all approaches, this one should be used in conjunction with other approaches as well. Having both teachers stay at the front of the room continuously does not provide for differentiated instruction. Indeed, it may complicate matters for students if each concept is explained in different ways just so each teacher feels they were able to "say something." In fact, with today's pacing plans, this may also lengthen all lessons so that it is simply not feasible to allow both teachers to have verbal input on each comment.

While Team Teaching is effective at times, there are certainly many times that regrouping students is more appropriate—or other times when students need to hear just one voice explaining a concept and might be confused by two. In addition, if co-teachers are merely "tag teaming"—in essence, a verbal ping-pong match—they may be simply doing together what one teacher could do alone. Make sure what you and your co-teacher are doing in front of the class together is something that really warrants two voices or a shared approach. Take a look at Figure 13.14 for an example of how two teachers might share and divide roles when Team Teaching. Don't forget to discuss the pros and cons provided in the EZ Reference snapshot in Figure 13.15 with your co-teacher. The more prepared you both are, the more likely you will be able to use Team Teaching effectively.

Remember: This approach may take the most *trust* and *respect*. Do you both feel comfortable if the other "jumps in" to provide support and alternative explanations if needed?

Ask yourselves as you plan: Will this lesson be more effective for students if they stay in the large group and we share the instruction? What can we do together using Team Teaching that we could not do alone?

Mrs. Hutchinson	Ms. Weichel
May take primary role of identifying state standards, grade level curriculum, and student skills that need to be addressed in lesson	May take primary role of reviewing IEPs, 504 plans, and behavior plans to consider possible adaptations needed
Collaborate with Ms. Weichel in planning instruction; is more responsible for seeing the "forest," class as a whole	Collaborate with Mrs. Hutchinson in planning instruction; is more responsible for seeing the "trees," individual students
Jointly deliver content instruction to the large group making accommodations as required	Jointly deliver content instruction to the large group making accommodations as required
Jointly evaluate the class to assess success and areas where further instruction is needed	Jointly evaluate the class to assess success and areas where further instruction is needed

Figure 13.14 Team Teaching in Action: What's My Role?

SOURCE: Murawski, W. W. (2008a).

Co-teachers use a Team Teaching approach to "share the stage" as they actively engage students.

Pros of This Approach	Cons of This Approach
This approach, more than all others, can help to demonstrate parity between co-teachers since both teachers are "sharing the stage."	Co-teachers who are not yet comfortable with one another or who do not yet trust or respect one another fully can find this approach the most difficult to use well.
During planning for this approach, both teachers tend to have more ownership because they know they will be actively engaged in front of the class with their partner; this can lead to improved planning and instruction.	This may take more planning on the part of teachers, which is always difficult due to time constraints; in addition, co-teachers have to give up control in order to be open to their partner's suggestions for instruction.
This approach enables co-teachers to do role plays, model discussions, conduct debates, facilitate games, model note taking, and use other interactive instructional approaches that are difficult to do well as a solo teacher.	Co-teachers have to be open to a variety of different types of instruction and have to be willing to plan accordingly. Many "traditional" teachers are unused to, and sometimes nervous about, using varied approaches.
Having both teachers engage actively with students simultaneously means both teachers have input on a lesson. This helps students, because if they don't understand something one person said, they may understand the way it's explained by the other.	Time is always a factor and co-teachers can't afford to have lessons take twice as long. Also, avoid having lessons become a "verbal ping-pong match" or "tag teaming" where they are merely breaking up who says what and going back and forth.
Having both teachers facilitate activities, such as games, independent or guided practice, etc., means that both can be walking around helping students so they don't have to wait as long to be included or to have questions answered.	Students report that a *con* of this approach is that "we can't get away with as much." (Yes, that's actually a *pro* for teachers.) The additional behavior management when teachers work together is a pleasant result of co-teaching.

Figure 13.15   Team Teaching Snapshot

14

Teaching the Seven Dwarves

UNDERSTANDING DIFFERENTIATION ■

_____ **Mission Impossible?** _____

Here is your mission (and you don't really have a choice of whether or not to accept it)

Your Mission: Teach students about long division

Your Class: The Seven Dwarves: Sneezy, Dopey, Doc, Bashful, Sleepy, Grumpy, and Happy (i.e., student who has allergies, student who has a learning disability, student who is gifted, student who has Asperger syndrome, student who has narcolepsy, student who has a behavioral disability, and student who has bipolar disorder and is in the manic phase)

Defining Differentiation

It is no longer expected that children who struggle with academics will be pulled to a special education class where their needs may or may not be met in a self-contained or resource setting. No Child Left Behind (NCLB) mandated schools to ensure that all children are provided with access to state standards curriculum, taught by teachers highly qualified in the subject matter (Hoover & Patton, 2004). The result of NCLB combined with the mandate for individualization from the Individuals with Disabilities Education Improvement Act (IDEIA) of 2004 is that as more children with disabilities are being included in general education classes, teachers are being expected to meet the very diverse needs of those students (Burstein, Sears, Wilcoxen, Cabello, & Spagna , 2004). McTighe and Brown (2005) address the question of how teachers can meet the requirements of a standards-based curriculum, while also differentiating for individual student needs.

So, what exactly is differentiation? Carol Tomlinson (2000), a professor at the University of Virginia and the guru of differentiation, clarified that differentiation is not meant to be a model of instruction nor is it an instructional strategy. Differentiated instruction is an approach designed to ensure "that what a student learns, how he/she learns it, and how the student demonstrates what he/she has learned is a match for that student's readiness level, interests, and preferred mode of learning" (Tomlinson, 2004, p. 30). There is no "magical recipe" for differentiation (Tomlinson, 2005) but essentially, differentiation involves "shaking it up" in the classroom to guarantee student motivation and learning. In essence, you are being asked to find a way to teach long division (or whatever other content you may have) in such a way that Sleepy stays awake, both Dopey and Doc are appropriately challenged, and Sneezy, Bashful, Happy, and Grumpy are all focused on the activity. No problem! Right? Um. *Right.*

Ask yourself this: Where did the concept of differentiation originate? Now go ask the teacher next door. After that, proceed down the hall, asking your fellow teachers. Go ahead. I'll wait. Let me know when you are ready.

Most teachers will claim ignorance, though a few will venture to guess. Inevitably, they will guess the field of special education. Most teachers are shocked when they find out that differentiation has its roots in gifted education. Go back down the hall and tell your neighboring teachers this because it helps to see that differentiation really is about mixing it up, challenging students at their appropriate levels, and recognizing and developing student strengths; it is not about watering down or slowing down the curriculum for students with special needs. It is about challenging students. It is about maximizing potential. Tomlinson's Web site (www.caroltomlinson.com) shares the following: "The idea of differentiating instruction to accommodate the different ways that students learn involves a hefty dose of common sense, as well as sturdy support in the theory and research of education (Tomlinson & Allan, 2000). It is an approach to teaching that advocates active planning for student differences in classrooms." Active planning: Heard that before? That's right. Be proactive in your approach to planning for student differences, and the students in your inclusive classes will be successful, just as you will be as co-teachers.

Teachers who want to be successful using differentiation recognize that their students will show up for class with a variety of abilities, interests, prior knowledge, and learning styles (Broderick, Mehta-Parekh, & Reid, 2005). In fact, Tomlinson's work repeatedly cautions teachers to prepare for students to have differences in their readiness, interests, and learning profiles. Flores (2007) summarized the literature related to these three areas.

Readiness. Readiness refers to the level of knowledge, understanding, and skills required for learning. This level is influenced by students' cognitive abilities, prior knowledge, and motivation. A student's readiness may vary throughout time. Activities are geared toward the student's readiness level, nevertheless ensuring that all students are being provided with the same concept (Brimijoin, Marquisee, & Tomlinson, 2003; Corley, 2005). Corley (2005) and Benjamin (2002) suggest the use of tiered performance tasks to focus on students' readiness. For instance, differentiating a lesson is not providing certain students with more difficult work and others with easier work; tiered performance tasks refer to enabling students to access the same content while allowing them to choose the tier activity level accordingly. Furthermore, another suggestion to address student readiness is grouping students in small-group sessions, peer tutoring, or coaching (Tomlinson, 2005).

Interest. Ginsberg (2005) states that "motivated students will surpass unmotivated students in learning and performance" (p. 218). Motivation arises when a student is interested in a certain topic that she is passionate about or has curiosity in (Stipek, 1988; Tomlinson, 2005). When a child experiences self-efficacy, it allows for the child to have more control of what he wants to learn (Tomlinson et al., 2003; Tomlinson, 2005). Also, Tomlinson (2000) emphasizes that student learning increases when students have the opportunity to connect their interests with the curriculum and life experiences. In addition, Pierce and Adams (2004) suggest using interest questionnaires to assess student learning interests. The literature demonstrates that engaging students in their learning increases their interest of academic success; for example, allowing students to select their own reading books increases their academic efforts (Carbonaro & Gamoran, 2002; Tomlinson et al., 2003).

Learning profiles. The concept of learning profiles refers to a student's preferred style of learning that can be affected by numerous factors, including learning style, intelligence preference, gender, and culture (Tomlinson et al., 2003). Corley (2005) suggests the following activities may be implemented in the differentiated instruction to address students' learning profiles: project-based learning, journals, role plays, videotape presentations, and oral histories. In addition, teachers can identify the students' learning styles, or teachers may consider using Howard Gardner's theory of multiple intelligences (Pierce & Adams, 2004).

Differentiating Curriculum

So now that we know what differentiation actually is—that it relates to identifying students' readiness levels, learning profiles, and interests, execution should be easy right? Well, not for teachers who have a class full of students who vary in their abilities, disabilities, interests, and needs. There are certainly numerous forms, worksheets, and inventories teachers can give students to assess their readiness, interests, and learning styles, but what should you do once you have that information? Gartin, Murdick, Imbeau, and Perner (2002) emphasize that there are three parts to curricula that teachers need to consider when designing lessons: content, process, and product.

Content. Content refers to what will be taught and what is going to be learned. Who determines the content? State standards certainly guide district and school decisions regarding textbook and content selection. Teachers also make decisions regarding what they will teach and what priorities they assign to different content. Planning for differentiated instruction does not mean choosing completely different content for students based on their various ability levels; on the contrary, teachers must make certain that all students have access to the same content. To differentiate by content, teachers need to determine what students know and what they will be able to learn. G. Wiggins and McTighe (2005) have done a good deal of work explaining a concept known as Understanding by Design (UbD). Under the umbrella of UbD, teachers are asked to look at their curriculum and determine the enduring understandings (e.g., "big ideas") and essential questions. For example, West Virginia elementary school teachers Patsy Dicken and Lynette Swiger created a lesson on geography for a third-grade social studies standard. Rather than merely identifying fact-related questions, such as *What is an island? What is a peninsula? How do they differ?* as their essential questions, these teachers' essential question included, "How does where I live influence how I live?" This is the type of enduring understanding we want our students to have as they leave schools. In addition, you can see how it would be easy to differentiate for students at the foundational (basic), grade level, and advanced levels based on that question. (To see all of their lesson plans, in addition to other examples of UbD lessons, go to the West Virginia Teach 21 Web site at http://wvde.state.wv.us/teach21/.) Determining content and essential questions is an excellent time to also consider students' readiness levels.

Process. The process of how content will be presented is easily as important as what that content is. Process refers to how instruction is presented and what activities are selected to ensure student understanding of a skill or concept (Broderick et al., 2005; Corley, 2005; Gartin et al., 2002). Co-teachers can choose to present information in a variety of ways. Using the five co-teaching approaches reviewed in the previous chapter, co-teachers may choose to present in a whole-group format (using One Teach, One Support), conduct a role play or skit for the class (using Team Teaching), get students into cooperative learning groups (through Station Teaching), break them into two equal groups (with Parallel Teaching), or select a small group for reteaching, preteaching, or enrichment (using Alternative Teaching). In addition to the manner in which content is presented by teachers, process also can differ based on the materials selected by teachers to augment the instruction. These may include graphic organizers, coaching, peer groups, visuals, manipulatives, audiotapes, assistive technology, large print, videos, discussions, and so forth. Determining process is an excellent time to consider students' interests and learning profiles, as their integration can lead to increased attention, motivation, and learning.

Product. Too often products are confused with grades. However, not every product needs to be graded. Wiggins and McTighe (2005) share that the purpose of grading is not merely to provide a score; the goal is to be able to represent a student's performance with reliability and validity given established performance standards. How then do we determine students' grades? We need to look at the evidence they present to demonstrate the knowledge, skills, and key concepts they have acquired. Evidence can vary in nature and products should be flexible in nature, taking into account students' readiness, interests, and learning profiles. Let students have choices in how they wish to demonstrate their learning and you may be surprised. Students may choose to write a song, rap, poem, story, essay, blog, or book report; construct a diorama, poster, collage, or drawing; do an interpretive dance, monologue, skit, dramatic reading, or oral presentation; create a Webquest, PowerPoint, or video game; or work collaboratively with a group to demonstrate their collective understanding of the content.

I recently added a joke to my national presentations that I think demonstrates the impact product can have on grading practices. After teaching participants the three key aspects required for true co-teaching (you know, co-plan, co-instruct, co-assess), I ask them what grade they would get if I tested on that content. I make sure that everyone in the audience says they would get an "A" even if I have to review the content repeatedly, show it on the board, etc. Once everyone feels comfortable with the content and says they would get an A if tested, I let them know that their great state of (name of state here) has developed a new policy that ensures everyone is tested fairly. Rather than having students do a paper-and-pencil test, which teachers seem to be rallying against given some students' difficulty with that task, the state has agreed to test students differently. Now all students will be assessed on their content knowledge using classical opera. Yep, opera. I then ask my audience members, knowing that they will be assessed on the same content (co-plan, co-instruct, co-assess) but using opera as the method of assessment, which of them will now get an A as their grade. Only the rare few raise their hand. I get a few hands for Bs, a couple Cs and Ds, and an overwhelming amount of exuberant hands indicating that they will get an F on the assessment. When I ask who would prefer to take an F now rather than getting up in front of their peers to sing opera (even though they know the content), the majority of my audience consistently raises their hands. I then point out to them that within the space of a few minutes, a group of educated teachers just went from confident individuals who knew their content to a group of individuals willing to take an F rather than embarrass themselves. I ask them to put themselves in the shoes of students who have repeatedly failed assessments. As elementary teachers, we have to remember that even young students know what their strengths and their weaknesses are. It often does not matter if we tell them, "You know this stuff. I'm behind you. I know you can pass." Their experiences are that they do not test well, or read well, or write well, or do "school" well. So they ask themselves, why even try? This is exactly how we reacted when faced with opera as our product of assessment. Following that activity, I ask teachers how they would prefer that I assess their knowledge of the three key requirements for true co-teaching. As you may expect, I have a variety of responses, including multiple-choice test, essay, paper, oral presentation, skit, drawing, PowerPoint, observation, teaching others, and—in just one case—opera.

Best Practices for Differentiation

"A teacher who acknowledges that all students require special attention to some degree and their uniqueness in interests, abilities, and attitudes is undoubtedly the best teacher" (George, 2005, as cited in Flores, 2007). Pierce and Adams (2004) emphasize the need for teachers to have explicit classroom management techniques, planned activities, flexible use of time, a supportive learning environment, and a variety of cooperative learning arrangements. While any teacher would probably look at that list and think it states the obvious, not all teachers are able to manage it all alone; working with a co-teacher makes differentiation that much more manageable. Check out Wormeli's books (2003, 2004) on differentiation. They are practical and provide many strategies that co-teachers can use on a daily basis. In addition, Flores (2007) reviewed the literature and identified the following as helpful for ensuring successful differentiation in the inclusive classroom.

- *Create a learning climate.* Students need to feel respected, accepted, valued, safe, included, and able to take risks. In fact, isn't this true of teachers also? We want to work in an environment that makes us feel respected, valued, and safe. Administrators, parents, and other teachers impact our school climate. In the classroom, though, co-teachers are the ones who can make or break this climate through their actions. One of my favorite quotes is by Dr. Haim Gainott (1995), highlighted in Figure 14.1.

I have come to a frightening conclusion.

I am the decisive element in the classroom.

It is my personal approach that creates the climate.

It is my daily mood that makes the weather.

As a teacher, I possess tremendous power to make a child's life miserable or joyous.

I can be a tool of torture or an instrument of inspiration.

I can humiliate or humor, hurt or heal.

In all situations, it is my response that decides whether a crisis will be escalated or de-escalated, and a child humanized or de-humanized.

Haim Gainott (1995)

Figure 14.1   The Power of the Teacher

- *Identify different learning profiles and abilities.* Recognizing students' abilities, needs, and strengths (rather than focusing on disabilities) is key. Gardner's (2006) Multiple Intelligences (MI) theory, Bloom's Revised Taxonomy, Lavoie's Motivation scales, and Levine's Neurodevelopmental Constructs are four methods of identifying and supporting students' strengths and their different ways of learning.
- *Use strategies to adapt to student learning needs.* Be open to identifying modifications, adaptations, and research-based strategies that may help different students access the content, always ensuring that instruction is authentic, relevant, and rigorous.
- *Group students flexibly.* Three of the co-teaching approaches involve regrouping students (Alternative, Parallel, and Station). Co-teachers are encouraged to allow students to work collaboratively with others to focus content learning and to improve social skills.
- *Enable curriculum compacting.* Allow students to demonstrate prior learning through preassessments that will then enable them to move forward, further exploring the content in new ways that promote depth and breadth of content knowledge and skills.
- *Design tiered lessons.* Lessons can be tiered vertically (e.g., a task all must do, one that some can do, and one that a few can do) or horizontally (e.g., a complex task for 100 points, or two tasks for 50 points each, four for

25 points each, or 10 for 10 points each). Providing flexibility and choice encourages student motivation and challenges students at their appropriate levels.

- *Provide ongoing and regular feedback.* One way to do so is to use learning contracts with students who would benefit from the structured and concrete nature of the written agreement between teachers and student. Ongoing assessments that include observations, portfolios, discussions, questionnaires, reflections, and so forth are ways to collect student feedback to enable co-teachers to plan instruction to more effectively meet students' diverse needs.

Considering Student Learning Styles

Another activity I do when working with teachers is to have them self-identify their learning styles. Overwhelmingly, teachers are visual and auditory learners. I then share with them the data that state 50 percent of students are kinesthetic and tactile learners, 32 percent are visual learners, and 18 percent are auditory learners. How do most teachers teach? They lecture, orate, narrate, talk, instruct, speak, address, teach, discuss, inform, clarify, and otherwise "say and spray." Occasionally, they throw an overhead or PowerPoint up to provide a visual. I am partly joking here and partly serious. Go into most classrooms and you will see students sitting, listening, and (maybe) taking notes. While elementary classrooms (especially early elementary) may look more active, consider what students have to look forward to. Those students who enjoy school because they excel at recess, playtime, and kinesthetic activities will be stifled as they progress in school. Middle school teachers are trying to prepare students for high school (where they will have to sit and take notes) and high school teachers are trying to prepare students for college (where they will have to sit and take notes). I'm not saying that lecture is evil. There is certainly a time and place when it is necessary and might even be the most appropriate way to provide information to students. Interestingly, however, I now find as a college professor, that my students (most of whom are teachers) do not want to sit for the whole time, nor do they want to take notes. Instead, they ask me to provide them with copies of the PowerPoint via e-mail, handouts, or WebCT. They want more applied strategies and ideas, and request time to talk with their peers about how the subject matter we've read about relates to their actual situations. They want to have classes offered online so they can learn at a time that works better for their own style. In fact, Centers for Teaching and Learning in higher education encourage professors to mix it up, to engage students, to find ways to let them work collaboratively, and to recognize, allow for, and even embrace student differences (Bess and Associates, 2000; Murawski, 2002b). Many universities even offer classes that are co-taught, teach about co-teaching, and encourage their own faculty to model best practices themselves (Murawski, 2002b). Interesting, isn't it? Change: It is *a'coming!* Let's hope we are all ready for it.

There are many learning style inventories available online and in print. It makes sense for teachers to provide these types of inventories (on learning styles, interests, multiple intelligences, and so on) early in the year. The more information teachers have about their students, the better they can differentiate and meet their diverse needs. One of the problems, however, is that busy teachers get excited to do these activities in the beginning of the school year, collect the information, and then promptly file the results somewhere, never to be seen again. The next time students need to be grouped, teachers will look for those results, and when they can't find them quickly, they will simply return to tradition and say to the kids, "Just get in groups." This defeats the purpose of collecting that helpful data. Find a way to collect the information and keep it in a place where you can refer to it frequently. I consulted on the CTSS (Co-teaching Solutions System) software. One of its nifty features is that the program provides a learning styles inventory to download and give to students and then will take the results and automatically cluster students by auditory, visual, and kinesthetic/tactile learners. Because this is a software program, the results are easily accessible and always available for lesson planning.

A myriad of materials are currently available on differentiation tips and strategies. It is important for co-teachers to be familiar with differentiation as it is the core of why we are working together. We need to understand differentiation and how it fits with Universal Design for Learning (Stanford & Reeves, 2009). Our challenge is to find ways to take our core content, our inflexible pacing plans, our rigorous standards, and our diverse class of students and find a way to make them come together seamlessly. Simple. Or maybe not. I haven't yet found the magic powder that will accomplish all of that, but I have identified some strategies that will help motivate students and move your content forward.

■ PRACTICAL STRATEGIES FOR DIFFERENTIATION

Contemporary Timelines

Many students have difficulties with sequencing information. This activity helps kinesthetic learners find a way to remember the sequences of events, facts, or concepts. Co-teachers should each take a piece of string and stand across the room from each other, holding the string. Each student gets a sentence strip with information on it and a paper clip. Tell students that the teacher on the students' left is "first" or "a long time ago." The teacher on the students' right is "last" or "now." (It's also helpful to post a sticky note with this information on it on the teachers' chests, foreheads, or hats.) Explain the directions to students, then have them get up and paperclip their information in place on the string in the order in which it occurred. It is helpful to time this activity to ensure that students use their time wisely and don't just dally. You will find that it is utter chaos and talking for the three to five minutes you give the activity; students will be discussing and arguing with each other to determine what goes where and when.

I call the activity Contemporary Timeline because it's more fun (and more likely to work) if you start with information the students might actually know. *People, Us Weekly,* and *Entertainment Weekly* are good sources for this information, as are Nickelodeon and the Disney Channel. Find out from students what topics or people they are currently interested in or know a lot about. For example, if you use information about things that occurred with your own students, you might have the following on sentence strips:

| Stella broke her arm. |
| Jehaan went to China for a week to see family. |
| Kiernan won the Spelling Bee. |
| Sam's dad, the stuntman, visited our class. |
| Grace and Kaleb went to California. |
| William brought a spider to Show and Tell. |

You get the drift. Put information on the strips that the students are bound to know, and that you sort of wish you didn't know. Once students have fun with the activity and are able to have success at it, you can use the activity to help teach the sequencing of content. For example,

Reading: Plot of a story

Math: Order of operations

Science: Steps in scientific method

Social studies: Dates in history

Magic Tablecloth

Another excellent way to make learning kinesthetic takes just two little items: a plastic tablecloth and some spray adhesive. Tape the tablecloth to a wall, window, or door, and then spray the tablecloth with the adhesive. You now have a surface on which various and sundry papers will stick magically.

Tips for the Tablecloth. Get the cheap version. Dollar store tablecloths are the best. Avoid vinyl or heavier tablecloths. Any color is fine. You will be able to use this tablecloth many, many times. When removing the tablecloth from the wall, don't bother to try to pull off the tape; it will just rip the tablecloth. Instead, merely fold the tape back and use new tape next time. This is definitely a time when function is more important than appearance. Also, when folding the tablecloth for multiple uses, fold the sticky side out.

Tips for the Adhesive. Although other companies sell a stronger spray adhesive, I've found that they can be almost too sticky. Papers do not come off easily. Instead, I recommend the 3M Artists' Adhesive, which you can generally find at major home supply, hardware, and craft stores. Put a light spray all over the tablecloth; you will find that over time, the tablecloth will become more tacky and work even better. You won't need to respray every time you use it, but you may find it works better on day two than on day one.

Uses for the Tablecloth. You can have students display index cards, postcards, full pieces of paper, or even light construction paper on the tablecloth. Following are some ideas for its use:

- Displaying student work
- Answering KWL (What I Know, What I Want to Know, and What I Learned) questions anonymously on index cards
- Grouping students by card responses
- Sequencing information
- Manipulating parts of a math equation
- Diagramming sentences or doing daily oral language (DOL) activities
- Posting pictures to help learn foreign language vocabulary or concepts
- Creating a dynamic word wall
- Displaying the content standards, big ideas, or essential questions for the lesson
- Collaborating with other students to create a visual of the parts of a cell
- Labeling a picture to learn new vocabulary

Worksheet Wonder

This technique is so easy that it's almost embarrassing. Have you ever had a day when you didn't have time to plan the perfect lesson? Once or twice at the most, right? Well, if the day comes when you are relegated to having students complete a worksheet, and you know that the motivation factor will be low, here's a simple solution. Cut your worksheet into individual problems or questions and put the parts into a paper bag. Pair up students (do this strategically so that students are complementary to one another's skills) and have them each pull a part of the sheet out of the bag and ask their partners to complete the skill, problem, or question. You have just turned a worksheet into a game that involves collaboration, social interaction, kinesthetic activity, and peer support. Good for you! (By the way, don't overdo this one. After a while, students get the gist and realize it is still a worksheet.)

Quiet Manipulatives

Think about the student who is always driving you insane by tapping his pencil on the table, doodling, or fidgeting. Rather than letting this get to you, consider that this student may actually have a bodily-kinesthetic or musical intelligence. I know that doesn't help when you and your co-teacher are trying to teach, but it may help you feel better about providing that student with a quiet manipulative. This should go without saying, but do tell the student that the manipulative is contingent on it remaining in his hands and not getting thrown across the room. I know many teachers who have found that having a box of little manipulatives available for students allows them to self-identify a need; if a student takes one just because it is fun and keeps his attention from wandering, so be it. What works as a quiet manipulative?

- Small Koosh ball
- Squeezy balls (also great for hand strengthening)
- Wikki Stix
- Pieces of string

- Play dough or modeling clay
- Paper clips
- Pieces of Velcro stuck to the bottom of the desk to touch (Here I must interject; do not use both sides of the Velcro. That would be incredibly disturbing. Just use one side of the Velcro so students have something to touch under the desk, other than the typical pieces of old gum.)
- For more ideas, talk to an occupational or physical therapist; I'm sure they'll have many ideas.

Masks

All you need for this technique is a printout of the work you want students to complete and a manila folder. If your goal is to have all students in the room work on listening to directions rather than racing ahead to do the work, have a class set of manila folders and cut the front page so that when the worksheet is put inside the folder, you can fold back the top part to only reveal the directions. That way students will have to read along and wait before starting the rest of their work; if they fold back the bottom half, you and your co-teacher will easily be able to see them and react accordingly.

Two other uses of masks are for students who become easily overwhelmed by the sight of a full page of work and for students who appear to have learned helplessness. For the first, cutting the folder in halves or thirds enables the teachers to limit the work the student is given at a time, without cutting up each individual worksheet. For the second, students who tend to ask questions about each problem ("Teacher! Teacher! Teacher!") or who wait for teacher assistance too frequently can be provided with the mask and be told that they need to complete the first section within a certain number of minutes without asking for additional assistance from either teacher. When that section is completed, only then is the student allowed to raise her hand and ask for someone to review her work and give assistance if needed. This increases her independence, while concurrently increasing her work output.

Peer Dictation

Three needs motivate students, and these three needs increase as students get older.

1. Students *need* to be social (even students who are not good at being social).

2. Students *need* to get out of work (which is why "senioritis" starts at about fourth grade).

3. Students *need* to avoid humiliation (at all costs). This is why many students will opt not to do the work at all rather than attempt and fail.

Given those needs, create ways to engage students in social activities that make the students think they are getting out of something (though they really aren't), and which avoid student humiliation. An activity that meets these three criteria is the use of peer dictation. How does it work?

1. Tell students they will be required to answer a question, write an essay, or respond to a journal question (whichever you choose).

2. After they have groaned a bit, pair them up strategically and give them numbers (1 or 2). This is yet another example of when it comes in handy to have two teachers; you will need to discuss who should be with whom to ensure that you will not be putting any students in potentially humiliating situations.

3. Once they are paired, tell Student 1 that she will not have to write at all for this assignment. Watch her cheer.

4. Then tell Student 2 that he will not have to think at all for this assignment. Watch him smile as he recognizes his comfort zone.

5. Finally, explain to students that those who are 1s will "dictate" their responses to their partners. Those who are 2s will "scribe" the responses for their peers.

Caveat: If your students are too young to actually write words, you can also do this with pictures, inventive spelling, or cut and paste. Feel free to differentiate based on the readiness levels of your students.

Both parties (if you and your co-teacher have paired them well) will love this activity. Why? Because (1) it's social, (2) they feel like they are getting out of work, and (3) it is a safe activity that avoids humiliation. To ensure that students do avoid humiliation, feel free to include additional differentiation strategies, such as allowing some students to use computers, AlphaSmarts, spell checkers, dictionaries, thesauruses, cut-and-paste pictures, whisper phones, and so forth. Do students really "get out of work"? Certainly not. Consider the typical student journal response. If I ask a student to write about his perfect day, he'll write, "The perfect day was yesterday. It was good. The end." Doing this activity actually increases the thinking we get out of one student and the writing we get out of the other. Ultimately it is a fun activity that pleases both students and co-teachers in the end.

15

Are We Successful Yet?

CO-ASSESSING US AND THEM ■

When you read the word *assess*, do you think immediately of grading? Most teachers do. Grading is certainly an aspect of assessment, especially as it relates to the traditional classroom, but it is by no means the only—or even the most important—aspect of assessment. As Bigge, Stump, Spagna, and Silberman (1999) attest, "Assessment is much more than administering tests and achieving scores. It is gathering information to make decisions" (p. 151). As such, it is important that this chapter deals with assessing both the students and the adults. To put it back in terms of our marriage analogy: If we want a happy home life, we need to make sure that our children are doing well, but we can't forget to take care of our adult relationships as well. We need to gather information to make decisions about what we need to continue to do—or stop doing—in order to ensure that we and our students experience success. Thus, this chapter touches on the types of assessments we might consider for the diversity of needs the students in our co-taught classes have, in addition to addressing how co-teachers can take time to evaluate their own progress.

Many books and articles on inclusion, strategies, collaboration, and co-teaching avoid the issue of assessment altogether, while others give general tips but don't discuss the issues related to two teachers assessing together. Assessment can certainly be daunting, especially when there are often different beliefs regarding what constitutes assessment and what constitutes success. Figure 15.1 identifies some of the various activities in which co-teachers may engage for the co-assessing aspect of their relationship. Spend a few minutes with your partner to see which you are doing and which you have not yet addressed.

Co-teachers need to be on the same page regarding assessing and grading.

Check ☑ the statements you and your co-teacher are doing.
Look at the ones you are *not* doing.
Should you be doing those?
Co-assessing may include

☐ Sharing information on standardized assessments
☐ Jointly determining what curriculum-based measures should be given
☐ Developing teacher-made assessments with modified versions as needed
☐ Sharing in the workload of daily grading
☐ Creating individual assessments for guiding instruction
☐ Collecting data on behavior, academics, social and study skills
☐ Documenting parental contacts and sharing that responsibility
☐ Charting or graphing student progress for individuals or classes
☐ Providing formative and summative evaluations to students, with modifications (such as reading aloud) conducted as needed on a shared basis
☐ Completing daily, weekly, or other regular progress reports
☐ Measuring progress toward meeting individualized education program (IEP) goals and objectives
☐ Jointly determining final grades for students with and without disabilities
☐ Providing one another with regular feedback on what is and is not working in the class, from your unique perspective
☐ Inviting others (co-teachers, mentors, administrators, researchers) to observe your shared class to provide you both with helpful and ongoing feedback for improvement

Figure 15.1 Co-Assessing Checklist

SOURCE: Murawski, W. W. (2008a).

Student Assessment

Before we talk more about how co-teachers need to self-assess, let's focus on the students. It is *imperative* that co-teachers discuss early in the relationship how they will assess students. General educators can take the lead on providing information on how to assess the general curriculum, and special educators can take the lead on providing ways to modify for special needs; however, assessment decisions should not be made completely independently. It's also important that we keep in mind that assessment is so much more than grading—even though as students get older, grades do take on more importance than before (Murawski & Dieker, 2004). Bowe (2005) reviewed the literature and clarified the difference between related key terms. He spelled out the following:

- *Assessment* is the gathering of information to make decisions. . . . Assessment includes measurement, evaluation and grading.
- *Measurement* is the phase of assessment in which numbers are assigned.
- *Evaluation* is the making of judgments about those numbers.
- *Grading* is the conversion of those evaluations into symbols to communicate with students, families, and educators. (p. 353, bullets added)

Co-teachers need to share the load for each aspect of assessment. That does not mean we need to sit down next to each other and grade each piece of paper together; that would be a colossal waste of time. It does, however, mean that we need to discuss what we think are the best ways to determine student improvement and learning in the classroom. Given that assessment is gathering information, we need to jointly determine what information we want to gather and what decisions need to be made. We need to determine what areas need to be measured, how they should be measured, by whom, when, and for what purpose. We need to discuss how we want to evaluate students and their progress, and finally we need to determine how we will work together to determine the grades for the students in our class.

There are two tips to co-assessing students that should serve as the cornerstone to this aspect of co-teaching.

- There is no one right way to assess students. They are different learners, and they will require different modes of assessment.
- It is not "You grade *your* kids" and "I'll grade *mine*." They are *our* kids, and we will assess them together.

There is not one specific way in which teachers should assess diverse learners. Each school has its own culture that needs to be respected when discussing matters related to inclusion (McLesky & Waldron, 2002); assessment is certainly one of these burning issues. Teachers will feel differently and need to be open to one another's individual frames of reference. Compromise will frequently be necessary. Discuss options and possible adaptations up front and, in some cases, obtain administrative support for assessment decisions beforehand. Read articles and texts related to co-assessing and co-grading. Start with the book *Fair Isn't Always Equal: Assessing and Grading in the Differentiated Classroom* (2006) by Rick Wormeli. Wormeli describes various grading and assessing issues related to the differentiated classroom and provides teachers with numerous suggestions, techniques, and tips.

In Part III: The Wedding, I mentioned the need to see if every assignment addressed the co-teachers' HALO (high achievers, average achievers, low achievers, and other). Wormeli (2006) takes that a step further. In his book, he provides numerous explanations for how to differentiate proactively so that the resulting assessments are valid. He emphasizes that "assessment guides practice" (p. 20). He goes on to write, "Instructional decisions are based not only on what we know about curriculum, but also on what we know about the specific students we serve. We have to be diligent, however. Dividing students into flexible groups, for example, might be creative or break up boring lesson routine, but it only becomes true differentiated instruction when we assign students to different groups based on something we know about those students" (p. 20). Wormeli's text provides readers with strategies for backwards planning, designing substantive assignments that avoid *fluff*, creating appropriate assessments and tests and with numerous tips for how to determine grading that is valid, reliable, and fair. Co-teachers would be wise to read this text and discuss the issues with which they agree or disagree.

Given the wide variety of assessment types educators need to be aware of—formal, informal, formative, summative, authentic, performance, projects, portfolios, rubrics, observations, dialogues, tests, papers, alternative, self-assessment, and so on—it is critical for co-teachers to sit down and discuss the various types of assessments they have experienced and with which they feel comfortable and uncomfortable. It's also a great time to try new things. In addition to the types of assessments available, there are also numerous tasks involved in ongoing assessment. Figure 15.2 provides strategies that will aid co-teachers in their planning for co-assessment.

Student Grading

Despite my emphasis that assessment entails much more than grading, the reality in most schools is that students receive a letter grade upon completion of most assignments which in turn results in a letter grade for the class overall. Dr. Lisa Dieker writes, "In a perfect world, all letter grades would disappear, and all general and special educators would agree on an alternate way of addressing the unique learning and assessment needs of all students" (2007, p. 139). While Dr. Dieker's book addresses a variety of assessment techniques and grading options for secondary educators, her accompanying DVD through National Professional Resources (NPR) (www.nprinc.com) provides schools with additional information on inclusion and differentiation strategies that, though focused on secondary students, can be adapted and applied to elementary situations as well. Another resource through NPR appropriate for elementary educators is the *Winning Strategies* DVD by Rebecca Hines and Lisa Dieker.

Strategies for Co-Assessment

- Create criteria charts prior to an assignment to model expectations for students; get student input and participation in creating charts
- Use rubrics to provide clear expectations and assess consistently
- Create regular assessment cards to monitor and document progress on goals and objectives, as well as specific behaviors
- Include social skills, study skills, and organizational techniques in instruction related to an assignment
- Establish a structure for grading regular assignments (e.g., weekly spelling quizzes or chapter tests)
- Avoid bias by rotating the grading of all students between co-teachers
- Ensure reliability by having one co-teacher grade a particular part of an assignment for all students
- Use portfolios or other methods of collecting permanent product data for authentic assessments
- During co-planning, discuss how it will be determined if students met the objective and if the standard was addressed for all; establish what adaptations may be needed for individual students
- Create "must do" and "may do" charts to ensure that students always have something to do
- Create individualized folders that provide work for students who finish early
- Consider enrichment and acceleration opportunities for students who are high-achieving or gifted; encourage critical thinking and creative problem-solving in their assessments
- Establish a method of student to teacher feedback (e.g., a comment box) to allow students to assess teachers
- *Be creative*. Work together to remember that quality assessments do not need to be pencil and paper tasks. Figure out how you can use both teachers to maximize the outcomes.

EZ Reference

Figure 15.2 Strategies for Co-Assessment
SOURCE: Murawski, W. W. (2008a).

Struyk and colleagues (1994) did research with educators a while ago to determine what types of grading adaptations teachers felt most comfortable with given an inclusive classroom. While there are multiple options for grading, the most important tip for co-teachers to remember is that they need to determine their grading options *together* if they want to succeed. The continuum in Figure 15.3 depicts what teachers in Struyk et al.'s study reported as most to least effective. Despite the relative age of this research, I have found that teachers still respond similarly in what they consider appropriate options when grading students with special needs. Starting at the bottom of the continuum in Figure 15.3, teachers were least happy with passing students with disabilities

EZ Reference

Grading Options	
How teachers rate various grading adaptations:	
• Provide separate grades for process and for product • Base grades on amount of individual improvement • Weight individual assessments differently (e.g., classwork is more than homework; projects are weighted more than tests) • Base grades on academic or behavioral contracts • Base grades solely on meeting individual IEP goals and objectives • Adjust grades after the fact, based on student ability • Adjust grades based on modified grading scale (for some, 90–100 = A, for others 93–100 =A) • Base grades on less content covered than the rest of the class • Base grades solely on effort (i.e., if they try, they pass) • Base grades solely on attendance • Pass students with disabilities no matter what	**Most Helpful** ↑

Figure 15.3 Grading Options
SOURCE: Adapted from Struyk et al. (1994).

regardless of their efforts or work or even solely due to their attendance and efforts. Given today's climate of NCLB, standards, and assessment, teachers are much more aware of the need for students to demonstrate content mastery. The next four options relate to providing individual modifications and would obviously need to be decided proactively and jointly. One of the items that jumped out at me related to adjusting grades after the fact. The following scenario depicts a situation that happens all too often.

Jason: Hey there, Brenda. Are you ready for the Christmas break? Did you get your grades in already?

Brenda: Oh, I'm ready all right. I am a bit ticked though. I just had to go in and change some grades for the students I have in my class with Mr. Wishnowski.

Jason: What do you mean you had to change grades? I thought you were co-teaching with him?

Brenda: Well, "co-teaching" is in air quotes. I'm in there every day, but I don't get to do anything. Mr. W just likes me to walk around or stay near the kids who are being too wiggly that day. He wouldn't let me make any accommodations for some of my students, so—no surprise here—they failed. That's just not fair to them, so I had to go back in and change their grades to a C.

Anyone else cringing? There are so many things wrong with this scenario and yet I have seen it happen time and again. First of all, clearly what Brenda is doing in that class is "in-class support" at best; it is not co-teaching. She mentioned that she doesn't "*get to* do anything" and that "he wouldn't *let* [her] make any accommodations" (emphasis added). She doesn't "get to"? He wouldn't "let" her? Those words certainly emphasize that there is no parity in that classroom. Remember, co-teaching is supposed to entail equality and shared decision making; the general education teacher is not in a position to allow or disallow the special educator to do certain things and neither is the special educator. They need to make these decisions jointly. In addition, what about the students with special needs in the class? They have suffered through an entire semester without the accommodations to which they are legally and ethically entitled. Their motivation will decrease each time they experience failure and then, to make matters even more confusing for them, they will end up with a C rather than the F they knew they were getting. No wonder so many students with special needs say they have "no clue" how they are graded. Will this type of "grading modification" help the students? Of course not. Will it help the teachers' relationship? Definitely not. Clearly there are no positives to this type of behavior; it should not even be considered an option for co-assessing. Why then does it continue to be a fall-back option for so many teachers? Instead, teachers should consider assessing specific students (especially those with significant learning or behavioral disabilities) based on their individualized education program (IEP) or a contract.

The final three options at the top of the chart are the ones teachers in Stryuk et al.'s (1994) study reported liking the most. The "weighting work" option is a mere mathematical calculation. Students still complete the homework, classwork, projects, and tests like everyone else, but their results are weighted differently. For example, students who do not test well might be encouraged to spend more time demonstrating their learning through homework and classwork if their grading scale was adapted. (See Figure 15.4.)

Most Students' Grading Scale	Some Students' Grading Scale
Tests and quizzes = 50 percent	Tests and quizzes = 20 percent
Major project = 30 percent	Major project = 30 percent
Homework and classwork = 20 percent	Homework and classwork = 50 percent

Figure 15.4 Adapting the Weighting of Assignments

The next item from the Struyk et al. study involves basing grades on individual improvement. Ask any teacher about a student in his class and he will most likely be able to define that student by a letter grade: "Oh, he's a B student." That same teacher might spend hours doing the math required to add, multiply, or divide all the grades in the grade book and guess what? Nine times out of ten, the teacher will be right. That's because we as teachers generally know the amount of effort and the ability that each student possesses. If we were to work collaboratively to truly differentiate our instruction, we would be able to look at each student individually and determine his grade based on his individual improvement. That way, the child with Down syndrome who is in our sixth-grade class and performed well beyond expectations (though perhaps not at grade level mastery) might still get an A. On the other hand, a typical learner might receive a C in the class if he only produced average work for his ability level and work output. Working together to determine grades may also help us to avoid any potential bias.

The final option on the continuum is the one teachers reported liking best—the concept of averaging process and product grades. The best example I have for this one involves two of my own former students—Jose and Samantha (names changed). Jose was a student who was highly gifted, in addition to having attention deficit/hyperactivity disorder and an emotional and behavioral disorder. Samantha was a young lady who carried the label of learning disability, but only after her parents fought to have the old MMR (mild mentally retarded) label removed. Samantha was sweet and loving but not strong academically. When my co-teacher and I assigned a task and asked students to complete it by the end of the lesson for a grade, Samantha worked diligently on it—but her product was always objectively inferior to her peers. Jose, on the other hand, messed around for the majority of the time and then whipped something together in the last few minutes. His product, however, surpassed the standards we set. In this scenario, Samantha would get an A for process but perhaps a D for product; her resulting grade on the assignment would be a B–. Jose would receive an F for process and an A for product, resulting in a C for his grade. In this case, both students would see that their efforts and outcome were rewarded accordingly.

Remember what I said earlier about the two tips to co-assessing.

- There is no one right way to assess students. They are different learners, and they will require different modes of assessment.
- It is not "You grade *your* kids" and "I'll grade *mine*." They are *our* kids, and we will assess them together.

The key to all of this is that you and your colleague sit down—before the students enter the class for the first time—and discuss your options for assessing and grading. You may need to make some changes as you get to know your students throughout the school year, but at least you will have proactively identified some options for assessment alternatives. Being clear about your grading methodologies will help you avoid issues later on. You don't want to be those parents at the soccer game: the dad insisting the child demonstrate technical skill, while the mom is saying, "Don't worry, honey. Just go out there and have fun." If you are going to co-parent, you need to send one consistent message to students about what constitutes success in your shared class.

Once that message has been determined, be sure parents are made aware of your decisions related to assessing and grading as well. If some students will be assessed differently than others, parents also need to know so they won't be surprised and so they can support your efforts in the classroom. The more adults who are working collaboratively to ensure student success, the more likely the students will be successful.

Putting It Together

Now that we've reviewed assessment as the big picture and grading as the sometimes necessary evil of assigning a letter grade to an evaluation, let's consider what that might look like in practice. I have selected one national standard for science, math, and language arts to demonstrate how co-teachers might co-assess. In Figure 15.5, I have provided an example standard, how the standard might need to be spiraled for certain students in terms of objectives, and how that student might have his or her learning assessed and subsequently graded. While doing this activity for *each* lesson and *each* student is certainly not reasonable, given teachers' already overloaded schedules and time requirements, keep in mind that the majority of students will not need these adaptations. This should, however, help co-teachers consider those students (with and without identified disabilities) who appear to be struggling for a variety of reasons.

For those teachers who enjoy the use of technology and its propensity to save time and make work easier, the Co-Teaching Solutions System (CTSS) Co-teachers' Toolbox also provides features that can assist in co-assessing. First of all, the lesson plan worksheet has a drop-down menu of state-specific standards that also provide an option for teachers to spiral standards. For example, if you are co-teaching fifth grade language arts but have a student in your class who is at the first grade reading level, you don't want to ask him to simply color while everyone else is doing a reading assessment. By entering the fifth grade standard, identifying first grade as your lowest academic level in class, and then clicking on "View Continuum Standards," the program will identify for you the standards that lead from the first grade to the fifth grade standard you selected. In addition, there is a rubric maker and a Student Self-Assessment Run Chart (based on the Baldridge Model of high-performing schools). Each of these options also aids in co-assessing.

Identify the Standard That Will Be Addressed			

Language Arts—focuses on the general skills and strategies of the writing process

During co-planning, establish the continuum of needs and how the standard will be co-taught to meet those various needs. Also establish during this time, how students will be assessed based on meeting that standard.

Name	Objective and Assessment Option	Evaluation	Grade
Veronica Schiller Kiernan Farrell Bronte Rassan	Write an essay that employs a strong thesis sentence, supports, and transitions to argue against a popularly held belief	**Met objective** 3 pp essay against hunting 2 pp against Pluto as dwarf planet 2 pp against uniforms	A- A A
Typical Lesson 20 students	Write a three-paragraph essay that demonstrates strong understanding of thesis sentence, supports, and transitions	**Will vary** Some students will use computers, will need more time, other supports	**Will vary**
Julia Desser Ramon Aguilar	Using a graphic organizer & assistive technology, write a three-paragraph essay that demonstrates understanding of thesis sentence, supports, and transitions	**Met objective** One paragraph was weak Needs work on transitions	A- B+
Jim Sanodi	From three options, select the sentence that captures the main idea (thesis sentence)	**Met objective** Selected correct sentence 9/10 times, given different readings	A-

Identify the Standard That Will Be Addressed			

Science—focuses on the nature of scientific inquiry

During co-planning, establish the continuum of needs and how the standard will be co-taught to meet those various needs. Also establish during this time how students will be assessed based on meeting that standard.

Name	Objective and Assessment Option	Evaluation	Grade
Saundy Pickery	Using a variety of in-class materials, be able to create an object that will transmit sound (similar to article on early scientists)	**Met objective** Exceptionally creative project	A
Typical Lesson 24 students	Given a short article on early scientists, read and answer questions on worksheet	**Will vary by student** Evaluate questions answered correctly on worksheet	**Will vary**
Alex Glasidid Rachel Barrister Ramon Aguilar	Given a short article on early scientists, listen to article on tape and answer questions on worksheet	**Met objective** Answered 8/10 questions correctly Answered 10/10 questions correctly Answered 7/10 questions correctly	B- A C
Jim Sanodi	Given a picture in the article on scientists, be able to ask at least five questions about it	**Met objective** Required prompting for 3/5 questions	C

Identify the Standard That Will Be Addressed			
Mathematics—focuses on a variety of strategies in the problem-solving process			
During co-planning, establish the continuum of needs and how the standard will be co-taught to meet those various needs. Also establish during this time how students will be assessed based on meeting that standard.			
Name	**Objective and Assessment Option**	**Evaluation**	**Grade**
Saundy Pickery and Samson Vieth	*Given real-world materials and a budget, work together to determine the best combination of buying, leasing, or renting a car and house*	**Met objective** *Orally presented their determination to class and explained how they got their results*	A
Typical Lesson 24 students	*Given real-world materials and a budget, work in small groups to determine which items to buy from a catalogue so that the total does not exceed the budget (including tax)*	**Will vary by student groups** *Evaluate questions answered as group and individually ask student to explain solution as "ticket out the door"*	**Will vary**
Rachel Barrister *Ramon Aguilar* *Alex Glasidid*	*Given real-world materials and a budget, work in small groups to determine which items to buy from a catalogue so that the total does not exceed the budget*	**Met objective** *Group assessment of learning; ticket out the door modified to be concrete problem to solve*	B+ B A
Jim Sanodi	*Working in small group with others, his objective is to identify which items are more expensive (from three choices)*	**Met objective** *Identified 2/3 correct; needed prompting from group on third item*	B

Figure 15.5   Assessing by Standards

SOURCE: Murawski, W. W. (2008a).

Assessing Adults

Now that we've worked together for a while to determine how our students are doing, it is also time for us to self-assess. K. Wiggins and Damore (2006) write, "All too often, unfortunately, attempts at a collaboration process create an environment where participants view themselves as survivors rather than friends and professional colleagues" (p. 49). To move beyond being survivors, we need to go through the stages that Norris (1997) and Gately and Gately (2001) describe. The only way to do that is to self-assess. What are those stages?

- Forming
- Storming
- Norming
- Performing

Do these stages look familiar? They should. Consider them in the context of our marriage analogy.

- *Dating.* We meet. We begin to get to know each other. We start to be seen as a couple. (*Or* in the real world, we are *formed* as a couple by our administrator whether we had input or not. This, of course, will change once your administrator has a chance to read all the Matchmaker, Matchmaker chapters of this text.)
- *Engagement.* We are committed to one another (whether we like it or not). We begin to S.H.A.R.E. our preferences, pet peeves, and comfort zones. We *storm* through issues as we establish how we will present ourselves to the students.
- *Wedding.* It all begins to come together. The marriage is official, and we set *norms* for our class rules, procedures, sharing of materials and space, and distributions of roles and responsibilities. No honeymoon night though; the analogy doesn't carry that far.
- *Marriage.* The longer we are a married couple, the more we are able to work out our differences and be a team. We are able to finally *perform*, tweaking lessons as we learn from our mistakes, collaborating to meet individual student needs, and starting to, if not look alike, at least act alike.

Short-Term Assessments

As we work to enhance our collaborative relationship, there are both short- and long-term activities we can do to improve. For any of these to have any impact, however, both co-teachers need to be open to feedback and have a desire to improve. The right attitude is far more important than the right skills, for if you don't have the right attitude, it is not likely you will employ the skills you have.

Daily. For co-teachers who work together on a daily basis, such as co-teaching language arts for the second–third grade split, it is important to be open to quick suggestions, feedback, and constructive criticism. Being able to debrief quickly on how a lesson went is helpful. This does not need to be a lengthy process; class is about to start. It does, however, need to be a question that is asked at the end of each lesson: "Is there anything we need to discuss later?" If there is time for a brief chat, you can ask each other, "How do we think it went?" Be open to your co-teacher saying that a part of the lesson wasn't as effective as you might have thought or that something you taught didn't go over very well. Being defensive won't help the situation. If you don't have time to discuss it in detail then, simply say, "Okay. Let me think about that, and we can talk about it at our weekly meeting." For teachers on a varied schedule, these quick checks would occur after whatever lesson is co-taught. You might also agree to a regular quick daily e-mail debrief, as long as you are consistent with it.

Weekly. Co-teachers need to give an honest evaluation to each other on a regular basis regarding how they each think the week went. This should include how the students are doing, as well as how each feels regarding the co-planning, co-instruction, and co-assessment. Again, it is critical that co-teachers are honest with one another, or there will not be any improvement over time. As I previously mentioned, early in the relationship is the ideal time to give one another feedback; there is still time to change bad habits before they become too ingrained. You may think that later you will have a better relationship (and you might) but by waiting you may miss an opportunity for change.

Discuss how you will give one another feedback. This can make a big impact on a relationship. Those who know me know I am a "need it now" kind of gal. I tend to want to know the issues immediately and solve them (often too) quickly. After a lesson, I tend to want to do a debrief with my co-teachers right away and at length if possible. I have had as many different responses to this as I have had co-teachers. For example, Linda would want to chat with me right away, and we would get excited about what we could do for the next time. We would jump right in, not always thinking it through but quickly deciding in the middle if we needed to change something. Sally was always up for a quick debrief, but preferred to do a more in-depth one when she was not rushed for time. She was also more reflective and really analyzed our proposed changes to determine if they would have any negative consequences. Michael didn't care to debrief at all after the lesson, but was up for talking about the overall gestalt of the week when we met for our weekly planning session. He was a strong personality and knew his content well, but was open to trying new things provided that I had a good rationale for why a change should be made. With Tim, however, I had to be very careful. Tim was more territorial and defensive about change. He had been teaching a long time, and it was already a stretch that he was moving into our co-taught model. The fact that I had been a general education teacher was what convinced him that I could actually teach a class and that, even though I was a special education teacher, I did not intend to water down the content, slow it down for *those* kids, or plan to give them all the answers. When we were debriefing, I had to be very careful about how I would present my feedback. I often found that I had to do the time-honored technique of finding ways to make him think it was his idea. I made sure that my feedback did not appear to criticize his teaching or techniques, but rather offered up alternatives as "newfangled ideas" that I learned in my university courses that might be fun to try.

In addition to having a variety of communication preferences in content (lots of feedback, lots of reflection, etc.), you may also have to consider feedback format. Some of my co-teachers preferred to debrief immediately after class in person, while others preferred to e-mail or call one another later. I now use a lot of e-mail, text, and IM (instant messaging) with my current co-teacher.

Another helpful resource for both planning and self-assessment by co-teachers is the Co-Teaching Lesson Plan Book (www.nprinc.com). Throughout the text are boxes titled Reflective Framework. These boxes provide questions to help guide co-teachers as they progress throughout the school year together. Asking each other these questions, and responding honestly, will help co-teachers determine where they are struggling and where they are strong. In addition, for each week of instruction, there is a column titled Performance Data and Notes, wherein co-teachers can also document items that need future discussion.

Long-Term Assessments

There are additional techniques for collecting data on how the co-teaching relationship is going. These may require more commitment and reflection than the daily or weekly communications. Following are some of the options co-teachers may consider when they are really ready to improve:

- Invite mentors or other teachers into the classroom to observe you both in action. Ask them to take notes on the interaction and relationship between the two of you and on the pedagogical (i.e., teaching) elements of the classroom, as opposed to the content. You don't need someone to teach you more math; you want someone to help you learn to teach math better together.

- Ask administrators to provide you both with the time and opportunity to go out together to observe veteran co-teachers. Be sure to set up the situation so that you'll have time to debrief with the co-teachers you observe in addition to being able to talk as a team about what you liked or didn't like.

- Videotape yourselves co-teaching on a regular basis and watch the tapes together (popcorn and soda recommended). Notice that I did say "on a regular basis." The rationale for that is that kids (and teachers) tend to "perform" when it is a unique event. Once the kids get used to being videotaped, they will be more natural—and so will you.

- Use an official problem-solving process to work you both through issues. Using formal steps to identify a problem, analyze, brainstorm solutions collaboratively, and then determine how and when you will resolve it can be empowering to both teachers. These issues may be student centered that you both share but can't seem to resolve, or they can be issues related to your co-teaching relationship (e.g., we disagree on grading issues).

- Select someone on staff you both respect to serve as your "marriage counselor." I recommend that this person not be an administrator, if possible. In an effort to obtain feedback rather than evaluation, I suggest selecting someone from the faculty who is less likely to make judgments and more likely to provide support and an ear to listen. Arrange to meet with this person once a semester (or more if needed) merely to talk about your co-teaching situation openly but with some guidance. Have these meetings set up in advance so it doesn't look like you are meeting with the "counselor" only when there are issues you can't work through. It's not easy to facilitate open conversations between two adult colleagues, so choose wisely and make sure it is someone who (1) you both equally respect and select and (2) is willing to serve in this role. Be sure to thank your colleague for acting in this role by buying her dinner, flowers, or a Starbucks gift card and thanking her publicly at a staff meeting. Or better yet, offer to do the same for her and her co-teachers.

Want More on This Topic?

For more information on the administrator's role in this, see Chapter 17, Matchmaker, Matchmaker.

- Complete official questionnaires that require you to analyze your co-teaching relationship and respond honestly. Fill these out individually first, then together. There are a few different ones that are available and will be helpful.

  o DeBoer and Fister (1995) have a Collaborative Teaching Questionnaire available in their text.
  o Adams, Cessna, & Friend (1993) created the CO-ACT (Colorado Assessment of Co-Teaching).
  o Dieker (2001) published the Secondary Co-Teaching Practices Checklist in her article on the effective practices of secondary co-teaching teams.
  o Gately and Gately (2001) provided a checklist for co-teachers in their article in *Teaching Exceptional Children.*
  o Magiera and Simmons (2005) self-published their Magiera-Simmons Quality Indicator (QI) Model of Co-teaching.
  o Co-Teaching Solutions System Observation System (different from the CTSS Co-Teachers Toolbox) is a software system that allows co-teachers to self-assess what they do in the classroom on a typical basis and then to compare those responses to what is observed in the co-taught classroom. Figure 15.6 displays an example of some of the items included in the CTSS observation checklist.

Figure 15.6 CTSS Observation Checklist

SOURCE: Murawski, W. W., & Lochner, W. W. (2007).

16

Playing Nicely With the Other Parents

■ CO-TEACHING'S ROLE WITH OTHER SCHOOL-IMPROVEMENT INITIATIVES

A frequent and legitimate concern of teachers is that there are so many initiatives that come and go in schools. It is difficult to determine which initiatives are going to stay and which are going to be a comet—coursing brightly for a short period of time and then disappearing altogether, or at least until they reappear years later. As Lisa Dieker and I stated in our article in *Teaching Exceptional Children* (Murawski & Dieker, 2004), "Faculty . . . are well acquainted with change. New mandates or approaches are often introduced at the beginning of a school year with the announcement that they are to be implemented immediately. This 'ready, fire, aim' approach negates what we know about change needing time and professional buy in" (p. 53). Knowing this, where does co-teaching fit in? Is it another comet, or is it here to stay? Regardless, how do we as teachers reconcile its use when we are faced with so many other new mandated initiatives each school year?

The concept of co-teaching between general and special educators started more than 15 years ago and has only increased in use over the years, with a huge boost after No Child Left Behind (NCLB) was enacted in 2001 and the Individuals with Disabilities Education Improvement Act was reauthorized in 2004. Given this legal support and the fact that co-teaching is a service delivery option tied to the increase of inclusion, a philosophy that has gathered strength since early 1970s, I feel very comfortable stating with authority that co-teaching is not going away any time soon. In fact, it is only increasing as a means by which students are given services in the general education classroom.

Do schools seem to wax and wane in their use of co-teaching? Definitely. I have been to many schools where teachers pull me to the side to say, "You know, I used to do this 10 years ago. Then we got a new administrator and it just stopped, and I was back to my self-contained classroom." Shifts in policy, focus, administration, and priorities all impact the use of co-teaching and other inclusive practices. That said, I find it to be a powerful message that we keep coming back to co-teaching as a viable option for meeting so many school needs. As a teacher, I like to identify the initiatives that are not likely to disappear and then ensure that I am at the forefront of their induction at my school.

How does co-teaching relate to the variety of educational initiatives that are impacting today's educational culture? Because co-teaching is a method of teacher collaboration by which needs can be met, co-teachers who work well together generally find that their collaborative relationship makes the infusion of new requirements easier. Some of the more well-known initiatives elementary schools are undertaking include Reading First, cooperative learning, 21st-century technology, Universal Design for Learning, and Response to Intervention. Let me explain how co-teaching fits in with each of these recommended programs, approaches, strategies, or initiatives.

READING FIRST ■

Reading First is a federally funded reading program that was established with the passage of NCLB in 2001. The Reading First initiative is based on the findings of the National Reading Panel, which was composed of researchers, teachers, child development experts, parents, and leaders in elementary and higher education. These individuals reviewed the literature and research on effective reading practices and identified as the top five components: phonemic awareness, phonics, vocabulary, fluency, and comprehension (Reading First, 2008). Reading First was created as a program designed to promote the use of instructional techniques supported by research-based, scientifically supported reading practices, especially in the nation's highest need schools, for students in first, second, and third grades.

Reports on Reading First's success with students is mixed. Some reports cite achievement data from state educational agencies stating that "Reading First students from nearly every grade and subgroup have made impressive gains in reading proficiency" (Reading First, 2008, p. 1). They emphasize that states report that students in all grades have identified reading improvement, teachers spent more instructional time on reading, schools have flexibility in their use of reading programs, and subgroups like students with disabilities and English language learners are increasing their reading comprehension skills. On the other hand, a recent congressionally mandated independent evaluation of Reading First was not as laudatory. That study, which included 13 states and was conducted for the 2004–2005 and 2005–2006 school years, reported that there were no statistically significant differences in reading comprehension between students who were and were not in Reading First programs. While the study did find that Reading First schools did increase the instructional time spent on the five components identified as critical by the

National Reading Panel (phonemic awareness, phonics, vocabulary, fluency, and comprehension), there was no significant difference in students' reading test scores. This report has led to a renewed criticism of the program by some. The *Washington Post* ran an article immediately after the report become public, stating that "the conclusion is likely to reignite the longstanding 'reading wars.' Critics say that Reading First places too much emphasis on explicit phonics instruction and doesn't do enough to foster understanding" (Glod, 2008, A01). On the other hand, many educators, including former Education Secretary Margaret Spellings, remain avid fans of Reading First and support its use in the classroom, repeatedly emphasizing its foundation in research-based practices.

Regardless of whether or not your school is a Reading First school, you are certainly implementing some kind of reading program with students. The need to focus on phonics, vocabulary, fluency, and comprehension is one that takes time in the classroom and often requires individual time with a student. When co-teachers take this into account, they can work collaboratively to use various approaches to improve reading skills with students. For example, they can introduce phonics and vocabulary by role-playing using the Team Teaching and One Teach, One Support approaches; they can work on comprehension by doing small group reading discussions while in Parallel or Station groups; and they can spend more individual time with students working on fluency using the Alternative Teaching approach.

Co-teachers in elementary schools can use a variety of approaches to help students develop their reading skills.

COOPERATIVE LEARNING ■

Having students work together in collaborative, cooperative, and heterogeneous groups is not a new concept. It is, however, a concept that some elementary teachers often have difficulty implementing effectively in the classroom. Research has identified that cooperative learning is helpful for students with disabilities (D. Fuchs et al., 2001), students who are English language learners (Bahamonde & Friend, 1999; Greenwood, Arreaga-Mayer, Utley, Gavin, & Terry, 2001), and students who are at risk for school failure (Gardner et al., 2001). Cooperative learning is considered a research validated teaching method, which can "facilitate active learning, promote social interaction, and help develop social skills for most students, especially students with special needs" (Choate, 2004, p. 42). Sounds great, doesn't it? Why then do we see so many students even at the elementary level sitting in their individual chairs, listening to a teacher pontificate, for much of their school day? Why do so many teachers steer clear of cooperative learning groups?

Reasons abound. First of all, in elementary school, we are essentially working with "human balls of energy." It can be hard for a student who is still learning social skills to have to apply them to an academic situation. For some, being with peers automatically equals playtime—the rougher and louder, the better. Other students are more comfortable working alone and don't have the interest or ability to work with others. Putting these students together—on purpose—may seem like a bad idea. Second, as students work together, the noise and chaos levels rise. The teacher's blood pressure may follow suit. Third, teachers recognize that as students work in small groups, personality traits emerge. One overachieving student may surface in each group; this is the student who ends up taking over the assignment and doing it all herself in order to ensure that it is done well and that the group gets a good grade. The other students take a "cool by me" approach and let her do the work.

An additional difficulty is that cooperative groups take organization and structure to work effectively. Teachers need to know how to get them in groups, how to ensure that they are productive, how to limit the noise levels, how to differentiate appropriately, how to get them to transition for stations, and how to get them to produce quality work during this activity. That is a lot to do. Most importantly, though, I emphasize that, given the research support for collaborative

Want More on This Topic?

Go back to Chapter 13, Working Together to Wrangle the Li'l Rascals and reread the strategies provided for differentiation and group work.

learning groups, teachers should embrace this technique. Is it easy to do when you have a 1:20 teacher-student ratio? No, but when you are co-teaching, it becomes that much easier. Thus, this is an instructional initiative that clearly benefits from the use of co-teaching.

TWENTY-FIRST-CENTURY TECHNOLOGY ■

The use of technology is no longer an elective. It is a requirement. An imperative. A critical aspect of all we do in today's schools. We have teachers who struggle to create PowerPoint presentations and who avoid checking e-mail, while students enter the classroom e-mailing from their cell phones. When my son was three, he said, "Who are you texting, Mommy?" I shouldn't have been shocked; on a daily basis, I'm sure I say, "Just a sec, hon. I'm texting Daddy," more times than I'd like to know. He sees my phone come out and says, "Take a picture of me!" Sadly, I have colleagues whom I doubt even know that phones have the capability of taking pictures. Now that he's four and three-quarters, he is using the mouse deftly and is able to Google dinosaurs at will. His comfort with the computer is astounding. My girlfriend's daughter, at three years old, was walking around the house with her fake cell phone saying, "www dot www dot www dot." When asked what she was doing, she responded, "Checking my e-mail." Our children are digital natives, while so many of us are digital immigrants. We are new to this environment; we came here from somewhere else. Our students were born here.

Given this dichotomy, how can we bring 21st-century education into the schools? How can we be the ones who provide students with the 21st-century skills they will need to succeed? "Emerging technologies and resulting globalization provide unlimited possibilities for exciting new discoveries and developments such as new forms of energy, medical advances, restoration of environmentally ravaged areas, communications, and exploration into space and into the depths of the oceans. The possibilities are unlimited" (21stcenturyschools.com). Well, they *should* be unlimited; unfortunately, they can be limited—by teachers unwilling or unable to provide access to those skills and technologies. Herein comes the benefit of co-teaching.

One of the identified benefits of co-teaching is that teachers can gain from one another's expertise. Another is that we can divide and conquer. Yet another is that we can facilitate more interaction and engagement among our students. Let's translate that in terms of 21st-century technology. First of all, a special educator who is concerned that he does not have the same level of content as his general education co-teacher may want to take on the role of technology expert. He can find ways to incorporate technology into lessons on a regular basis. He can keep the class Web site up to date, continuing to add links that would challenge higher-achieving or motivated students and those who would provide additional information and support to struggling students. He can create and disseminate a digital newsletter to parents and community members. He can be the one to take half the class to the computer lab, while the general educator stays with the other half in the classroom to start an assignment. Thus, the value of the special educator is increased, and the skills developed in taking on this role are easily adaptable to any future class in which the special educator co-teaches.

If neither teacher feels adept at technology, co-teaching is the perfect opportunity to develop those skills. Co-teachers can select skills they want to use in the classroom and then divide the workload. One will offer to learn more about video streaming, while the other will learn more about podcasting or how to do a webquest. The two can then come back together and teach each other the new skills. Each can take the lead on that activity as he teaches it to students. Thus, each of us has the opportunity to be the "expert" in something technologically related, while the other is in the role of "novice" or "learner." This is also a great time to show students that you are willing to learn new things and to share the role of expert.

Facilitating appropriate interactions between students and increasing their active academic engagement are two of our goals as co-teachers. The use of technology can certainly help with accomplishing both goals (Kim, Woodruff, Klein, & Vaughn, 2006), but this is more difficult when working in isolation. As co-teachers, we can have students collaborate to create and edit digital videos, research information on the Web, download lyrics to compare to poems read in class, and even just word process their own stories. Computer stations, Alphasmarts, calculators, and other technological devices make an excellent independent station for students when we are working in groups. We can videotape group work and debrief with students, not only on their content and results but also on their social interaction, collaboration, and communication skills. Working together, we can determine what activities are appropriate for all, for most, and for some. We can pair students so that one student is stronger in content and one is stronger in the technological skills. We can more easily address students' kinesthetic and tactile learning modalities. We can collaborate to prepare our students by creating real-world activities, which are interdisciplinary, integrated, project-based, and address those skills identified as critical for the 21st-century learner, including collaboration, critical thinking, oral communications, written communications, technology, citizenship, career-orientation, and content-based learning (www.21stcenturyschools.com).

Last, but unfortunately not least, another selling point for teachers is the need for supervision with regard to technology. It is so hard to police the use of this much technology, both to protect our students and to keep them honest. When I was in school, kids passed notes. This required proximity. Now they can text—no adjacent contact required. When I was in school, kids would look at the paper of the kid at the next desk. Now they can look at the paper of any other kid in the world. Another set of eyes will not eliminate this concern, but it will certainly help. The more we know about technology, the more it will help.

Effective co-teachers include technology for every age.

■ UNIVERSAL DESIGN FOR LEARNING

Universal Design for Learning (UDL) is a concept that stems from universal design in architecture (Stanford & Reeves, 2009). As the Americans with Disabilities Act (ADA) was passed and buildings needed to "come to code" to allow access for individuals with physical disabilities, more and more venues were required to add ramps, railings, and larger bathrooms. Those who were creating new buildings realized that it made intuitive sense to have these structures available right from the start. Not only did it ensure that the building was ADA compliant, but they were also structures that were accessible to all individuals. Think about it. Steps are accessible to only some, ramps are accessible to all. I'm not only talking about individuals who are in wheelchairs; what about someone who sprained his ankle recently, a small child, an elderly gentleman, or someone with asthma or whose breathing is difficult? Each of these individuals would be able to access a ramp or an elevator, but only some can use the steps. Acrey, Johnstone, and Milligan (2005) write,

> Universal design is found everywhere and the general public often takes it for granted. Examples include curb cuts that increase accessibility for wheelchair users, in addition to facilitating ease of movement for people with bicycles, shopping carts or baby strollers. Around the house, utensils and tools with large grips prevent blisters and make jobs easier. Although people with fine-motor difficulties were the intended users of such utensils, they have become very popular with nondisabled users. (p. 23)

The concept of proactively designing materials that are accessible to all from the beginning quickly merged into education (Thousand, Villa, & Nevin, 2007). Instead of special educators taking exorbitant amounts of time to redesign, modify, adapt, or accommodate materials for a select group of students with special needs, wouldn't it make more sense to design those materials initially so that all children could benefit? Herein lies the benefit of co-teaching with a special service provider. Special service providers are trained in working with students with special needs, including gifted, English language learners, or students with physical, emotional, and cognitive or attentional difficulties. As you collaborate to determine instruction and create materials, you will more easily be able to embrace UDL (Universal Design for Learning).

The long-term benefits of this are enormous. Instead of having to adapt a test, lesson, video, or other material when you get a student with a visual disability next year or a student who is deaf the year after that or a student in a wheelchair three years from now, you will have lessons that are universally designed and more readily accessible to the masses of students you will have over the years. We as teachers are always complaining that we do not have time; this is the perfect example of when collaborating with others can save time. I suggest that teachers work not only with their co-teachers but also with the other teachers in their grade and subject area to share resources and jointly create UDL lessons and materials.

RESPONSE TO INTERVENTION ■

Response to Intervention or Response to Instruction (more commonly known as RTI) was initially conceptualized as a different way to identify learning disabilities in children. Now, for many, it is seen as a method of providing instructional supports to students at all levels, thereby reducing the number of children identified for special education. RTI involves having multiple levels, circles, or tiers of intervention—ranging from whole group instruction to small group intensive intervention. Its implementation impacts all teachers and students, both in general education and special education. The RTI approach is new to schools and emphasizes proactive instruction, ongoing assessment, data-based decision making, and intensive instruction for struggling students. Most of the research on RTI implementation has been at the elementary school level and has been in the area of reading; that said, however, RTI is increasingly being supported nationwide as a support model for K–12 education.

Dr. Claire Hughes and I wrote an article for *Preventing School Failure* (2009) to help clarify how co-teaching fits into the RTI picture. In that article, we state,

> When meeting the needs for RTI implementation, teachers will need to actively collaborate with their colleagues to make sure (a) that lessons are research-based, (b) that they address the wide variety of needs in the general education classroom, (c) that they ensure access to the general education curriculum for diverse learners, (d) that ongoing data collection and progress monitoring is occurring and (e) that students in Tiers II and III are able to receive specialized and more individualized instruction in small groups. Co-teaching becomes a very powerful means of meeting the goals of RTI. (p. 69)

Aspects of RTI can be daunting; not the least of which because it is considered a general education initiative, meaning that students are to receive the individualized support and progress monitoring in the general education classroom by the general education classroom teacher, even if a special educator is unavailable. Students who struggle are no longer sent out of the classroom to be evaluated for alternative programs (e.g., Special Education, ELL), but rather are kept in the general education classroom as various interventions are tried and their results documented.

D. Fuchs and Fuchs (2007), who have done a lot of work in the area of RTI, clarify that in the first tier of the RTI model, all students should be provided with a scientifically based program in the general education classroom (2007). In addition, students need to be assessed at least three times a year on an established benchmark. "In Tier I, the underlying assumption is that all students in the general education classroom are getting quality instruction (i.e., research-based) that will be effective for approximately 80 percent of the students" (Murawski & Hughes, 2009, p. 69). What does this mean for teachers? It means they need to know what constitutes quality, research-based instruction, while also making time for regular assessments and data collection. I can't think of a better time to be collaborating with a special service provider. Many special educators believe that the majority of children with mild to moderate disabilities (e.g., learning disabilities, attention deficit/hyperactivity disorder, emotional disabilities) can have their needs met in the general education classroom if instruction and curricular materials are universally designed. Using research-based methods for instructing all students will help meet the criteria for RTI as well as UDL, thereby also meeting the goals of inclusion. How best to do all this? Co-teach, of course. For specific examples of what this might look like using the five approaches with the three RTI tiers, check out the Murawski and Hughes (2009) article in *Preventing School Failure* titled "Response to Intervention, Collaboration, and Co-Teaching: A Necessary Combination for Successful Systemic Change."

Alone, addressing all the components required for RTI is daunting. Together, however, you and a co-teacher can easily manage to address these components. The following lesson plan will help you see how co-teachers would be able to work collaboratively to address various criteria for success, even given a very academically or behaviorally diverse group of students.

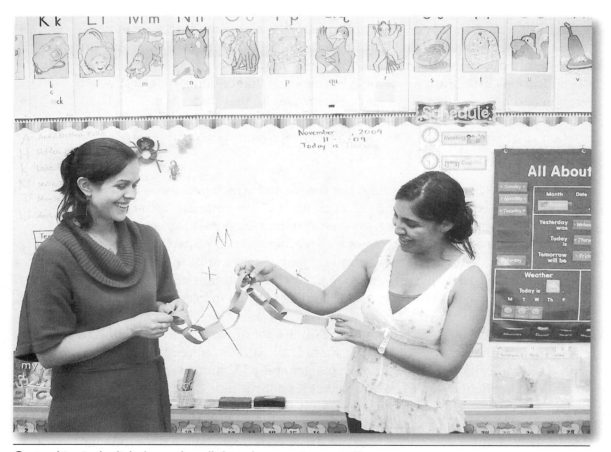

Co-teaching is the link that makes all the other practices possible.

Co-Teaching Lesson Plan					

Subject Area: Math

Grade level: 4th

Content Standard: Students will demonstrate an understanding of the relationships of fractions and decimals.

Lesson Objective: Students will be able to identify and solve problems with fractions and decimals.

Essential Questions: When might I need to use fractions and decimals in the real world?

Key Vocabulary: Fractions, decimals, greatest common factor, least common denominator

Preassessment: Day before: Quick check on who already knows how to find and solve equations with decimals and fractions

Materials: Calculators and computer lab with internet access to www.kidshealth.org/recipes; adapted materials

Lesson	Co-Teaching Approach	Time	General Education Teacher	Special Service Provider	Considerations
Beginning	☑ *Team*	9–9:10 a.m.	In a large group, teachers introduce lesson to students by doing a role play. GET acts like someone who doesn't understand why she has to know fractions and decimals and SET gives examples like cooking and sports. They then tell kids that they will be doing these activities today in groups.		Have groups already created and posted. Have Web site and examples ready.
Middle	☑ *Parallel*	9:10–9:30 a.m. 9:30–9:50 a.m.	Group One (in computer lab): Students pretend they are having a sleepover and have to find recipes online and then adapt them for if 5 or 15 kids show up. Groups Swap	Group Two (in classroom): Students receive various sports examples and have to work in pairs to convert fractions to decimals and vice versa. Groups Swap	Have a variety of examples to link to student interests. Have a picture board for Brandon and more advanced work for Stella.
End	☑ *Alternative*	9:50–10 a.m.	Work with identified small group of students to reteach main concepts of fractions and decimals.	Facilitate sharing of different recipes and how students approached math problems with large group out loud.	Have manipulatives ready for small group.

Figure 16.1   Co-Teaching Lesson Plan

SOURCE: Format compliments of www.2TeachLLC.com. Software version available at www.coteachsolutions.com

Self-Assessment 4

Will We Be Able to Celebrate Our Anniversary?

You've almost completed your first year of co-teaching. Congratulations! Answer the following questions independently and then share your responses with your co-teacher to see where you agree or disagree. Feel free to take time to talk about these areas as you compare your responses.
I benefited from this co-teaching arrangement. Agree ☐   Disagree ☐
My co-teacher benefited from this co-teaching arrangement. Agree ☐   Disagree ☐
Students with special needs benefited from this co-teaching arrangement. Agree ☐   Disagree ☐
Students without special needs benefited from this co-teaching arrangement. Agree ☐   Disagree ☐
In terms of *co-planning,* I felt our strengths were In terms of *co-planning,* I felt our weaknesses were
In terms of *co-instructing,* I felt our strengths were In terms of *co-instructing,* I felt our weaknesses were
In terms of *co-assessing,* I felt our strengths were In terms of *co-assessing,* I felt our weaknesses were
For future co-teaching situations, I would really like to keep or change the following:
I would like to be in this co-teaching arrangement again next semester or next year. Agree ☐   Disagree ☐
If not, why not?
If not, what would you like to do instead?

17

Matchmaker, Matchmaker

The Role of the Administrator

IS IT TIME FOR A DIVORCE? ∎

Supervising Co-Teaching

Prior to determining the success or failure of a co-teaching program, administrators need to supervise co-teachers and provide ongoing feedback. Unfortunately, many administrators responsible for supervising and evaluating teachers are not familiar with the role each teacher should play in a co-taught relationship. Co-teaching is a relatively new service delivery option for servicing students with disabilities in the general education classroom and, unless they have done it themselves or received quite a bit of training in the subject, administrators may feel at a loss in terms of providing feedback and evaluation. In fact, Dr. Katherman (2005) cites one of his administrators who said, "Supervising co-teaching is like herding cats." It can certainly be a daunting process.

In order to effectively assess co-teaching and give teachers helpful feedback, administrators need to be aware themselves of what co-teaching entails. They need to ensure parity between the two teachers, encourage both educators to actively engage with students at all times, and need to confirm that teachers (especially special educators) have consistent schedules. The latter is important so that special educators are not constantly called away from the co-taught class for individualized education program (IEP) meetings, discipline problems, or parent phone calls. Administrators need to demonstrate their understanding that both teachers are equally responsible for the co-taught class and must therefore be present consistently. Each of these items has been discussed in earlier Matchmaker, Matchmaker chapters of this text. In addition to this book, another excellent reference for administrators interested in tips for evaluating co-teachers is the article "This Doesn't Look Familiar: A Supervisor's Guide to

Observing Co-Teaching" (Wilson, 2005) in *Intervention in School and Clinic*. For a clear, one-page synopsis of the five most important aspects to ensuring a quality co-teaching program, see the article I published in *The School Administrator* (September 2008) titled "The Five Keys to Co-Teaching in the Inclusive Classroom." It's pithy and, therefore, an easy one to disseminate to administrators.

Collecting Data on Co-Teaching Improvement

Assessment related to co-teaching involves both the evaluation of how well the teachers are doing in their collaborative efforts, as well as how well students are learning. Change takes time as we all know, and it is important to document how co-teachers and students in the co-taught classes are doing so that evidence-based decisions can be made (Boscardin, 2005). Rash decisions are never a smart move in education. Administrators should encourage teachers to communicate with one another frequently regarding how they feel the relationship is progressing and what can be done to improve. The supervision and feedback of co-teachers will also help with the assessment of their progress. In addition, however, administrators need to promote the active engagement by co-teachers in regular co-planning, co-instruction, and co-assessment. Without these elements, the desired benefits of co-teaching are much less likely to be obtained. I have seen two teachers in the same room together, each having a wonderful time joking with the other, while providing no real value to students. Just because teachers are enjoying what they are doing doesn't necessarily mean they are improving instruction for students. It helps, but it's no guarantee. It is important to be able to identify what the "value added" is of co-teaching versus just having one teacher in the classroom.

In addition to the importance of scheduling time or finding time for teachers to co-plan, administrators are also strongly encouraged to ask teachers to share their lesson plans with them. Doing so accomplishes a variety of goals: it ensures that teachers are using their time to co-plan, it provides motivation to teachers to co-plan, it provides documentation of co-planning (which is helpful with parents as well), and it gives administrators information from which they can learn more about what is happening in the co-taught classroom. Looking at a co-taught lesson plan should help the administrator see if co-teachers are planning for co-instruction or if one teacher has been relegated to the role of assistant.

Classroom observations are also a key technique for observing co-instruction and giving feedback. While there are paper forms available for interviewing and observing co-teachers in action, such as Magiera and Simmons's (2005) *The Magiera-Simmons Quality Indicator Model of Co-Teaching*, most traditional observation tools are not designed with co-teachers in mind. Walk-through observations are typically set up merely to observe one teacher in action. A software available for observing co-teachers and collecting data on their actions over time (for walk-through length or longer observations) is the CTSS Observation System (www.coteachsolutions.com). The CTSS Observation System is designed to be loaded on a laptop or handheld device and includes a narrative and checklist option.

The CTSS Observation Checklist provides items for observers to "look for," "listen for," and "ask for" to help determine co-teaching effectiveness. It provides quantitative results immediately and can analyze observation data across individuals, classes, subjects, grades, schoolwide, and individual criteria. Another helpful feature is that it can archive results and provide historical data for administrators who are willing to collect data over a period of years. Using this type of system enables administrators to be explicit in their expectations with co-teachers. Administrators and other observers are encouraged to give co-teachers copies of these checklists so the expectations for observation are clear. While not every approach will be used each day, nor will every lesson include every component on the list, having the items observers will be looking for, listening for, and asking for in advance helps co-teachers meet those expectations.

After assessing whether teachers are co-planning and co-instructing, administrators need to also provide support for co-assessing. When working with kids with and without disabilities, co-teachers need to use both traditional and alternative, authentic assessments. Rather than admonishing teachers for not sticking to pacing plans or traditional lecture formats, administrators should recognize that, while access to the general education curriculum is critical, if students are not able to absorb the content in ways that are meaningful to them (which frequently do not include more traditional methods), they will not demonstrate improvement on standardized tests or other methods of assessment. Thus, allowing students to listen to tests on tape or have the tests read to them, using portfolios instead of only pencil-and-paper tests, and finding ways to support multiple intelligences are all ways that may actually improve student learning and outcomes. It is critical that students with disabilities have modifications and accommodations to which they are entitled throughout the school year; administrators need to ensure teachers are not merely adjusting grades after the fact as a pseudo accommodation. It sends the wrong message to students and does not improve learning.

When Is Divorce a Wise Option?

Although I do not generally advocate divorce, there are times when it may be the best choice for all involved, and if it is done well, it can result in an amicable decision for all parties. However, while divorce may be the end result in some cases, it is always worthwhile to first attempt to save the marriage. If adults can't find a way to get along in the classroom, what are we modeling for our students?

Students are obviously the litmus test for whether a new approach is effective in school or not. If students are not learning, responding negatively to a pair of co-teachers, or somehow otherwise negatively impacted by the co-teaching arrangement, it is certainly time to reevaluate this team. Be aware, however, in research I conducted with students and teachers at the elementary level (Murawski, 2006), I found that while students usually liked the co-teaching arrangement, saying "we don't have to wait as long for help," they also did not like "that we don't get away with as much with two teachers." Therefore, if students are railing against having two teachers because they are finally being held to appropriately high standards and being presented with appropriately challenging work, while being asked to demonstrate appropriately required behavior, this may not be a team you want to split. On the other hand, if students can tell that the teachers do not get along, that they continually disagree with one another and go behind each other's back, if students can play one teacher against another or complain that they are stigmatized by only working with the same teacher, it may be time to reconsider that arrangement. It may also be time to consider additional professional development with teachers on the skills of collaboration and communication.

One of the real challenges I have seen related to co-teaching is that teachers who do not want to work with *those* kids or *those* teachers demonstrate in their actions that they will not accommodate for kids or collaborate with other adults. By doing so, administrators and other teachers often reinforce their behavior by removing *those* kids from their classes and not having them work with other teachers (who would rather not work with them anyway). Thus, the naysayers are rewarded by being able to shut their door, work in isolation, and only have children without special needs in their classes. While I am not advocating making these individuals work with someone else or putting students in their classes who would then experience failure, I do suggest that they not receive preferential treatment. If teachers who are making a concerted effort at making co-teaching work are given the best classrooms, schedules, and materials; are allowed to work with higher-achieving students as well; or are allowed to avoid extra duties, this will help demonstrate to others that while co-teaching takes effort, it can be worth it. This should also reduce the number of teachers who try to get a "divorce" when they see their colleagues being given the "easier" classes, students, and assignments by not agreeing to co-teach.

One administrator told me about a couple of teachers at her school who had been co-teaching together for four years. They were considered the model for co-teaching for the district and many novice co-teaching teams were told to go and watch them teach to get a feel for what co-teaching should look like. The administrator shared with me that this team had come to her multiple times during their first year of co-teaching, each of them separately begging to be released from the commitment. Instead of allowing them to go their own ways immediately, the administrator did some "counseling." She met with them both in her office and asked them to come in with a list of their concerns. They did so, and in the ensuing conversation, the three of them were able to work out an agreeable situation—one that involved some compromise, some accommodation, and a lot of collaboration. The result is that four years later, this team not only functions extremely well together, but they are happy that they were never granted their separation.

Thus, before signing any divorce papers, administrators need to be sure to gather all the facts. If teachers see that you are quick to separate teams who complain or don't want to work together, they will quickly follow suit. Working in isolation is preferable for many teachers because they are simply not used to the collaborative approach. That doesn't mean they won't get used to it or even improve over time. If teachers are struggling, prior to separating them, try the following:

- *Provide professional development on co-teaching.* Send both teachers together to receive training on how to most effectively co-teach. The Bureau of Education and Research (www.ber.org) is well known for its teacher-friendly and innovative sessions on a variety of educational topics, including co-teaching and inclusion. Other information on professional development for co-teaching can be found at www .2TeachLLC.com, www.ber.org, www.corwinpress.com, and www .ideasforeducators.com.

- *Provide training and practice in the art of problem solving.* Teachers who have been trained in how to formally problem solve are often able to work out their own problems. They do need to know the steps of problem solving and then practice those steps together. Using formal steps helps remove the emotionality and personal nature of the issue.

- *Create a co-teaching support group.* I spent a week with Granada Hills Charter High School in California (the largest charter high school in the nation) doing professional development when they first decided to pilot a co-teaching program. At the end of the week, one of the general education science teachers stood up and said to the rest of the group, "Guys, let's make a deal. If any of us are getting upset about our partners or the co-teaching in general, let's vent to another person in this room. Otherwise, people who are not in the co-teaching program will only hear and remember the negatives and they won't understand." I was impressed. They ended up meeting as a group once a month for lunch to share, vent, ask questions, help with ideas, and so forth. Their co-teaching program is still going strong.

- *Have teachers visit other classes and interview co-teachers to see how they have worked out their issues.* When teams see how other co-teachers are working together and benefiting from the arrangement, this can provide the incentive needed to make things work. At the elementary level, this is much more powerful if co-teachers get to see another team who is teaching the same content or grade as their own; for a fifth-grade team who co-teaches language arts to watch a kindergarten team during calendar time is less powerful.

- *Facilitate the identification of a mentor (aka marriage counselor).* To avoid the administrator having to serve as marriage counselor, it is helpful if co-teachers select an individual at the school whom they both respect. Asking that individual to help them sort their differences allows the issues to be vented and addressed, without it becoming a formal affair or escalating beyond an acceptable point. As the administrator, see if you can support that arrangement by working out times for the "counselor" to get together with the team during or after school hours.

- *Ask teachers to share their concerns separately.* If no marriage counselor is available, having teachers individually share their concerns prior to bringing them together is another option. This will allow you to hear both sides first and then, when they come together, you can help facilitate a shared decision. In this case, you may want to review the characteristics and suggestions for collaborative consultation; see Kampwirth's (2006) *Collaborative Consultation in the Schools.*

- *If necessary, have co-teachers create an alternative plan.* The students in the co-taught class still have needs that have to be met. If teachers are unable to collaborate in the same room to meet those needs, see if they have alternate suggestions. For example, is it a personality issue that can be fixed by having a different special education teacher in the room? Is it a control issue that needs to be addressed by staff development over time and that in the short term might be ameliorated by having a paraprofessional provide in-class support instead of trying to have parity with a special education teacher? Is it a problem that is bigger and requires the special educator and the students with special needs to be removed; if so, to where, and how can this decision be shared with parents?

When is divorce acceptable? If you answer yes to any of the following questions, you may consider dissolving the partnership.

- Have both of the teachers come to you, together or separately, on multiple occasions to ask for a divorce? Do their concerns seem justified?
- Have students or parents spoken to you on multiple occasions indicating their concern that the team is not a strong match? Are they able to provide you with specific examples?
- Have you observed in the classroom over multiple occasions and recognized a lack of communication or collaboration between teachers? Have you tried to discuss this with teachers to no avail?
- Have you observed in the classroom over multiple occasions and wondered why there are two teachers in the room if they both are not active with kids? Have you provided strategies, yet they are not being implemented?
- Have the teachers indicated to you that they do not think two teachers are necessary for that group of students? Is there another class that could benefit from an additional adult?
- Has the team worked together for a full year and no longer has a group of students they would need to share this year? Are the services of the special educator needed elsewhere?
- Have you provided professional development, problem-solving strategies, a marriage counselor, individual counseling sessions, and other supports to no avail?
- Do teachers continue to resist improving and learning? Is it clear that they just do not like each other or do not even want to make it work?

If you are answering yes to many of these questions, it may be time to allow teachers to part ways. Be sure to make it clear to co-teachers that the split is being made in the best interest of the students and that you are not giving up on the expectation of teacher collaboration. How are we to expect children to learn to collaborate if we as adults and role models are not able to "play nicely" ourselves?

BUILDING AN EFFECTIVE PROGRAM: ■
MAKING MORE MATCHES

Administrators set the tone in a school. Research has demonstrated time and time again that administrative support for new initiatives can make or break their success (Walther-Thomas, 1997). Specifically, research on inclusive practices also supports the need for administrative support and guidance if they are to be effective (Murawski & Dieker, 2004; Spencer, 2005; Wilson, 2005). Teachers look to their administrators when determining if they should embrace a new practice or philosophy or if they should resist. It is often not difficult to ascertain if a practice has true administrative support or if teachers who choose not to implement or accept a new practice do so with their administrators' quiet support. We have all had those administrators who told us that we are supposed to be engaging in a particular practice (wink, wink, nudge, nudge), and we got the hint that if the superintendent or someone similar asks us, we knew the correct response. We also knew we didn't actually have to go any further than that.

For co-teaching to be accepted in a school, and for it to be implemented with integrity in order to achieve valid and positive outcomes, administrators must recognize those actions they can take to support co-teaching. What can be done to demonstrate to educators, parents, and students that this is a service delivery option with merit and that it deserves to be fully integrated into the fabric of an inclusive school? These actions include understanding the nature of co-teaching, providing guidance in the logistics of co-teaching, and ensuring that best practices are being utilized in co-planning, co-instructing, and co-assessing for the benefit of all children. They also include celebrating those individuals who are succeeding at implementing new approaches and sharing those successes with the community at large.

I have been working frequently with the State of West Virginia over the past few years. Dr. Lynn Boyer, state executive director of special programs, recognized the importance of involving administrators in their statewide efforts at improving co-teaching practices. She hired me to come out and conduct multiple staff development trainings for administrators throughout the state. In addition, the state department personnel have worked tirelessly to create publications, Web site information, presentations, and new policies to disseminate best practice information on co-teaching. Recently I completed a statewide survey of the co-teachers (Murawski, Boyer, Melchiorre, & Atwill, 2009). With 2,700 co-teachers reporting, one of the most notable results we found was that 85 percent of those co-teachers stated that their administrators supported or greatly supported their co-teaching efforts. Eighty-five percent! To me, that truly demonstrates the efforts made by the state department to include administrators in this process have been successful. While there is still much work to be done, at least we know that we are indeed including all key individuals as we move forward. Let's hope this focus and support continues!

Administrators should continually remind themselves of the five keys critical to the positive creation, implementation, and maintenance of a co-teaching program. Copy the card in Figure 17.1 and keep it posted in your office or share it with other administrators.

Five Keys to Establishing a Co-Teaching Program

1. Know what co-teaching is and when it is needed.
2. Recognize that co-teaching is a marriage and you are the matchmaker.
3. Make scheduling a priority.
4. Planning is critical.
5. Monitor success, give feedback, and ensure evidence-based practice.

Figure 17.1 Administrative EZ Reference

SOURCE: Murawski, W. W. (2008b).

If you are interested in continuing to build your co-teaching program, involve your stakeholders and assess your collaborative efforts. K. Wiggins and Damore (2006) provide a rubric that identifies three distinct levels of development—initial, emerging, and effective—related to the elements of collaboration. While their rubric is not specific to co-teaching, the elements they measure (i.e., positive attitude, team process, professional development, leadership, resources, and benefits) are certainly crucial to the success of any collaborative program.

Consider creating a Co-Teaching Improvement Education Plan (Co-Teaching IEP) for your school site, such as that provided in Figure 17.2. This will resemble an IEP in nature. Your first step is to determine where you are currently in terms of co-teaching. Is it happening at all? Just in a few pockets of the school? Is it considered successful? If so, by whom? Is there agreement? If not, why not? Be sure to come to an agreement regarding your present level of performance as it relates to inclusion, collaboration, and specifically co-teaching at your site. You want inclusion and collaboration to be embraced schoolwide, rather than the pet project of one or two teachers. What you *don't* want is to overhear a teacher say, "We had a great inclusion program . . . but she left."

The second step is to determine your goals: What is it you want to see happen this year? Next year? In five or 10 years? Do you as the administrator have the same goals as your teachers, parents, and students? If not, why not? How do they differ and how are they similar? Can you come to a consensus? Once a focus group of stakeholders has identified these goals, bring them to your students, parents, faculty, and staff to make sure the goals are embraced by the larger community as well.

Assessing Co-Teaching Effectiveness

Strategies for the Program Level

It is always important to assess and evaluate what is working and what is not working in order to determine how better to improve. All individuals engaged in the co-teaching process need to be involved in the creation of a co-teaching individualized education program (IEP). The co-teaching IEP would allow participants and observers to determine the following:

1. What is our current status in terms of co-teaching? What is working? What are our barriers? This is our *present level of performance*.

2. Where do we want to be and what do we want to occur over time? This is where we determine our *goals* and our *timelines*.

3. How do we intend on getting to our goals? These become our *benchmarks* and *activities for improvement*.

Administrators who want to support co-teaching success need to have the correct vision, skills, incentives, resources, and action planning (Thousand, Villa, & Nevin, 2006a). They need to be engaged in the creation, maintenance, and improvement of the co-teaching program, being sure to address those five most important keys to success (Murawski, 2008b).

The importance of data collection cannot be emphasized enough. Since the No Child Left Behind Act (NCLB), schools have emphasized "evidence-based practice." Thus, it is not sufficient for co-teachers to say, "Yes, we planned together." Instead they will need to be able to produce evidence of that planning. Lessons should be clearly co-planned, classes should be clearly co-taught, and learning should be clearly co-assessed. It is the administrator's job to oversee each of these activities to provide teachers with the support and feedback they need to improve their attitudes, their skills, and their results.

RESOURCES FOR ADMINISTRATORS TO HELP ASSESS CO-TEACHING

- Wilson, G. L. (2005). "This doesn't look familiar: A supervisor's guide to observing co-teaching." *Intervention in School and Clinic, 40*(5), 271–275.

- Thousand, J. S., Villa, R. A., & Nevin, A. I. (2006, May). "What special education administrators need to know about co-teaching." *In CASE Newsletter, 47*(6), 1–3, 5.

- Murawski, W., & Lochner, W. (2007). *Co-Teaching Solution System* (CTSS) Observation System. Available at www.coteachsolutions.com.

- Murawski, W., & Carter, E. (2008). *The role of the administrator in supporting co-teaching: Staff development module*. Available at www.2TeachLLC.com.

Figure 17.2 Creating a Co-Teaching IEP for the School

SOURCE: Murawski, W. W. (2008a).

A successful co-teaching program at our school will

- Involve ☐ all ☐ most ☐ some ☐ a few of our special education teachers and staff
- Involve ☐ all ☐ most ☐ some ☐ a few of our general education teachers and staff
- Involve ☐ all ☐ most ☐ some ☐ a few of our special education students
- Involve ☐ all ☐ most ☐ some ☐ a few of our general education students

- What would a quality co-teaching program look like for our students? _____
  _____
  _____

- What would a quality co-teaching program look like for our teachers? _____
  _____
  _____

Figure 17.3 Defining Our Terms for Successful Co-Teaching

Finally, identify the steps you will need to take, the resources you will need, and the time frame that will be required to meet your goals. Based on this information, what goals are likely and which ones appear lofty? Who needs to be involved to ensure success? By what measure will you be identifying success? Use the questions in Figure 17.3 to guide your conversation regarding success.

Please don't forget my earlier caution about "baby steps." Building a quality co-teaching program takes time and both top-down and bottom-up support (McLesky & Waldron, 2002). Let your successful co-teaching teams share the benefits they experienced with others at your school and in your district; encourage them to present at conferences or publish action-research articles on their experiences. Work out the issues related to scheduling and planning time with a pilot group. Once you have a solid foundation, begin to grow your program and watch as other educators ask to be a part. Be selective but always supportive. Above all, remind yourself and others that the purpose of everything we are doing in schools—including co-teaching—is about the *kids*. We collaborate for our students' welfare and success. Their changing and diverse needs are why we are changing our methods of instruction. It is our students that make our work in schools necessary and worthwhile. And it is our students who will recognize—and often let us know outright—if we are successful or not in these endeavors.

Ultimately, everything we do in schools, including co-teaching, is to benefit the ***kids.***

Appendix

Keeping the Honeymoon Going

RESOURCES TO KEEP ■ FRESH AND MOTIVATED

Every couple has a time when they go through a rough, or dry, patch. A time when the relationship feels like there is nothing new or different. While I am definitely a proponent of keeping teaching teams together over the space of a few years so they can really get to know one another and hone their co-teaching skills, it is not healthy for any one teacher or teaching team to get complacent in their teaching. We need to always challenge ourselves to move with the times, to improve, to encourage one another, and to recognize that students have ever-changing needs. Too often, however, the common complaint is, "We've got no time for that. We are barely keeping our heads above water so when we have the opportunity to use materials or lessons we used last year (or for the last 20 years, in some cases), we do it."

Luckily for us all, there's the Internet. What did teachers do before it? I really don't know. The Net provides teachers with so many ways to learn, improve, and share with one another so that we are not reinventing the wheel every time we teach or plan. I have done some preliminary searching to save you some time, but I do strongly suggest that you both challenge each other regularly to find new, different, and exciting teaching ideas, strategies, materials, and technologies. Following are some Web sites I have found helpful over time. *Please, keep in mind that sites do change, and if some of these addresses no longer work, I apologize. Don't use the excuse of a nonworking site to stop looking for strategies for improvement.* Now's the time to surf the Web! Also, there are so many Web sites available that provide excellent resources that I could not include them all. If you find more that you think are especially useful, please let me know about them and definitely share them among your colleagues at school. Collaboration is the name of the game, and these Web sites will certainly aid you in your efforts to include, collaborate, differentiate, teach, guide, inspire, and avoid burning out while doing it all.

Sites Related to Disability and Inclusion

Web Sites	Description
www.inclusion.com	Workshops, books, media, and links
www.paulakluth.com	Articles, resources, and links related to inclusive schooling, especially for children with autism
www.uni.edu/coe/inclusion	University of Northern Iowa inclusion site
www.inclusive-solutions.com	Services, resources, links, and materials
www.inclusiveschools.org	Inclusive Schools Network, a Web-based resource on inclusion
www.landlockedfilms.com	Videos and documentaries related to disabilities
www.kidstogether.org	Information and resources on disabilities
www.disabilitysolutions.org	Resources for individuals and families with Down syndrome
www.disabilityisnatural.com	Kathie Snow's Web site with resources, materials, and staff development
www.thenthdegree.com	T-shirts, signs, pins, etc. related to inclusion
www.wrightslaw.com	Web site on laws and policies related to disabilities
www.marilynfriend.com	Dr. Marilyn Friend's Web site with books, videos, etc. related to inclusion/collaboration
www.tash.org	International organization for persons with severe disabilities and their families
www.cec.sped.org	Council for Exceptional Children, the largest international organization related to disabilities
www.tsa-usa.org	Tourette Syndrome Association Web site
www.ldanatl.org	Learning Disability Association national Web site
www.ncld.org	National Center on Learning Disabilities Web site
www.ldonline.org	Resources for working with individuals with Learning Disabilities
www.geocities.com/SEN_resources	Special education needs resources site
www.forumoneducation.org	Information and videos on inclusive education
www.aft.org/psrp/careeredpara.htm	Information for paraprofessionals in education
www.nichcy.org	National Dissemination Center for Children with Disabilities
www.nrcld.org	National Research Center on Learning Disabilities

Sites to Help Plan Differentiated Lessons

Web Sites	Description
www.edhelper.com	Games, units, lessons, and printables
www.writedesignonline.com/organizers	All kinds of graphic organizers to download
www.allkindsofminds.org	Lessons, staff development, and resources related to neurodevelopmental constructs and different learning profiles
www.azpromisingpractices.com	Arizona Department of Education Web site, links to teaching tools and lesson plans
wvde.state.wv.us/teach21	West Virginia Department of Education Web site, lessons, instructional guides, etc. related to 21st-century technology and skills
www.rtinetwork.org	RTI Network, RTI resources and links
www.jimwrightonline.com/php/rti/rti_wire.php	RTI Wire, RTI resources and info
www.ala.org/gwstemplate.cfm?section=great websites&template=/cfapps/gws/default.cfm	Great Web sites for kids
www.internet4classrooms.com/di.htm	Information on differentiated instruction, learning styles, multiple iIntelligences
www.teachervision.fen.com	Teacher lessons, printables, and more
www.thegateway.org	Gateway to 21st-century skills and lessons
www.ala.org/ala/aasl/schlibrariesandyou/ k12students/k12students.cfm	American Librarians Association, ask a librarian almost anything
www.ipl.org/youth/projectguide	Guides for science projects and fairs
www.un.org/Pubs/CyberSchoolBus	History, international and current events
www.sitesforteachers.com	Hundreds of teacher Web sites listed
www.abcteach.com	Tons of ideas and printables
www.funbrain.com	Tons of ideas, games, and printables
www.aplusmath.com	Math related games and lessons
www.k12.aleks.com	Online tutoring in subject area content
www.askjeeves.com	Find just about anything

(Continued)

Sites to Help Plan Differentiated Lessons (Continued)

Web Sites	*Description*
www.nationalgeographic.com	*National Geographic videos, information, maps, etc.*
www.sparknotes.com	*Study Guides for literature and more*
www.specialneedsinmusic.com	*Helpful lessons for students who struggle in music*
www.lessonplancentral.com	*Tons of lessons, Web links, ideas and more*
www.timesaversforteachers.com	*Some cost but many helpful forms*
www.chem4kids.com, www.physics4kids.com, www.biology4kids.com, www.geography4kids.com, www.cosmos4kids.com, and www.numbernut.com	*Help make different content accessible*
www.teachplanet.net	*Printables, lessons,and links to other content sites*
www.tolearnenglish.com	*For English language earners*
www.math-worksheet.org	*Hundreds of free math worksheets*
www.fctd.info	*Helpful resource on assistive technology and families*
www.historyforkids.org	*Excellent resource for history information and links*
www.dy-regional.k12.ma.us/wixon/hotlist_ancient_civ.htm	*Impressive source of information and links related to ancient civilizations*
www.2TeachLLC.com	*Dr. Wendy Murawski's Web site for professional development resources and includes free co-teaching lesson database*
www.co-teachsolutions.com	*Free 14 day trial of co-teaching software, CTSS Teachers' Toolbox and Observation System*
www.pent.ca.gov	*California Positive Environments Network of Trainers, behavior staff development*
www.pbis.org	*National Technical Assistance Center on Positive Behavior Interventions and Supports*
www.tolerance.org	*Helpful for teachers and students to learn about tolerance issues*
www.teachkind.org	*Humane education materials and resources on , social justice*
www.stopbullyingnow.hrsa.gov	*Resources for teachers and students to stop bullying in schools*

References

Acrey, C., Johnstone, C., & Milligan, C. (2005). Using Universal Design to unlock the potential for academic achievement of at-risk learners. *Teaching Exceptional Children, 38*(2), 22–31.

Adams, L., & Cessna, K. (1993). Metaphors of the co-taught classroom. *Preventing School Failure, 37,* 28–31.

Adams, L., Cessna, K., & Friend, M. (1993). *Colorado assessment of co-teaching* (CO-ACT). Denver: Colorado Department of Education.

Alper, S., Schloss, P. J., Etscheidt, S. K., & MacFarlane, C. A. (1995). *Inclusion: Are we abandoning or helping students?* Thousand Oaks, CA: Corwin.

Austin, V. A. (2001). Teachers' beliefs about co-teaching. *Remedial and Special Education, 22,* 245–256.

Bahamonde, C., & Friend, M. (1999). Teaching English language learners: A proposal for effective service delivery through collaboration and co-teaching. *Journal of Educational and Psychological Consultation, 10*(1), 1–24.

Barley, Z., Lauer, P. A., Arens, S. A., Apthorp, H. S., Englert, K. S., Snow, D., & Akiba, M. (2002). *Helping at-risk students meet standards: A synthesis of evidence-based classroom practices.* Aurora, CO: Mid-continent Research for Education and Learning.

Batshaw, M. L., Pellegrino, L., & Roizen, N. J. (2007). *Children with disabilities* (6th ed.). Baltimore: Paul H. Brookes.

Bauwens, J., & Hourcade, J. J. (1997). Cooperative teaching: Pictures of possibilities. *Intervention in School and Clinic, 33*(2), 81–85, 89.

Bauwens, J., & Hourcade, J. J., & Friend, M. (1989). Cooperative teaching: A model for general and special education integration. *Remedial and Special Education, 10*(2), 17–22.

Beninghof, A. (2008). Presentation entitled *Co-teaching that works: Effective strategies for working together in today's inclusive classrooms (grades K–12).* Bureau of Education and Research: Seattle, WA.

Benjamin, A. (2002). *Differentiated instruction: A guide for middle and high school teachers.* Larchmont, NY: Eye on Education, Inc.

Bess, J. L., and Associates (2000). *Teaching alone, teaching together: Transforming the structure of teams for teaching.* San Francisco: Jossey-Bass.

Bigge, J. L., Stump, C. S., Spagna, M. E., & Silberman, R. K. (1999). *Curriculum, assessment, and instruction for students with disabilities.* Pacific Grove, CA: Wadsworth Publishing.

Boe, E. E., Cook, L. H., & Sunderland, R. J. (2008). Teacher turnover: Examining exit attrition, teaching area transfer, and school migration. *Exceptional Children, 75*(1), 7–31.

Boscardin, M. L. (2005). The administrative role in transforming secondary schools to support inclusive evidence-based practices. *American secondary Education, 33*(3), 21–32.

Bottge, B. A., Heinrichs, M., Mehta, Z., & Hung, Y. (2002). Weighing the benefits of anchored math instruction for students with disabilities in general education classes. *Journal of Special Education, 35,* 186–200.

Boudah, D. J., Schumaker, J. B., & Deshler, D. D. (1997). Collaborative instruction: Is it an effective option for inclusion in secondary classrooms? *Learning Disability Quarterly, 20*(4), 293–315.

Bouris, R., Creel, H., & Stortz, B. (1998). Improving student motivation in secondary mathematics by the use of cooperative learning. *Master's Action Research Project, Saint Xavier University and IRI/Skylight*. Retrieved June 20, 2008, from http://www.eric.ed.gov

Bowe, F. (2005). *Making inclusion work*. Columbus, OH: Pearson.

Brimijoin, K., Marquisee, E., & Tomlinson, C. A. (2003). Using data to differentiate instruction. *Educational Leadership, 60*(5), 70–73.

Broderick, A., Mehta-Parekh, H., & Reid, K. D. (2005). Differentiating instruction for disabled students in inclusive classrooms. *Theory Into Practice, 44*(3), 194–202.

Burstein, N., Sears, S., Wilcoxen, A., Cabello, B., & Spagna, M. (2004). Moving toward inclusive practices. *Remedial and Special Education, 25,* 104–105.

Calhoon, M. B., & Fuchs, L. S. (2003). The effects of peer-assisted learning strategies and curriculum-based measurement on the mathematics performance of secondary students with disabilities. *Remedial and Special Education, 24,* 235–245.

Carbonaro, W. J., & Gamoran, A. (2002). The product of achievement inequality in high school English. *American Educational Research Journal, 39,* 801–827.

Carroll, D. (2001). Considering paraeducator training, roles, and responsibities. *Teaching Exceptional Children, 34*(2), 60–66.

Choate, J. S. (Ed). (2004). *Successful inclusive teaching: Proven ways to detect and correct special needs* (4th ed.). San Francisco: Pearson.

Chopra, R. V., Sandoval-Lucero, E., Aragon, L., Bernal, C., Berg de Balderas, H., & Carroll, D. (2004). The paraprofessional role of connector. *Remedial and Special Education, 25,* 219–231.

Cohen, D. K., Raudenbush, S. W., & Ball, D. L., (2003). Resources, instruction, and research. *Educational evaluation and policy analysis, 25,* 119–142.

Conderman, G., Bresnahan, V., & Pedersen, T. (2009). *Purposeful co-teaching: Real cases and effective strategies*. Thousand Oaks, CA: Corwin.

Conderman, G., Johnston-Rodriguez, S., & Hartman, P. (2009). Communicating and collaborating in co-taught classrooms. *TEACHING Exceptional Children Plus, 5*(5) Article 3. Retrieved August 14, 2009, from http://escholarship.bc.edu/education/tecplus/vol5/iss5/art3.

Cook, L., & Friend, M. (1995). Co-teaching: Guidelines for creating effective practices. *Focus on Exceptional Children, 28*(3), 1–12.

Cook, L. & Friend, M. (2007). *Interactions: Collaboration Skills for School Professionals* (5th ed.). Boston: Allyn & Bacon.

Corley, M. A. (2005). Differentiated instruction adjusting to the needs of all learners. *Focus on Basic, 7*(C), 13–16.

Correa, V. I., Jones, H. A., Thomas, C. C., & Morsink, C. V. (2005). *Interactive teaming: Enhancing programs for students with special needs* (4th ed.). Columbus, OH: Pearson-Merrill Prentice Hall.

Cross, L., & Walker-Knight, D. (1997). Inclusion: Developing collaborative and cooperative school communities. *Educational Forum, 61*(3), 269–77.

Damer, L. K. (2001). Inclusion and the law. *Music Educators Journal, 87*(4), 19–22.

DeBoer, A., & Fister, S. (1995). *Working together: Tools for collaborative teaching*. Longmont, CO: Sopris West.

Dieker, L. A. (1998). Rationale for co-teaching. *Social Studies Review, 37*(2), 62–65.

Dieker, L. A. (2001). What are the characteristics of "effective" middle and high school co-taught teams? *Preventing School Failure, 46*(1), 14–23.

Dieker, L. A. (2004). *The co-teaching lesson plan book: Academic year version* (3rd ed.). Whitefish Bay, WI: Knowledge by Design.

Dieker, L. A. (2007). *Demystifying secondary inclusion: Powerful school-wide and classroom strategies*. Port Chester, NY: Dude Publishing, National Professional Resources.

Dieker, L. (2008). *Urban Collaboration Leadership Institute*. [Unpublished paper.] Newton, MA: Education Development Center.

Dieker, L. (2009). Urban collaboration leadership institute. Newton, MA: Education Development Center. Unpublished paper.

Dieker, L. A., & Barnett, C. A. (1996). Effective co-teaching. *Teaching Exceptional Children, 29*(1), 5–7.

Dieker, L. A., & Murawski, W. W. (2003). Co-teaching at the elementary level: Unique issues, current trends, and suggestions for success. *The High School Journal, 86*(4), 1–13.

Dieker, L. A., & Murawski, W. W. (2005, June). *Classrooms for Excellence*. Presentation to Baldwin County, Alabama teachers and administrators.

Downing, J. A. (2008). *Including students with severe and multiple disabilities in typical classrooms: Practical strategies for teachers* (3rd ed.). Baltimore: Paul H. Brookes.

Downing, J. E., Ryndak, D. L., & Clark, D. (2000). Paraeducators in inclusive classrooms: Their own perceptions. *Remedial and Special Education, 21*, 171–181.

Emmer, E. T., Evertson, C., & Worsham, M. E. (2002). *Classroom management for elementary teachers* (6th ed.). Boston: Allyn & Bacon.

Fattig, M. L., & Taylor, M. T. (2008). *Co-teaching in the differentiated classroom: Successful collaboration, lesson design and classroom management (grades 5–12)*. San Francisco: Jossey-Bass.

Fennick, E. (2001). Co-teaching an inclusive curriculum for transition. *Teaching Exceptional Children, 33*(6), 60–66.

Fennick, E., & Liddy, D. (2001). Responsibilities and preparation for collaborative teaching: Co-teachers' perspectives. *Teacher Education and Special Education, 24*, 229–240.

Flores, S. (2007). *Co-planning for success: Effective strategies for today's co-taught classrooms*. Unpublished Master's thesis. California State University, Northridge.

Foley, R. M., & Mundschenk, N. A. (1997). Collaboration activities and competencies of secondary school special educators: A national survey. *Teacher Education and Special Education, 20*, 47–60.

French, N. K. (2002). Maximize paraprofessional services for students with learning disabilities. *Intervention in School And Clinic, 38*(1), 50–55.

Friedman Narr, R., Murawski, W. W., & Spencer, S. (2007, Spring). Fostering independence in students with special needs. *The Ladder*, pp. 9–10.

Friend, M. (2000). Myths and misunderstanding about professional collaboration. *Remedial and Special Education, 21*, 130–132.

Friend, M., & Cook, L. (2003). *Interactions: Collaboration skills for school professionals* (4th ed.). White Plains, NY: Longman. (Instructor's manual by W. Murawski, S. Kurtts, L. Cook, & M. Friend)

Friend, M., & Cook, L. (2007). *Interactions: Collaboration skills for school professionals* (5th ed.). White Plains, NY: Longman.

Friend, M., & Pope, K. L. (2005). Creating schools in which all students can succeed. *Kappa Delta Pi Record, 41*(2), 56–61.

Fuchs, D., & Fuchs, L. S. (2001). Responsiveness-to-interventions: A blueprint for practitioners, policymakers, and parents. *Teaching Exceptional Children, 38*(1), 57–61.

Fuchs, D., Fuchs, L. S., Thompson, A., Svenson, E., Yen, L., Al Otaiba, S., Yang, N., et al. (2001). Peer-assisted learning strategies in reading: Extensions for kindergarten, first grade, and high school. *Remedial and Special Education, 22*, 15–21.

Fuchs, L. (n.d.). *Mathematics intervention at the secondary prevention level of a multi-tier prevention system: Six key principles*. (Retrieved August 30, 2008, at http://www.rtinetwork .org/Essential/TieredInstruction/Tier2/ar/MathIntervention

Fullan, M.G. (1993). Why teachers must become change agents. *Educational Leadership, 50*(6).

Gaines, A. (2006). *Academic outcomes for students with disabilities educated in co-taught secondary mathematics classes.* Unpublished master's thesis. California State University, Northridge.

Gainott, H. (1995). *Teacher and child: A book for parents and teachers.* New York: Collier.

Gardner, H. (2006). *Multiple intelligences: New horizons in theory and practice.* New York: Basic Books.

Gardner, R., Cartledge, G., Seidl, B., Woolsey, M. L., Schley, G. S., & Utley, C.A. (2001). Mt. Olivet after-school program: Peer-mediated interventions for at-risk students. *Remedial and Special Education, 22,* 22–23.

Garrison, W. M. (2004). Profiles of classroom practices in U.S. public schools. *School Effectiveness and School Improvement, 15*(3), 377–406.

Gartin, B. C., Murdick, N. L., Imbeau, M., & Perner, D. E. (2002). *How to use differentiated instruction with students with developmental disabilities in the general education classroom.* Arlington, VA: Council for Exceptional Children.

Gately, S. E., & Gately, F. J. (2001). Understanding co-teaching components. *Teaching Exceptional Children, 33*(4), 40–47.

George, P. S. (2005). A rationale for differentiating instruction in the regular classroom. *Theory Into Practice, 44*(3), 185–193.

Gerber, P. J., & Popp, P. A. (1999). Consumer perspectives on the collaborative teaching model: Views of students with and without LD and their parents. *Remedial and Special Education, 20,* 288–296.

Giangreco, M. (1998). *Ants in my pants.* Minnetonka, MN: Peytral Publications.

Giangreco, M. F. (2003). Working with paraprofessionals. *Educational Leadership, 61*(2), 50–53.

Giangreco, M. F. (2007). *Absurdities and realities of special education: The complete digital set[CD].* Thousand Oaks, CA: Corwin.

Giangreco, M. F., Baumgart, D. M., & Doyle, M. B. (1995). How inclusion can facilitate teaching and learning. *Intervention in School and Clinic, 30,* 273–278.

Giangreco, M. F., & Broer, S. M. (2005). Questionable utilization of paraprofessionals in inclusive schools: Are we addressing symptoms or causes? *Focus on Autism and Other Developmental Disabilities, 20*(1), 10–26.

Giangreco, M. F., & Doyle, M. B. (2002). Students with disabilities and paraprofessional supports: Benefits, balance, and band-aids. *Focus on Exceptional Children, 34*(7), 1–12.

Giangreco, M. F., Edelman, S. W., & Broer, S. M. (2003). School-wide planning to improve paraeducator supports. *Exceptional Children, 70*(1), 63–79.

Giangreco, M. F., Edelman, S. W., Broer, S. M., & Doyle, M. B. (2001). Paraprofessional support of students with disabilities: Literature from the past decade. *Exceptional Children, 68,* 45–64.

Giangreco, M. F., Edelman, S., Luiselli, T. E., & MacFarland, S. Z. (1997). Helping or hovering? Effects of instructional assistant proximity on students with disabilities. *Exceptional Children, 64*(1), 7–18.

Giangreco, M. F., Edelman, S., MacFarland, & Luiselli, T. E. (1997). Attitudes about educational and related services provision for students with deaf-blindness and multiple disabilities. *Exceptional Children, 63*(3), 329-342.

Ginsberg, M. B. (2005). Cultural diversity, motivation & differentiation. *Theory Into Practice, 44*(3). 218–225.

Glod, M. (2008, May 2). Study Questions "No Child" Acts Reading Program, Lauded Program Fails to Improve Test Scores, *Washington Post,* A01.

Greenwood, C. R., Arreaga-Mayer, C., Utley, C. A., Gavin, K. M., & Terry, B. J. (2001). Class-wide peer tutoring management system: Applications with elementary-level English language learners. *Remedial and Special Education, 22,* 34–47.

Griffin-Shirley, N., & Matlock, D. (2004). Paraprofessionals speak out: A survey. *RE:view, 36*(3), 127–136.

Grossman, P., Wineburg, S., & Woolworth, S. (2001). Toward a theory of teacher community. *Teachers College Record, 103*(6), 942–1012. Retrieved July 31, 2008, from ERIC database.

Hallowell, E. M., & Ratey, J. J. (1995). *Driven to distraction: Recognizing and coping with Attention Deficit Disorder from childhood through adulthood.* New York: Simon & Schuster.

Haycock, K. (1998). Good teaching matters . . . a lot: How well qualified teachers can close the gap. *Thinking K-16, 3*(2), 3–14.

Hirsh, S. (2005). Professional development and closing the achievement gap. *Theory Into Practice* (Winter). Retrieved July 31, 2008, from http://findarticles.com/p/articles

Hohenbrink, J., Johnston, M., & Westhoven, L. (1997). Collaborative teaching of a social studies methods course: Intimidation and change. *Journal of Teacher Education, 48*(4), 293–301.

Hoover, J. J., & Patton, J. R. (2004). Differentiating standards-based education for students with diverse needs. *Remedial and Special Education, 25,* 74–78.

Hourcade, J. J., & Bauwens, J. (2001). Cooperative teaching: The renewal of teachers. *The Clearing House, 74,* 242–247.

Hourcade, J. J., & Bauwens, J. (2003). *Cooperative teaching: Rebuilding and sharing the schoolhouse* (2nd ed.). Austin, TX: Pro-Ed.

Huber, J. J. (2005). What works for me: Collaborative units for addressing multiple grade levels. *Intervention in School and Clinic, 40*(5).

Hughes, C. E., & Murawski, W. W. (2001). Lessons from another field: Applying co-teaching strategies to gifted education. *Gifted Child Quarterly, 45*(3), 195–204.

Hunt, P., Alwell, M., Farron-Davis, F., & Goetz, L. (1996). Creating socially supportive environments for fully included students who experience multiple disabilities. *JASH, 21*(2), 53–71.

Idol, L., Paolucci-Whitcomb, P., & Nevin, A. (1986). *Collaborative consultation.* Rockville, MD: Aspen Publishers.

Jackson, C. W., & Turnbull, A. P. (2004). Impact of deafness on family life: A review of the literature. *The Journal of Early Childhood Special Education,* (2), 167–184.

Jitendra, A, K., Edwards, L. L., Choutka, C. M., & Treadway, P. S. (2002). A collaborative approach to planning in the content areas for students with learning disabilities: Accessing the general curriculum. *Learning Disabilities Research and Practice, 17*(4), 252–267.

Johnson, D. W., & Johnson, R. T. (1999). *Learning together and alone: Cooperative, competitive, and individualistic learning.* Boston: Allyn & Bacon.

Jones, M. M., & Carlier, L. L. (1995). Creating inclusionary opportunities for learners with multiple disabilities: A team-teaching approach. *Teaching Exceptional Children, 27,* 23–27.

Kampwirth, T. J. (2006). *Collaborative consultation in the schools: Effective practices for students with learning and behavior problems* (3rd ed.). Columbus, OH: Pearson/Merrill Prentice Hall.

Katherman, H. (2005). Supervising co-teaching: Moving beyond a staffing arrangement. Retrieved August 26, 2008, at http://web.wm.edu/ttac/corner/2005novdec.htm

Katsiyannis, A., Yell, M. L., & Bradley, R. (2001). Reflections on the 25th anniversary of the Individuals with Disabilities Education Act. *Remedial and Special Education, 22,* 324–334.

Kauffman, J. M., Mostert, M. P., Trent, S.C., & Pullen, P. L. (2005). *Managing classroom behavior: A reflective case-based approach* (4th ed.). Boston: Allyn & Bacon.

Kavale, K. A., & Forness, S. R. (2000). History, rhetoric, and reality: Analysis of the inclusion debate. *Remedial and Special Education, 21,* 279–296.

Keefe, E. B., & Moore, V. (2004). The challenge of co-teaching in inclusive classrooms at the high school level: What the teachers told us. *American Elementary Education, 32*(30), 77–88.

Kim, A., Woodruff, A. L., Klein, C., & Vaughn, S. (2006). Facilitating co-teaching for literacy in general education classrooms through technology: Focus on students with learning disabilities. *Reading and Writing Quarterly, 22*(3), 269–291.

Koppang, A. (2004). Curriculum mapping: Building collaboration and communication. *Intervention in School and Clinic, 39*(3), 154–161.

Lamar-Dukes, P., & Dukes, C. (2005). Consider the roles and responsibilities of the inclusion support teacher. *Intervention in School and Clinic, 41*(1), 55–61.

Lipsky, D. K. (2005). Are we there yet? *Learning Disability Quarterly, 28*(2), 156–158.

Magiera, K. A., & Simmons, R. J. (2005). *The Magiera-Simmons quality indicator model of co-teaching.* Fredonia, NY: Excelsior Educational Service.

Magiera, K., Smith, C., Zigmond, N., & Gebauer, K. (2005). Benefits of co-teaching in secondary mathematics classes. *Teaching Exceptional Children, 37*(3), 20–24.

Marzano, R. J., Pickering, D. J., & Pollock, J. E. (2001). *Classroom instruction that works: Research-based strategies for increasing student achievement.* Alexandria, VA: Association for Supervision and Curriculum Development.

Mastropieri, M. A., & Scruggs, T. E. (2007). *The inclusive classroom: Strategies for effective instruction* (3rd ed.). Columbus, OH: Pearson/Merrill Prentice Hall.

Mastropieri, M. A., Scruggs, T. E., Graetz, J., Norland, J., Gardizi, W., & McDuffie, K. (2005). Case studies in co-teaching in the content areas: Successes, failures, and challenges. *Intervention in School and Clinic, 40*(5).

McLeod, J., Fisher, J., & Hoover, G. (2003) *The key elements of classroom management: Managing time and space, student behavior, and instructional strategies.* Alexandria, VA: Association of Supervision and Curriculum Development.

McLesky, J., & Waldron, N. L. (2002). School change and inclusive schools: Lessons learned from practice. *Phi Delta Kappan, 84,* 65–72.

McTighe, J., & Brown, J. (2005). Differentiated instruction and educational standards: Is détente possible? *Theory Into Practice, 44*(3), 234–244.

Miller, K. J., Wienke, W. D., & Savage, L. B. (2000). Elementary and middle/Flexible cooperative groups in co-taught mathematics. educator's pre and post training perceptions of ability to instruct students with disabilities. *Rural Education Quarterly, 19,* 3–14.

Müller, E., & Burdette, P. (2007). High school reform: Integration of special education. In Forum. Retrieved June 2009 from http://www.projectforum.org/docs/HighSchool Reform-IntegrationofSpecialEducation.pdf

Murata, R. (2002). What does team teaching mean? A case study of interdisciplinary teaming. *The Journal of Educational Research, 96*(2), 67–77.

Murawski, W. W. (2002a). Demystifying co-teaching. *The CARS+ Newsletter, 22*(3), 17–19.

Murawski, W. W. (2002b). Including co-teaching in a teacher preparation program: A vital addition. *Academic Exchange Quarterly, 6*(2), 113–116.

Murawski, W. W. (2003). School collaboration research: Successes and difficulties. *Academic Exchange Quarterly, 7*(3), 104–108.

Murawski, W. W. (2005a). Addressing diverse needs through co-teaching: Take "baby steps!" *Kappa Delta Pi Record, 41*(2), 77–82.

Murawski, W. W. (2005b). A glimpse into the inclusive classroom. *The Autism Perspective Magazine, 1*(2), 34–36.

Murawski, W. W. (2006). Student outcomes in co-taught secondary English classes: How can we improve? *Reading and Writing Quarterly, 22*(3), 227–247.

Murawski, W. W. (2008a). *Co-teaching for success: Effective strategies for working together in today's inclusive classrooms.* Bellevue, WA: Bureau of Education and Research.

Murawski, W. W. (2008b, September). Five keys to co-teaching in inclusive classrooms. *The School Administrator, 27.*

Murawski, W. W. (2009). *Collaborative Teaching in Secondary Schools: Making the Co-Teaching Marriage Work!* Thousand Oaks, CA: Corwin.

Murawski, W. W. (in press). *Chapter Three: Collaboration and Communication with Families. Working with families of children with special needs: Family and professional partnerships and roles.* with Nancy Sileo and Mary Anne Prater (Eds.). (Publication date 2010).

Murawski, W. W., Boyer, L., Melchiorre, B., & Atwill, K. (2009, April). *What is happening in co-taught classes? One state knows!* Presentation to American Educational Research Association (AERA), San Diego, CA.

Murawski, W. W., & Carter, E. (2008). *The role of the administrator in supporting co-teaching: Staff development module.* Winnetka, CA: 2 TEACH LLC

Murawski, W. W., & Dieker, L. A. (2004). Tips and strategies for co-teaching at the secondary level. *Teaching Exceptional Children, 36*(5), 52–58.

Murawski, W. W., & Flores, S. (2007). *Co-planning for success.* Staff Development Module. Winnetka, CA: 2 TEACH LLC.

Murawski, W. W., & Hughes, C. E. (2009). Response to intervention, collaboration, and co-teaching: A necessary combination for successful systemic change. *Preventing School Failure, 53*(4), 67–77.

Murawski, W. W., & Lochner, W. W. (2007). *Co-teaching solution system* (CTSS) [Software]. Shepherdstown, WV: Wide River Educational Consulting from http://www.coteachsolutions.com.

Murawski, W. W., & Sherman, B. (2007). *The role of the paraprofessional in the inclusive classroom.* Staff Development Module. Winnetka, CA: 2 TEACH LLC.

Murawski, W. W., & Swanson, H. L. (2001). A meta-analysis of co-teaching research: Where are the data? *Remedial and Special Education, 22,* 258–267.

National Association of Elementary School Principals. (2004). *Breaking ranks II: Strategies for leading high school reform.* Reston, VA: Author.

National Reading Panel. (2008). Reading First Downloaded on November 20, 2008, from http://www.ed.gov/programs/readingfirst/support/foundations.tml

Norris, D. M. (1997). *Teachers' perceptions of co-teaching in an inclusive middle school: A look at general and special education teachers working together with students with learning disabilities.* Unpublished dissertation. George Mason University, Fairfax, VA.

O'Rourke, I. (2007). Flexible cooperative groups in co-taught mathematics. Unpublished Master's thesis. California State University, Northridge.

Pickett, A. L., & Gerlach, K. (Eds.). (2003). *Supervising paraeducators in educational settings: A team approach* (2nd ed.). Austin, TX: Pro-Ed.

Pierce, R. L., & Adams, C. M. (2004). Tiered lessons: One way to differentiate mathematics. *Gifted Child Today, 27*(2), 58–65.

Pugach, M. C., & Johnson, L. J. (1995). A new framework for thinking about collaboration. In *Collaborative practitioners, collaborative schools* (pp. 27–43). Denver, CO: Love Publishing.

Pugach, M. C., & Wesson, C. L. (1995). Teachers' and students' views of team teaching of general education and learning-disabled students in two fifth-grade classes. *The Elementary School Journal, 95*(3), 279–295.

Purcell, J. H., & Leppien, J. H. (1998). Building bridges between general practitioners and educators of the gifted: A study of collaboration. *Gifted Child Quarterly, 42*(3), 172–181.

Rea, P. J. (2005). 20 ways to engage your administrator in your collaboration initiative. *Intervention in School and Clinic, 40*(5), 312–317.

Rea, P. J., McLaughlin, V. L., & Walther-Thomas, C. (2002). Outcomes for students with learning disabilities in inclusive and pull-out programs. *Exceptional Children, 72*(2), 203–222.

Renzaglia, A., Karvonen, M., Drasgow, E., & Stoxen, C. C. (2003). Promoting a lifetime of inclusion. *Focus on Autism and Other Developmental Disabilities, 18*(3), 140–149.

Salend, S. J. (2008). *Creating inclusive classrooms: Effective and reflective practices* (6th ed.). Upper Saddle River, NJ: Merrill Publishing.

Salend, S. J., Johansen, M., Mumper, J., Chase, A. S., Pike, K. M., & Dorney, J. A. (1997). Cooperative teaching: The voices of two teachers. *Remedial and Special Education, 18*, 3–11.

Scruggs, T. E., Mastropieri, M. A., & McDuffie, K. A. (2007). Co-teaching in inclusive classrooms: A meta-synthesis of qualitative research. *Exceptional Children, 73*, 392–416.

Sherman, B. B. (2007). *Ensuring collaboration and support of paraprofessionals in an inclusive setting.* Unpublished Master's thesis. California State University, Northridge.

Siegel, C. (2004). An ethnographic inquiry of cooperative learning implementation. *Journal of School Psychology, 43*(3), 219–239.

Sindelar, P. T., Shearer, D. K., Yendol-Hoppey, D., & Liebert, T. W. (2006). The sustainability of inclusive school reform. *Exceptional Children, 72*(3), 317–331.

Smith, T. E. C. (2005). IDEA 2004: Another round in the reauthorization process. *Remedial and Special Education, 26*, 314–319.

Snell, M. E., & Janney, R. (2000). *Teachers' Guides to Inclusive Practices: Collaborative Teaming.* Baltimore: Paul H. Brookes.

Sparks, D. (2000). Low incomes, high hurdles—Data and examples can explode old myths: An interview with Kati Hancock. *Journal of Staff Development, 21*(3), 37–40.

Sparks, D. (2003). Interview/Ron Ferguson: We care, therefore they learn. *Journal of Staff Development, 24*(4), 42–47.

Spencer, S. A. (2005). An interview with Dr. Lynne Cook and Dr. June Downing: The practicalities of collaboration in special education service delivery. *Intervention in School and Clinic, 40*(5).

Stanford, B. & Reeves, S. (2009). Making it happen: Using Differentiated Instruction, Retrofit framework, and Universal Design for Learning. *TEACHING Exceptional Children Plus, 5*(6) Article 4. Retrieved August 14, 2009, from http://escholarship .bc.edu/education/tecplus/vol5/iss6/art4

Stipek, D. E. P. (1988). *Motivation to learning.* Boston: Allyn & Bacon.

Struyk, L. R., Epstein, M. H., Bursuck, W., Polloway, E. A., McConeghy, J., & Cole, K. (1994). The homework, grading, and testing practices used by secondary schoolteachers for students with and without disabilities. *The Clearing House, 69*(1), 50–55.

Thousand, J. S., Villa, R. A., & Nevin, A. I. (2006). The many faces of collaborative planning and teaching. *Theory Into Practice, 45*(3), 239–248.

Thousand, J. S., Villa, R. A., & Nevin, A. I. (2006, May). What special education administrators need to know about co-teaching. *In CASE Newsletter, 47*(6), 1–3, 5.

Thousand, J. S., Villa, R. A., & Nevin, A. I. (2007). *Differentiating instruction: Collaborative planning and teaching for universally designed learning.* Thousand Oaks, CA: Corwin.

Tomlinson, C. A. (2000). Reconcilable differences? Standards-based teaching and differentiation. *Association for Supervision and Curriculum Development, 58*(1), 6–11.

Tomlinson, C. A. (2004). Sharing responsibility for differentiating instruction. *Roeper Review, 26*(4), 29–34.

Tomlinson, C. (2005). Quality curriculum and instruction for highly able students. *Theory into Practice, 44*(2), 160–166.

Tomlinson, C., & Allan, S. (2000). *Leadership for differentiation schools and classrooms.* Alexandria, VA: Association for Supervision and Curriculum Development.

Trautman, M. L. (2004). Preparing and managing paraprofessionals. *Intervention in School and Clinic, 39*(3), 131–138.

Trent, S. (1998). False starts and other dilemmas of a secondary general education collaborative teacher: A case study. *Journal of Learning Disabilities, 31,* 503–515.

Trent, S. C., Driver, B. L., Wood, M. H., Parrott, P. S., Martin, T. F., & Smith, W. G. (2003). Creating and sustaining a special education/general education partnership: A story of change and uncertainty. *Teaching and Teacher Education, 19*(4), 2003–219.

University of South Florida. Clearinghouse for Special Education Teaching Cases. Retrieved July 28, 2008, from http://cases.coedu.usf.edu/TCases/Thats.htm

Vaughn, S., & Bos, C. (2008). *Strategies for teaching students with learning and behavior problems* (7th ed.). Boston: Allyn & Bacon.

Villa, R. (2006, September) *Co-teaching and collaboration.* Presentation to teachers. San Bernardino, CA.

Villa, R. A., & Thousand, J. S. (2003). Making inclusive education work. *Educational Leadership, 61*(2), 19–23.

Villa, R. A., Thousand, J. S., & Nevin, A. I. (2007). *A guide to co-teaching: Practical tips for facilitating student learning* (2nd ed.). Thousand Oaks, CA: Corwin.

Villa, R. A., Thousand, J. S., Nevin, A. I., & Malgeri, C. (1996). Instilling collaboration for inclusive schooling as a way of doing business in public schools. *Remedial and Special Education, 17,* 169–181.

Walker, J. E., Shea, T. M., & Bauer, A. M. (2006). *Behavior management: A practical approach for educators* (9th ed.). Columbus, OH: Pearson/Merrill Prentice Hall.

Walsh. J. J. & Snyder, D. (1993, April). *Cooperative teaching: An effective model for all students.* Paper presented at the annual convention of the Council for Exceptional Children, San Antonio, TX. (ERIC Document Reproduction Service No. ED 361 930)

Walther-Thomas, C. S. (1997). Co-teaching experiences: The benefits and problems that teachers and principals report over time. *Journal of Learning Disabilities, 30,* 395–407.

Walther-Thomas, C., Korinek, L., McLaughlin, V., & Williams, B. (1999). *Collaboration for inclusive education: Developing successful programs.* Boston: Allyn & Bacon.

Ward, R. (2003). General educators' perceptions of effective collaboration with special educators: A focus group study. *Dissertation Abstracts International, 64*(03), 861A. (UMI NO. AA13083896)

Wasserman, L. (2008). A marriage made in math class. *Teacher Magazine, 2*(1), 17–19.

Weichel, W. A. (2001). An analysis of student outcomes on co-taught settings in comparison to other special education service delivery options for students with learning disabilities. *Dissertation Abstracts International, 62*(07), 2386. (UMI No. 3021407).

Weiner, H. M. (2003). Effective inclusion: Professional development in the context of the classroom. *Teaching Exceptional Children, 35*(6), 12–18.

Weiner, I., & Murawski, W. W. (2005). Schools attuned: A model for collaborative intervention. *Intervention in School and Clinic, 40*(5), 284–290.

Weinstein, C. S. (2003). *Elementary classroom management: Lessons learned from research and practice* (2nd ed.). San Francisco: McGraw-Hill.

Weiss, M. P. (2004). Co-teaching as a schoolhouse science: More questions than answers. *Learning Disabilities Research and Practice, 37*(3), 218–223.

Weiss, M. P., & Brigham, F. J. (2000). Co-teaching and the model of shared responsibility: What does the research support? In T. E. Scruggs & M. A. Mastropieri (Eds.), *Advances in learning and behavioral disabilities* (p. 217–245). Greenwich, CT: JAI Press.

Weiss, M., & Lloyd, J. W. (2002). Congruence between roles and actions of secondary special educators in co-taught and special education settings. *The Journal of Special Education, 36*(2), 58–68.

Weiss, M. P., & Lloyd, J. W. (2003). Conditions for co-teaching: Lessons from a case study. *Teacher Education and Special Education, 26,* 27–41.

Werts, M. G., Harris, S., Tillery, C. Y., & Roark, R. (2004). What parents tell us about paraeducators. *Remedial and Special Education, 25,* 232–239.

Wiggins, G., & McTighe, J. (2005). *Understanding by, design* (2nd ed.). Alexandria, VA: Association for Supervision and Curriculum Development.

Wiggins, K. C., & Damore, S. J. (2006). "Survivors" or "friends"? A framework for assessing effective collaboration. *Teaching Exceptional Children, 38*(5), 49–56.

Will, M. C. (1986). Educating children with learning problems: A shared responsibility. *Exceptional Children, 52*(5), 411–416.

Wilson, G. L. (2005). This doesn't look familiar! A supervisor's guide for observing co-teachers. *Intervention in School and Clinic, 40*(5).

Wischnowski, M. W., Salmon, S. J., & Eaton, K. (2004). Evaluating co-teaching as a means for successful inclusion of students with disabilities in a rural district. *Rural Special Education Quarterly, 23*(3), 3–14.

Wong, H. K., & Wong, R. T. (2004). *The first days of school: How to be an effective teacher.* Mountain View, CA: Harry K. Wong Publications.

Wormeli, R. (2003). *Day one and beyond: Practical matters for new middle-level teachers.* Portland, ME: Stenhouse Publishers.

Wormeli, R. (2004). *Differentiation: From planning to practices, grades 6–12.* Portland, ME: Stenhouse Publishers.

Wormeli, R. (2006). *Fair isn't always equal: Assessing and grading in the differentiated classroom.* Portland, ME: Stenhouse Publishers.

Yell, M. L., & Katsiyannis, A. (2004). Placing students with disabilities in inclusive settings: Legal guidelines and preferred practices. *Preventing School Failure, 49*(1), 28–35.

Zigmond, N. (2003). Where should students with disabilities receive special education services? Is one place better than another? *The Journal of Special Education, 27*(3), 193–199.

Zigmond, N. (2006). Reading and writing in co-taught secondary school social studies classrooms: A reality check. *Reading and Writing Quarterly, 22*(3), 249–267.

Zigmond, N., Magiera, K., & Matta, D. (2003, April). *Co-teaching in secondary schools: Is the instructional experience enhanced for students with disabilities?* Paper presented at the Annual CEC Conference, Seattle, WA.

Zigmond, N., & Matta, D. (2004). Value added of the special education teacher in secondary school co-taught classes. In T. E. Scruggs & M. A. Mastropieri (Eds.), *Advances in learning and behavioral disabilities.* (pp. 55–76). Greenwich, CT: JAI Press.

Index

Acrey, C., 246
Acronyms, 12 (figure)
Activities, disability awareness, 54–55 (figure)
Adams, C. M., 217
Adams, L., 238
Administrators
    articulating with secondary schools, 183
    building an effective program, 257–260
    communicating with, 81, 83 (figure)
    creating viable schedules, 174–183
    decision to use co-teaching, 62–65
    lack of support, 31
Allkindsofminds.org, 53
Alper, S., 14
Alternative teaching, 205–207, 208 (figure)
Americans with Disabilities Act (ADA), 246
Antiseptic bouncing, 131–132
Areas of expertise, 158
Assemblies, school, 154
Assessments
    importance of, 225, 226 (figure)
    long-term, 237–239
    needs, 98–99
    readiness for co-teaching, 57–58, 59–61
        (figure), 63, 107
    short-term, 236–237
    by standards, 233, 234–235 (figure)
    student grading in, 228–233
    of students, 38–39, 136–138, 227–233
    of teachers, 138–139, 235–239
Attendance procedures, 124
Attention deficit hyperactivity disorder
        (ADHD), 49
Auditory disabilities, 54 (figure)

Backwards planning, 158
Bad experiences, getting over, 49–50
Banked time, 153
Barley, Z., 34
Barriers
    to co-planning, 151–152
    to co-teaching, 30–31
Batshaw, M. L., 53
Bauer, A. M., 122
Bauwens, J., 24, 25
Behavior, student, 128–133, 134 (figure)
Behavior Management: A Practical Approach for
        Educators (Walker et al.), 122
Benefits
    to co-planning, 150
    to co-teaching, 28–29, 55–56
Benjamin, A., 214

Best practices, 87
    for differentiation, 217–219
Bigge, J. L., 225
Bos, C., 119
Bowe, F., 227
Boyer, L., 257
Bradley, R., 21
Broer, S. M., 32
Brown v. Board of Education, 17–18

Case studies, I Am Solely Responsible, 47–48
Cessna, K., 238
Chambers of Commerce, 96
Change, resistance to, 13
Child Find, 18
Children With Disabilities (Batshaw et al), 53
CHIME Institute, 3
Clark, D., 86
Class proportions, 177–179
Classroom Management for Elementary Teachers
        (Emmer et al.), 122
Classrooms
    analysis of inclusion, 60 (figure)
    caps on co-teaching, 110
    homework policies, 124–125
    in-class support, 23 (figure), 63
    instructional issues in, 135–136
    keeping appropriate proportions in,
        177–179
    learning climate in, 217–219
    management issues in, 121–133, 134
        (figure)
    materials policies, 125
    on-the-spot modifications in, 143
    "out-of-seat" policies, 125–126
    paraprofessionals in, 32–33, 86–89
    physical issues in, 119–121
    posting teacher names on, 119, 120 (photo)
    proactive management procedures in,
        122–128
    reactive responses in management of,
        128–133, 134 (figure)
    seating arrangements in, 121
    sharing materials in, 144–145, 146 (figure)
    sharing space in, 141–144
    teachers' personal space in, 120
    See also Schools
Classrooms for Excellence, 100–101
Class size caps, 110
Climate, learning, 217–219
Clustering, 178–179
Collaboration, 9–12

Collaboration for Inclusive Education:
Developing Successful Programs
(Walther-Thomas et al.), 119
Collaborative Planning and Collaborative
Teaching Videos: 2 Video Set, 85 (figure)
Commitment-phobic teachers, 13
Communication
   with administrators, 81, 83 (figure)
   with families, 92, 93 (figure), 94 (figure)
   with other educators, 81–84, 85–86 (figure)
   with stakeholders, 93–96, 97 (figure)
   with students, 89–92
   with support staff, 86–89
   tips, 45 (figure)
Community support, 93–96, 97 (figure)
Compacting, curriculum, 218
Components of co-teaching, 25–26, 27 (figure)
Comprehensive lesson planning, 168–170,
   170–172 (figure)
Computer skills, 154–155
Conflicts between co-teachers, 68–70
Consultation, 11 (figure)
Contact sheets, community stakeholder,
   97 (figure)
Contemporary timelines, 220–221
Content differentiation, 215–216
Continuum of service delivery options, 21–23
Cook, L., 3, 11, 22, 25, 26, 44, 103, 104, 194
Cooperative learning, 243
Co-planning, 35–36, 88–89, 110
   backwards, 158
   barriers to, 151–152
   benefits of, 150
   comprehensive lesson planning in,
      169–170, 171–172 (figure)
   creating time for, 152–156, 157 (figure), 179
   indirect support through, 149–150
   lesson plans, 166–168 (figure), 249 (figure)
   long-range, 156–158, 159–160 (figure)
   methods, 163–170, 171–172 (figure)
   with paraeducators, 150
   rationale for, 147–149
   recommendations for effective, 163–165
   short-range, 161–162, 163 (figure)
Corley, M. A., 214, 215
Corporate stakeholders, 95–96
Correa, V. I., 103
Co-teaching
   Alternative Teaching approach, 205–207,
      208 (figure)
   barriers to, 30–31
   benefits of, 28–29, 55–56
   caps on classes using, 110
   in the collaborative continuum, 22, 23 (figure)
   components of, 25–26, 27 (figure)
   conducted in same classroom at same time,
      33–34
   conducted with heterogeneous groups,
      34–35
   Cooperative Learning and, 243

data collection on, 252–253
defined, 11 (figure), 12–13, 24–26
determining whether to use, 62–65
do's and don'ts of, 31–41
effective, 26
ending, 253–257
ensuring parity in, 70–72, 73–74 (figure), 143
equality of teachers in, 32–33
frames of reference and, 42–48
getting over bad experiences with, 49–56
going in with eyes wide open to, 23–31
growing use of, 1, 2–4
identifying needs for, 78, 79–80 (figure)
incentives for, 111
in-class support versus, 23 (figure), 63–65
Internet resources for, 84, 85–86 (figure)
litmus test, 13 (figure)
maximizing the benefits of having two
   teachers in the classroom, 39–40
One Teach, One Support approach,
   195–197, 198 (figure)
Parallel Teaching approach, 198–200,
   201–202 (figure)
practical approaches to, 194–210, 211–212
   (figure)
professional development for, 50–52, 84, 85
   (figure), 255
Reading First and, 241–242
reflecting on progress and process in, 40–41
resources for, 261, 262–264
Response to Intervention (RTI) and, 247–248
role with other school-improvement
   initiatives, 240–241
self-assessments, 63, 107, 173 (figure)
setting roles and responsibilities in, 75–76,
   77 (photo)
Station Teaching approach, 202–203, 204
   (figure)
strategies for obtaining volunteers for,
   109–112, 113–115 (figure)
supervising, 251–252
support groups, 255
surveys on, 111–112, 113–115 (figure)
teacher actions during, 73–74 (figure)
teachers both assessing and evaluating
   student progress in, 38–39
teachers both engaged in substantive
   instruction in, 37–38
teachers planning for instruction together
   in, 35–36
Team Teaching approach, 209–210, 211–212
   (figure)
technology and, 243–245
terminology, 11 (figure), 64–65
Universal Design for Learning (UDL) and,
   14, 241, 246
videos, 84, 85 (figure)
worksheet for scheduling, 190–191 (figure)
See also Teachers
Co-Teaching Lesson Plan Book, 40, 154

Co-Teaching Solutions Systems, 85 (figure), 220, 233, 239
  co-planning and, 154–155, 156 (figure)
  data collection and, 253–254
Council for Exceptional Children, The (CEC), 85 (figure)
Curriculum differentiation, 215–217
Cutting edge schools, 87

Daily assessments, 236
Damore, S. J., 235, 258
Data collection, 252–253
DeBoer, A., 238
DeFur, S., 24
Designated Instructional Service (DIS) personnel, 111–112
Developmental disabilities, 54–55 (figure)
Dicken, P., 215–216
Dictation, peer, 224
Dieker, L.A., 3, 40, 57, 99, 100, 125, 152, 228, 238, 240
Differentiation
  best practices for, 217–219
  curriculum, 215–217
  defining, 213–215
  practical strategies for, 220–224
  readiness and, 214
Differentiation in Practice: A Resource Guide for Differentiating Curriculum, Grades K–5 (Tomlinson and Eidson), 119
Disability awareness activities, 54–55 (figure)
Do's and don'ts of co-teaching, 31–41
Downing, J. A., 86, 119
Doyle, M. B., 88, 150
Drasgow, E., 14
Driven to Distraction: Recognizing and Coping With Attention Deficit/Hyperactivity Disorder From Childhood Through Adulthood, (Hallowell and Ratey), 53
Dually certified teachers, 19
Dunn, L., 14

Education for All Handicapped Children Act (EAHCA), 6, 18
Education Trust, 84
Elementary and Elementary Education Act (ESEA), 18
Emmer, E. T., 122
English language learners, 243
Equality of teachers in co-teaching, 32–33
Etscheidt, S. K., 14
Evertson, C., 122
Expectations with schools that are successful with inclusion, 59–61 (figure)
Expertise, areas of, 158

Fair Isn't Always Equal: Assessing and Grading in the Differentiated Classroom (Wormeli), 228
Families, communication with, 92, 93 (figure), 94 (figure)

F.A.T. City, 53
Feedback, 219
First Days of School: How To Be An Effective Teacher, The (Wong and Wong), 119
Fisher, J., 122
Fister, S., 238
"Five Keys to Co-Teaching in the Inclusive Classroom, The," 253
Flores, S., 214, 217
Ford, G., 15
Forness, S. R., 14, 17
Frames of reference, 42–48, 148, 227
Free Appropriate Public Education (FAPE), 18, 21
French, N. K., 150
Friedman Narr, R., 22
Friend, M., 11, 24, 25, 26, 44, 84, 103, 104, 194, 238, 262
Fuchs, D., 247
Fuchs, L. S., 247

Gaines, A., 35
Gainott, H., 218
Gardner, H., 40, 132, 215, 218
Garrison, W. M., 35
Gartin, B. C., 215
Gately, F. J., 149, 235
Gately, S. E., 149, 235
General educators
  frames of reference, 43
  sharing co-teaching model with, 109
  surveys of, 113 (figure)
  See also Teachers
Gerlach, K., 86
Giangreco, M. F., 32, 88, 150, 206
Ginsberg, M. B., 215
Glorified aide status, avoiding, 74–75 (figure)
Goals
  individual team improvement, 103–106
  school-wide improvement, 98–101, 102 (figure)
Grading, student, 228–233
Granada Hills Charter High School, 3, 255
Grossman, P., 103

Hallowell, E. M., 53
HALO, 135, 228
Haycock, K., 84
Heterogeneous groups in co-teaching, 34–35
Hines, R., 228
Hirsch, S., 84
Homework, 124–125
Hoover, G., 122
Hourcade, J. J., 24
How to Co-Teach to Meet Diverse Student Needs, 85 (figure)
Hughes, C., 9, 10, 247, 248
Hunter, M., 151

I Am Solely Responsible case study, 47–48
Identification of needs for co-teaching, 78, 79–80 (figure)
Idol, L., 10
Imbeau, M., 215
Improvement goals, establishing, 98–101, 102 (figure)
Incentives for co-teaching, 111
In-class support, 23 (figure), 63–65
Including Students With Severe and Multiple Disabilities in Typical Classrooms (Downing), 119
Inclusion, 6–8, 10–11, 11 (figure)
    determining level of inclusiveness and, 58 (figure)
    expectations in schools that are successful with, 59–61 (figure)
    history and rationale of, 14–17
    laws related to, 1, 6–7, 8, 17–20
    principles of practices in, 16 (figure)
    research and texts on, 118–119
    self-assessment, 58 (figure)
Inclusion: Are We Abandoning or Helping Students? (Alper et al), 14
Inclusive Classroom: Strategies for Effective Instruction, The (Mastropieri and Scruggs), 119
Indirect support through co-planning, 149–150
Individualized education programs (IEPs), 14, 17, 18, 99, 196
    articulating with secondary schools about, 183
    classroom management and, 127
    grading and, 231
    meetings, 186, 187 (figure)
Individuals with Disabilities Education Act, 6, 15
    least restrictive environment (LRE) requirements, 21
Individuals with Disabilities Education Improvement Act, 1, 6–7, 8, 19, 21–22, 37, 50, 240
    definition of support staff, 86
    differentiation and, 213
Instructional issues, 135–136
Interactions: Collaboration Skills for School Professionals (Cook and Friend), 25, 26, 104, 138
Interest, student, 215
Internet resources for co-teaching, 84, 85–86 (figure)

Jackson, C. W., 92
Janney, R., 25
Job sharing, 11 (figure)
Johnson, L. J., 10
Johnstone, C., 246
Jones, H. A., 103

Karvonen, M., 14
Katherman, H., 251
Katsiyannis, A., 17, 18, 21
Kauffman, J. M., 122
Kavale, K. A., 14, 17
Key Elements of Classroom Management: Managing Time and Space, Student Behavior, and Instructional Strategies (McLeod et al), 122
Koppang, A., 158
Korinek, L., 119

Lavoie, R., 53
Learning
    climates, 217–219
    cooperative, 243
    disabilities, 55 (figure)
    styles, 215, 219–220
Least Restrictive Environment (LRE), 7, 11 (figure), 18–19
    communicating about, 93
    IDEA requirements, 21
Legislation, inclusion, 1, 6–7, 8, 17–20
Lesson planning. *See* Co-planning
Letters, parent, 93 (figure), 94 (figure)
Lipsky, D. K., 21
Litmus test, co-teaching, 13 (figure)
Lloyd, J. W., 24, 33, 64, 196
Long-range co-planning, 156–158, 159–160 (figure)
Long-term assessments of adults, 237–239

MacFarlane, C. A., 14
Magic tablecloth, 221–222
Magiera, K. A., 239, 253
Magiera-Simmons Quality Indicator Model of Co-Teaching, 239, 253
Mainstreaming, 11 (figure)
Management, classroom, 121–122
    proactive procedures in, 122–128
    reactive responses in, 128–133, 134 (figure)
Managing Classroom Behavior: A Reflective Case-Based Approach (Kauffman et al.), 122
Manipulatives, quiet, 222–223
Masks, 223
Mastropieri, M. A., 50, 119
Materials
    policies, 125
    sharing, 144–145, 146 (figure)
McCleskey, J., 17
McDuffie, K. A., 50
McLaughlin, V., 119
McLeod, J., 122
McTighe, J., 158, 215, 216
Meetings, scheduled, 153, 161–162, 163 (figure)
    IEP, 186, 187 (figure)
Mentors, 255

Methods, co-planning, 163–170, 171–172 (figure)
Mieliwocki, R. 129
Miller, K. J., 7
Milligan, C., 246
Modification reminder cards, 128 (figure)
Monitoring, 22, 23 (figure)
Montebello School District, 3
Morsink, C. V., 103
Mostert, M. P., 122
Murata, R., 150
Murawski, W. W., 10, 102, 123, 152, 175, 195, 248, 264
Murdick, N. L., 215

National Reading Panel, 241, 242
Needs
    assessments, 98–99
    identifying, 78, 79–80 (figure)
Nevin, A. I., 10, 25
No Child Left Behind, 1, 6, 19, 37, 43, 50, 230, 240
    continuum of options and, 21–22
    differentiation and, 213
    teaming creatively and, 179–180
Noninstructional time requirements, 184, 185 (figure)
Normalization, 14
Norris, D. M., 235
Novice teachers, 102 (figure)

One Teach, One Support approach, 195–197, 198 (figure)
O'Rourke, I., 34, 35
"Out-of-seat" policies, 125–126

Paolucci-Whitcomb, P., 10
Parallel teaching, 198–200, 201–202 (figure)
Paraprofessionals, 32–33, 86–89
    planning with, 150
Parents, communication with, 92, 93 (figure), 94 (figure)
Parity, ensuring, 70–72, 73–74 (figure), 143
Peer dictation, 224
Pellegrino, L., 53
Perner, D. E., 215
Personality or philosophical clashes, 30
Pet peeves, 68–70
Physical disabilities, 54 (figure)
Physical issues with classrooms, 119–121
Pickett, A. L., 86
Pierce, R. L., 217
Planning. See Co-planning
Positive behavior support (PBS), 131
Proactive procedures in classroom management, 122–128
Problem solving skills, 255
Process differentiation, 216
Product differentiation, 216–217

Professional development
    for co-teaching, 50–53, 84, 85 (figure), 255
    lack of, 30
    recruiting volunteers for co-teaching through, 109–110
Profiles, student, 158, 159–160 (figure)
Proportions of students with disabilities to those without, 177–179
    clustering, 178–179
Pugach, M. C., 10
Pullen, P. L., 122
"Pull out," special education, 23 (figure)

Quiet manipulatives, 222–223

Ratey, J. J., 53
Reactive responses in classroom management, 128–133, 134 (figure)
Readiness for co-teaching, assessing, 57–58, 59–61 (figure), 63, 107, 173 (figure)
Reading First, 241–242
Reference, frames of, 42–48
Regrouping, 120
Regular Education Initiative (REI), 11 (figure)
Reluctance to lose control, 30
Renzaglia, A., 14
Research projects by universities, 154
Resistance to change, 13
Resources
    co-teaching, 261, 262–264
    limited, 30
Response to Intervention (RTI), 247–248
Roizen, N. J., 53
Roles and responsibilities, setting, 75–76, 77 (photo)
Ryndak, D. L., 86

Scheduling
    creating viable schedules in, 174–183
    issues, 30
    keeping appropriate proportions in, 177–179
    master schedules in, 176
    meetings, 153, 161–162, 163 (figure)
    noninstructional time requirements, 184, 185 (figure)
    steps for, 188–189 (figure)
    worksheet for co-teaching, 190–191 (figure)
Schloss, P. J., 14
School Administrator, The, 253
Schools
    assemblies, 154
    establishing improvement goals for, 98–101, 102 (figure)
    schoolwide analysis of inclusion, 59 (figure)
    See also Classrooms
Scruggs, T. E., 50, 119
Seating arrangements, 121

Secondary schools, 183
Segregation, 17–18
Self-advocacy cards, 127 (figure)
Self-assessments, co-teaching, 57–58, 59–61
    (figure), 107, 173 (figure), 250
Self-contained, special education, 23 (figure)
S.H.A.R.E. worksheet, 69, 71 (figure),
    103–104, 118, 152
Sharing
    materials, 144–145, 146 (figure)
    space in classrooms, 141–144
Shaw, G. B., 118
Shea, T. M., 122
Short-range co-planning, 161–162, 163 (figure)
Short-term assessments of teachers, 236–237
Siegel, C., 35
Silberman, R. K., 225
Simmons, R. J., 239, 253
Sindelar, P. T., 14
Smith, T. E. C., 18
Snell, M. E., 25
Social mixers for teachers, 109
Spagna, M. E., 225
Special Connections, 85 (figure)
Special service providers
    frames of reference, 43–44
    noninstructional time requirements of, 184,
        185 (figure)
    surveys of, 114 (figure)
    See also Teachers
Speech and language disabilities, 55 (figure)
Spencer, S., 3, 44
Staff development. *See* Professional
    development
Stakeholders, communicating with, 93–96, 97
    (figure)
Standards, assessing by, 235, 234–235 (figure)
Station teaching, 202–203, 204 (figure)
Stoxen, C., 14
*Strategies for Teaching Students With
    Learning and Behavior Problems*
    (Vaughn and Bos), 119
Struyk, L. R., 229, 231
Students, 1–2
    assessing and evaluating progress of,
        38–39, 136–138, 227–235
    behavior, 128–133, 134 (figure)
    benefits of co-teaching for, 28
    clustering, 178–179
    communication with, 89–92
    continuum of options with, 21–23
    defiant, rude, and aggressive, 131–132
    emphasizing strengths of all, 132–133
    grading of, 228–233
    interest, 215
    learning styles, 215, 219–220
    least restrictive environments (LRE) for, 7,
        11 (figure), 18–19
    legislation affecting, 1, 6–7, 15–16
    normalization concept and, 14

physical limitations of, 120–121
profiles, 158, 159–160 (figure)
progression for meeting needs of, 17
readiness, 214
rights of, 15
talking in class, 129–130
violent, 133
See also Inclusion
Stump, C. S., 225
Supervision of co-teaching, 251–252
Support groups, co-teaching, 255
Support staff, 32–33, 86–89, 115 (figure)
Surveys, 111–112, 113–115 (figure)
Swiger, L., 216

Tablecloth, magic, 221–222
Talking in class, 129–130
Tardy policies, 128–129
*Teacher Collaboration: Opening the Door Between
    Classrooms*, 85 (figure)
Teachers
    actions during co-teaching, 73–74 (figure)
    areas of expertise, 158
    assessment of, 138–139, 235–239
    benefits of co-teaching for, 29, 55–56
    both assessing and evaluating student
        progress, 38–39
    both engaged in substantive teaching,
        37–38
    building teams of, 108–109
    communicating with administrators,
        81, 83 (figure)
    communicating with other, 81–84,
        85–86 (figure)
    communicating with support staff, 86–89
    computer skills of, 154–155
    co-teaching in the same classroom at the
        same time, 33–34
    different frames of reference, 42–48
    dually certified, 19
    equality in co-teaching, 32–33
    first day script, 91
    getting over bad experiences, 49–56
    individual team improvement goals,
        103–106
    maximizing the benefits of having two,
        39–40
    novice, 102 (figure)
    observations of and conversations with
        other teachers, 255
    partnered with only one other teacher,
        181–183
    personal space in classrooms, 120
    pet peeves, 68–70
    planning for instruction together, 35–36
    reflecting on progress and process, 40–41
    roles and responsibilities of, 75–76, 77
        (photo)
    sharing space, 141–144
    sharing their concerns, 255–256

short-term assessments of, 236–237
social mixers for, 109
staff development, 50–53
strategies for getting, 109–112,
    113–115 (figure)
tips for improving communication
    between, 45 (figure)
veteran, 102 (figure)
See also Co-teaching; General educators;
    Special service providers
Teaching, team, 11 (figure)
Teaching Exceptional Children, 239, 240
Team(s)
    creativity in forming, 179–181
    getting volunteers and building, 108–109
    improvement goals, individual, 103–106
    teaching, 11 (figure), 209–210,
        211–212 (figure)
Technology
    co-planning, 154–155, 156 (figure)
    co-teaching and, 243–245
Terminology, 11 (figure), 64–65
"This Doesn't Look Familiar: A Supervisor's
    Guide to Observing Co-Teaching,"
    252–253
Thomas, C. C., 103
Thousand, J. S., 25
Tiered lessons, 167–168 (figure), 218–219
Time
    creating co-planning, 152–156, 157
        (figure), 179
    lack of, 31
    noninstructional time requirements and,
        184, 185 (figure)
Timelines, contemporary, 220–221
Tomlinson, C.A., 119, 213
Training, lack of, 30
Trent, S. C., 122

Turnbull, A. P., 92
2 Teach LLC Website, 86 (figure), 170

Understanding by Design (UbD), 158,
    215, 216
Universal Design for Learning (UDL),
    14, 241, 246
Urban Collaborative Leadership
    Institute, 99

Vaughn, S., 119
Veteran teachers, 102 (figure)
Videos, co-teaching, 84, 85 (figure)
Villa, R. A., 25, 88, 163
Violence, 133
Visual disabilities, 54 (figure)

Waldron, N. L., 17
Walker, J. E., 122
Walther-Thomas, C., 119
Weapons, 133
Weekly assessments, 236–237
Weiner, I., 57
Weiss, M. P., 24, 33, 64, 196
Wiggins, G., 158, 215, 216
Wiggins, K., 235, 258
Williams, B., 119
Wineburg, S., 103
Wong, H. K., 119
Wong, R. T., 119
Woolworth, S., 103
Worksheet wonder, 222
Wormeli, R., 228
Worsham, M. E., 122

Yell, M. L., 21

Zigmond, N., 19

CORWIN
A SAGE Company

The Corwin logo—a raven striding across an open book—represents the union of courage and learning. Corwin is committed to improving education for all learners by publishing books and other professional development resources for those serving the field of PreK–12 education. By providing practical, hands-on materials, Corwin continues to carry out the promise of its motto: **"Helping Educators Do Their Work Better."**